THE GIFTED STUDENT

CONTEMPORARY PROBLEMS OF CHILDHOOD A Bibliographic Series
Series Editor: Carol Ann Winchell

THE GIFTED
STUDENT

AN ANNOTATED
BIBLIOGRAPHY

Jean Laubenfels

Contemporary Problems of Childhood, Number 1

GREENWOOD PRESS
Westport, Connecticut · London, England

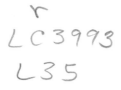

Library of Congress Cataloging in Publication Data

Laubenfels, Jean.
   The gifted student.

   (Contemporary problems of childhood; no. 1
ISSN 0147-1082)
   Includes indexes.
   1. Gifted children—Education—Abstracts. 2. Gifted
children—Education—Bibliography. I. Title. II. Series:
Contemporary problems of childhood; no. 1.
LC3993.L35   016.3719'5   77-82696
ISBN 0-8371-9760-0

Library of Congress Catalog Card Number: 77-82696
ISBN: 0-8371-9760-0

First published in 1977

Greenwood Press, Inc.
51 Riverside Avenue, Westport, Connecticut 06880

Printed in the United States of America

*To the gifted students in my classes who
made teaching challenging and exciting.*

To give a fair chance to potential creativity is a matter of life and death for any society. This is all-important, because the outstanding creative ability of a fairly small percentage of the population is mankind's ultimate capital asset, and the only one with which only man has been endowed.

Arnold Toynbee

CONTENTS

SERIES FOREWORD

The attention focused on children's problems has become increasingly
pronounced in the United States during the last two decades. Particular
interest and involvement have been directed toward certain problems:
pathological conditions, the handicapped child, the educationally and culturally deprived child, and various behavior disorders. This interest has produced a voluminous body of knowledge. One needs only a cursory perusal
through the literature to realize that it has now proliferated into an extensive, but unorganized, number of publications. Through modern technology,
masses of material have been flowing from the presses; given this plethora
of publication, it is frequently difficult to locate specific materials. A
Tower of Babel situation has developed in that some of this valuable information is unknown to the researcher who might wish to be aware of its
existence.

The purpose of *Contemporary Problems of Childhood* is to identify,
collect, classify, abstract, and index relevant material on the following
topics in need of systematic control: the gifted child, child abuse, behavior
modification techniques with children, the autistic child, the child with
dyslexia, and the hyperkinetic syndrome. Not only have these topics been
the subject of academe, but the mass media—magazines, newspapers, and
commercial and educational television specials—have recently devoted considerable attention to these problems. To bring some order to this discipline,
it was decided to issue a series of volumes, each considering one of these
topics and following the format of an earlier volume by this editor, *The
Hyperkinetic Child: A Bibliography of Medical, Educational, and Psychological Studies* (Greenwood Press, 1975). Volumes are intended to aid the
retrieval of information for educators, psychologists, physicians, researchers,
parents, and others interested in etiology, diagnosis, and management.

The volumes in the series are broad in scope, interdisciplinary, comprehensive in coverage, and contain retrospective and current citations. The
titles cited mainly reflect developments over the last decade, but some
earlier titles of relevance are included. Selection of citations is based on the

quality and direct applicability to the topic under consideration. For these publications only English-language sources are selected.

The entries are culled from extensive searches of manual and computerized information sources. Basic indexing and abstracting services, as well as many diverse and widely scattered sources, have been searched. Books, chapters in books, journal articles, conference reports, pamphlets, government documents, dissertations, and proceedings of symposiums are included. Since a bewildering variety of terminology exists for each subject, compilers have attempted to weed out unexplicitly defined topics.

Frontmatter contains appropriate introductory material: preface, contents, and a "state-of-the-art" message by a specialist in the area. Entries are classified and arranged alphabetically by author under the correct subject heading and appear only once in the bibliography.

Citations include complete and verified bibliographic information: author, title, source, volume, issue number, publisher, place, date, number of pages, and references. An attempt is made to annotate all citations that can be located, giving context, scope, and possible findings and results of the book or article.

Appendixes, author and key-word subject indexes, and journal abbreviations complete each volume.

It is hoped that the documentation provided by *Contemporary Problems of Childhood* will facilitate access to retrospective and current sources of information and help bring bibliographic control to this rapidly expanding body of literature.

Carol A. Winchell
General Editor
June 1, 1977

PREFACE

PURPOSE

There have been great fluctuations in interest in the gifted since Galton published the first significant research on the subject over one hundred years ago. The years following the Russians' successful launching of Sputnik saw a great concern with the gifted in this country, especially in the areas of mathematics, science, and foreign languages, which are considered vital to national defense. A variety of programs designed to identify, challenge, and accelerate the gifted were established with an eye to overtaking the Soviet Union in the race for scientific and technological superiority.

By 1956, however, the overriding concern with the educational plight of the culturally deprived had caused attention to shift from the gifted, who were considered able to succeed on their own, to the disadvantaged in need of compensatory education. There was a marked trend away from studies concerning gifted children to research on cognitive factors, creativity, and divergent thinking. Available resources were devoted to efforts to identify and develop potential in groups previously underrepresented in programs for the gifted.

With the publication in 1972 of the U.S. Office of Education's report, *Education of the Gifted and Talented,* attention was once again directed toward the gifted, and resources were made available for their special needs. Concern has centered recently on underachievement, which is estimated as high as 50 percent in our high schools and is affecting countless numbers of our most able students, and on creativity, a highly subjective quality that is difficult to both define and measure. Current researchers constantly stress the need to broaden the scope of giftedness to include areas other than the traditional academic ones and to find innovative ways of assessing potential among groups hitherto unrecognized.

A search of the literature reveals significant changes in terminology used to describe students of superior ability or achievement. The nineteenth-century term "genius" is out of fashion, and the more general "gifted" is now often replaced by "able," "talented," "rapid learners," "bright," and increasingly, "creative." Great differences in performances of student populations under study make necessary similar differences in requirements, standards, and objectives of programs designed for superior pupils and also determine the terminology used to describe them. This bibliography has attempted to select representative references on "giftedness" in its more traditional definition of superior intelligence or academic aptitude, with some attention to outstanding ability in specified fields such as leadership and aesthetic areas.

COVERAGE

The bibliography primarily covers the period of the past fifteen years since the 1961 publication of John Gowan's *Annotated Bibliography on the Academically Talented Student.* That volume provided a thorough review of materials published during the decade of the 1950s, thus updating the annotated bibliography in Paul Witty's definitive work *The Gifted Child* (1951). Although emphasis is on recent studies not previously described, an effort has been made to provide necessary background material by including earlier "classic" studies.

SCOPE

Since the subject is broad and the literature is vast, it has been necessary to be selective. Of the 1,300 references, a majority will be of special interest to teachers, administrators, counselors, school psychologists, and others working within an educational setting. However, an effort has been made to include some general selections for parents and some technical references for physicians interested in child development. The citations were selected after an extensive search of both manual and computerized information sources. Nearly 200 popular and professional educational, psychological, and medical journals were covered, as well as many abstracting and indexing sources. Also included are books, chapters in books, conference reports, government documents, pamphlets, and dissertations. Items excluded are anthropological studies, unpublished papers, foreign language references, personal correspondence, newspaper articles, and speeches.

ARRANGEMENT

Entries are grouped according to the major categories listed in the contents. Arrangement of entries within each category is determined primarily by evaluative judgment, each entry appearing only once under the most significant topic. When several subjects are covered in an article, placement has been under the subject given predominant focus or priority. Since there is much overlapping of subject, it is necessary to consult the Selective Key Word Subject Index for specific descriptors.

Within each section, arrangement is alphabetical by author. Entry numbers preceding the author's names run consecutively through the text.

THE ENTRIES

For monographs, the complete citation includes author, title, edition used, place, publisher, date, pages, inclusive pages of sections appearing as parts of larger works, and presence of bibliography. Journal citations contain author (three are given; et al. is used to indicate additional names), title of the article, journal abbreviation, volume number, issue number (in parentheses), inclusive pages, month, year, and usually the number of references. For dissertations, the user is referred to *Dissertation Abstracts International* with volume number, issue number, pages, and date given. Books and conference proceedings have been verified and entered in the bibliography under the U.S. Library of Congress *National Union Catalog: Author List* entry to facilitate retrieval for the user. Annotations are given for all entries except dissertations.

APPENDICES

Appendix A, Some Individuals and Organizations Concerned with the Gifted, alphabetically lists the various persons and associations interested in the gifted and their addresses. Appendix B, List of Instruments Useful in Identifying the Gifted, lists in order of frequency the most often used tests and measurment devices in assessment of the gifted. Appendix C, Audio-Visual Materials for Professional Use, alphabetically lists films, filmstrips, tapes, etc. providing information on the gifted. Appendix D, Media Aids for Student Use, alphabetically lists under type of media selected materials that teachers of the gifted can use for classroom or individual enrichment. Appendix E, Basic Bibliographic Tools, alphabetically lists major manual and computerized information sources consulted in locating and verifying the citations in this bibliography.

INDICES

The Author Index includes the personal names of all individuals in this volume who are cited as author, joint author, editor, or compiler, including up to three names per citation. Forenames, middle initials, and surnames are given in most cases. Numbers following the names refer to item numbers in the text.

The Selective Key Word Subject Index alphabetically lists important words in entry titles. The user may find it convenient to use the broader subject arrangement under subcategories in the contents, or this index may be consulted for more specific aspects of the topic. In general: only unique terms are given —alternate words for giftedness and other high frequency terms are omitted; phrases are used to put certain words in more meaningful contexts; and *see also* references are used to refer the reader to similar concepts. Numbers following the words refer to item numbers in the text.

The List of Journal Abbreviations alphabetically lists all journals cited in the text. Journal title abbreviations have been formulated according to the rules of the *American National Standard for the Abbreviation of Titles of Periodicals,* and the individual words of the title are abbreviated according to the forms given in the *International List of Periodical Title Word Abbreviations.*

ACKNOWLEDGMENTS

I should like to express my gratitude to the following Ohio State University faculty members for their invaluable assistance in the preparation of this manuscript: Dr. Thomas Stephens, Chairman of the Department for Exceptional Children, who wrote the introduction; Dr. Walter Barbe, Visiting Professor of Exceptional Children, who aided in the planning of the project; and Dr. Sidney L. Pressey, Professor Emeritus of Psychology, who shared his ideas on acceleration with me. Mention should also be made of several members of the Ohio State University Libraries, whose expertise was most helpful: Noelle Van Pulis, information specialist, Mechanized Information Center, for assistance with the key-word index; Ann Warmington, assistant professor, Health Sciences Library, for guiding me through the medical journals; Ross Poli, assistant professor, Mechanized Information Center, for assistance with computer searches; and Carol Winchell, my editor, for unflagging support and assistance in every phase of the preparation. Thanks also go to George Fichter, Coordinator of the Gifted Programs for the State of Ohio, for providing the resources of his ample professional library, and to Jean Stouder and Cindy Cleveland, my typists, whose careful attention to detail made this project possible.

INTRODUCTION

Three times in this century educators in the United States have focused their attentions of gifted children. Nationally, the first major wave of interest occurred in the 1920s, the second during what may be termed the "Sputnik Era" in the late 1950s and early 1960s. The current movement, which may simply be a resumption of the previous wave, followed a decline of interest as a result of an overemphasis on compensatory education, a prolonged war, and tragic domestic turmoil.

Attention in the 1920s was characterized by a fascination with verbal intelligence as measured primarily by the early editions of the Stanford-Binet test of intelligence. Lewis Terman's Genetic Studies of Genius[1] gave impetus to the movement and were the most noteworthy achievements in giftedness during that era. Of the many special programs started during that period, only one, the Cleveland Major Works Program, has continued without interruption to this day.

Giftedness was at one time relatively easily defined, and students were readily identified through the use of IQ measures. Since Terman's seminal studies, however, the concept of giftedness has changed.

Incidence figures for giftedness are related to definitions and identification methods. When IQ measures are used as cutoff scores, the number of students identified is the result of the minimum score and the test used. For example, using a Stanford-Binet IQ score of 180, Hollingworth (1942)[2] was daeling with an incidence figure of one in a million. But incidence figures using lower-IQ cutoff scores and/or more factors would result in a higher proportion of giftedness among the school-age population. During the Sputnik Era, broader definitions were used more often and frequently included special talents and abilities. As a result, as much as 15 to 20 percent of school populations were sometimes considered gifted and talented.[3]

Shifts in definitions of giftedness greatly influenced the identification of such children as well as educational programs for them. The more variables used in locating giftedness, the more diverse were the sample populations. Consequently, the period resulted in many different educational and instructional programs—single types of programming were no longer considered sufficient for meeting the educational needs of this special group of children. As with most changes, the broadening of giftedness had its pluses and minuses. On the plus side, the broader concept did call to school personnels' attentions the need for special consideration for many talented youth who otherwise would not have been assisted. Unfortunately, it also contributed to diluting the concept of the highly gifted as it had been originally developed by Terman and his associates. Many school programs tried to treat the lower-IQ students as academically gifted in association with the smaller number of the very bright.

Many school programs and administrative provisions that were rooted in the Sputnik Era continue to this day. Special provisions for secondary students, in particular, remain as a result of that attention. Notable among these is the Advanced Placement Program,[4] which permits high school students to receive college credit for selected courses. Admission to school at an earlier age has also continued in many instances.

But special provisions for the elementary school-aged child seemed to have diminished as movement into the third cycle of attention began. Current programs for the gifted cannot yet be characterized clearly since attention is now on the rise and has not yet be characterized clearly since attention is now on teristic of this era may be a reduction in the use of standardized measures for identification purposes. If this does prove to be one of the hallmarks of the present movement, it can be attributed to the disfavor into which tests have fallen. Our tendency to base scientific decisions on political issues may contribute to a further dilution of giftedness. Measures of intelligence should be considered as types of achievement tests. Their results would then be viewed as performance data (which they are) rather than as measures of intelligence.

The author's coverage has accurately captured the essentials of the period between the Sputnik Era and the new and emerging phase. Few publications reviewed here are remarkable, however, with occasional exceptions. Among the noteworthy ones is the effort by Stanley[5] and his associates in studying mathematically and scientifically precocious youth, conducted at Johns Hopkins University. Unfortunately, few innovative educational programs can be found. The governors' schools, which grew out of the Sputnik Era, have continued at a reduced level, but their value has yet to be fully measured.

People with special abilities continue to surface. But often they are not served adequately by the educational establishment. By drawing attention to the educational needs of such individuals, the author, editor, and publisher are contributing to the day when the sun will shine more brightly for gifted children and youth.

Thomas M. Stephens
Professor & Chairman, Faculty for Exceptional Children,
College of Education, The Ohio State University, Columbus, Ohio
February, 1977

NOTES

1. Terman, Lewis M., et. al. *Genetic studies of genius,* Vol. 1.
   Stanford: Stanford University Press, 1925.
2. Hollingworth, L. *Children above 180 IQ.* Yonkers: World, 1942.
3. Fliegler, L., and Bish, C. "The gifted and talented." *Review of Educational Research* 29 (1959): 408-450.
4. Gerritz, E. M., and Haywood, E. R. "Advanced placement: Opinions differ." NEA Journal 54: January, 1965.
5. Stanley, Julian C.; Keating, Daniel P.; and Fox, Lynn H., eds. *Mathematical talent: Discovery, description, development.* Baltimore: The Johns Hopkins University Press, 1974.

SAMPLE BOOK ENTRY

① ②   ③
19 Barbe, Walter B., and Renzulli, Joseph S., eds. *Psychology and education of the gifted.*
2nd ed. New York: Wiley, 1975. 481p. (Bibliography)
         ④   ⑤   ⑥   ⑦   ⑧

⑨ A textbook or supplementary reader for those preparing to work with the gifted.
Divided into five parts: "Introduction to the study of the Gifted," "Characteristics
of the Gifted and Creative," "Identification and Measurement of Giftedness," "Developing and Encouraging Giftedness," and "Teaching the Gifted."

1. Item number
2. Author (s)
3. Title of book
4. Place of publication
5. Publisher
6. Date of publication
7. Number of pages
8. Presence of bibliography
9. Annotation

SAMPLE JOURNAL ENTRY

① ②   ③
732 Fox, Lynn H. "Facilitating educational development of mathematically precocious
youth." *J Spec Educ* 9(1): 63-77, Spring, 1975. (5 References)
         ④   ⑤   ⑥   ⑦   ⑧

⑨ Seven case studies of mathematically precocious males are presented, with ideas for
educational counseling and individualization of school programs for the gifted.

1. Item number
2. Author (s)
3. Title of article
4. Name of journal (abbreviation)
5. Volume and issue number
6. Inclusive pagination
7. Month and year of publication
8. Number of bibliographical references
9. Annotation

THE GIFTED STUDENT

I

General Introductory Material

A. Historical

1 Abraham, Willard. Common sense about gifted children. New York:
      Harper, 1958. 268p. (Bibliography)
A general book for the layman dealing with various topics concerning the
gifted child.

2 Albert, Robert S. "Genius: present-day status of the concept and
      its implications for the study of creativity and giftedness." Am
      Psychol 24(8): 743-53, August, 1969. (75 References)
The author investigated the bibliography on genius and some allied concepts to gain a sense of the comprehensiveness of behavioral, medical,
and social sciences interests in genius from 1927-1965. A second aim of
the study was to determine the conceptual emphases placed in the study
of genius, creativity, and giftedness as well, and how these three
topics might be related in the literature.

3 Havighurst, Robert J.; Stivers, Eugene; DeHaan, Robert F. A survey
      of the education of gifted children. Chicago: The University of
      Chicago Press, 1955. 114p. (Bibliography)
Criteria for a good educational program for gifted children are identified. Then a list of school systems, individual schools, institutions
and organizations known for a current program of unusual merit for the
education and development of gifted children is offered.

4 Hollingworth, Leta S. Gifted children: their nature and nurture.
      New York: Macmillan, 1926. 374p.
A definitive study of what had been learned about gifted children during
the 20's.

5 Parnes, Sidney, J., and Brunelle, Eugene A. "The literature of crea-
      tivity, Part I." J Creat Behav 1(1): 52-109, Winter, 1967. (0
      References)
The research literature on creativity and giftedness during the year
prior to publication of Guilford's The Nature of Human Intelligence
equaled the amount reported during the previous decade, and this literature, in turn, equaled in volume the research reported from Galton's
time (1869).

6 Passow, A. Harry; Goldberg, Miriam L.; Tannenbaum, Abraham J.; et al.
      Planning for talented youth. New York: Teachers College, Columbia
      University, 1955. 84p. (Bibliography)
A publication of the Talented Youth Project under the auspices of the
Horace Mann-Lincoln Institute of School Experimentation.

7 Shertzer, Bruce, ed. <u>Working with superior students: theories and
      practices</u>. Chicago: Science Research Associates, 1960. 370p.
This volume is a compilation of papers touching on the most important
aspects of helping talented youth. Many of the leaders in education of
the gifted are represented.

8 Sumption, Merle Richard, and Luecking, Evelyn M. <u>Education of the
      gifted</u>. New York: Ronald, 1960. 499p. (Bibliography)
Deals with an overview of the gifted, identification, research, guidance,
teachers, present practices, preschool, elementary, secondary, and
college programs for the gifted. Also discusses role of the community.

9 Terman, Lewis M., and Oden, Melita H. <u>The gifted group at mid-life,
      genetic studies of genius</u>, V. 5. Stanford, California: Stanford
      University Press, 1959.
In 1921, Dr. Lewis Terman began his study of gifted youngsters who were
then about eleven years old. This volume, the fifth in his <u>Genetic
Studies of Genius</u> series, presents data of those same gifted people in
their mid-life. His data is enlightening, and presents the evidence that
their intellectual and social vigor was not yet in sight. Terman can be
considered the father of the gifted child movement, and his longitudinal
study is the basis for much of today's theory.

10 Wall, W. D. "Highly intelligent children, Part I." <u>Educ Res</u> (U.K.)
      2(2): 101-10, February, 1960. (0 References)
Part I deals with the psychology of the gifted--recognition, wastage,
difficulties of high ability, and importance of mental and physical
health.

11 Wiseman, Stephen. <u>Intelligence and ability: selected readings</u>.
      Baltimore: Penguin, 1967. 368p.
Adopting a historical approach, the author presents a selection of readings dealing with man's intellectual powers, their nature, form and
structure.

12 Witty, Paul A. "The education of the gifted and the creative in the
      U.S.A." <u>Gifted Child Q</u> 15(2): 109-16, Summer, 1971. (23
      References)
Gives historical perspective, deals with identification of creative,
differences between gifted and creative, and promising trends in education of the gifted.

13 ————. "The gifted and the creative pupil." <u>Education</u> 82(8):
      451-59, April, 1962. (61 References)
A comprehensive review of studies on the gifted, focusing on those done
during the 50's. Some significant trends may be noted, including increased interest in providing more stimulating programs for verbally or
academically gifted students and an emphasis on creativity.

14 ————. "Twenty years in education of the gifted." <u>Education</u>
      88(1): 4-10, September/October, 1967. (25 References)
Dr. Witty reviews the progress that has been made in recognizing and
providing for gifted children and points out certain areas in which
further study is needed.

B. 1961 to Date

15 Abraham, Williard. "The early years: prologue to tomorrow." Except
    Child 42(6): 330-35, March, 1976. (0 References)
The growth of special education is historically reviewed from the 19th
century to the present. Trends in concern for the gifted are noted.

16 Adler, Manfred. "Cycles of interest in the gifted student." Clear-
    ing House 41(8): 476-78, April, 1967.
Adler reminds readers that the current surge to identify and adequately
educate the gifted pupil is not an exclusive innovation of the sixties.
It has received attention at various times over the past forty years.
He relates interest in the gifted to economic cycles.

17 Anderson, Kenneth E., ed. Research on the academically talented
    student. Washington, D.C.: National Education Association, 1961.
    92p. (Bibliography)
One of the publications of the NEA project on the academically talented
student, this report was done to provide assistance to school personnel
who are responsible for research on the talented. Chapters include:
"Introduction to Research," "Illustrative Research on Individual Characteristics," "Educational Practice," and "The Status and Needs of
Research."

18 Barbe, Walter B., ed. Psychology and education of the gifted:
    selected readings. New York: Appleton-Century-Crofts, 1965. 534p.
The aim of this book is to present an overview of the outstanding literature on the psychology and education of the gifted. Much of it is on an
advanced level and may be used as a basic text for a course on the
gifted.

19 Barbe, Walter B., and Renzulli, Joseph S., eds. Psychology and
    education of the gifted. 2nd ed. New York: Wiley, 1975. 481p.
    (Bibliography)
A textbook or supplementary reader for those preparing to work with the
gifted. Divided into five parts: "Introduction to the Study of the
Gifted," "Characteristics of the Gifted and Creative," "Identification
and Measurement of Giftedness," "Developing and Encouraging Giftedness,"
and "Teaching the Gifted."

20 Barbe, Walter B., and Stephens, Thomas M., eds. Attention to the
    gifted--a decade later. Columbus, Ohio: State of Ohio Department
    of Education, 1962. 61p.
This monograph is a tenth anniversary presentation of the Ohio Association for the Gifted. It contains papers presented by many nationally
recognized leaders in the field of the gifted at the Association's semi-
annual meetings.

21 ————. Educating tomorrow's leaders. Columbus, Ohio: State of
    Ohio Board of Education, 1961. 156p.
Includes a number of the speeches given by leading educators in the field
of the academically gifted to various groups in Ohio. Covers the philosophy of education of the gifted, an evaluation of recent research on the
gifted, and effective programs carried out in Ohio.

22   Barnes, Fred P.   "Rediscovering the wheel."   Ill Sch Res   10(1):
     3-10, February, 1973.
A reprint of a somewhat satiric article used as a reminder that useful
educational research avoids the pitfall of pointlessly dwelling on the
obvious.

23   Barron, Frank.   Creativity and personal freedom.   Princeton, New
     Jersey: Van Nostrand, 1968.   322p.
A comprehensive account of research done with the support of the U.S.
Public Health Service, the Ford Foundation, the Carnegie Corporation,
and the Rockefeller Foundation.   More than 5,000 individuals took part
in the research.   Chapter 2, "Uses, and the Danger of Abuses, of Research
on Creativity," and Chapter 17, "Intelligence Quotient, Personality, and
Originality," have implications for teachers and counselors of the gifted.

24   Birch, Jack W., and Reynolds, Maynard C.   "The gifted."   Rev Educ
     Res   33(1):   83-98, February, 1963.   (Bibliography)
Reviews major research from 1959 to 1963 on high I.Q. pupils, as well as
the creative and talented.

25   Bish, Charles E.   "The academically talented."   NEA J   50(2):   33-37,
     February, 1961.
The director of the NEA Project on the Academically Talented Student
attempts here to aid teachers in recognizing and providing special programs for these gifted youth.

26   ———.   "The academically talented project, gateway to the present."
     Gifted Child Q   19(4):   271, 282-89, Winter, 1975.   (12 References)
The author, former director of the Carnegie NEA Academically Talented
Project, presents a valuable historical record of the developments and
accomplishments of the project.

27   Bloom, Benjamin S.   Stability and change in human characteristics.
     New York: Wiley, 1964.   237p.   (Bibliography)
Deals with physical characteristics, intelligence, interests, attitudes
and personality, environment, implications of stability, and change in
the human.   Relates research findings to posited ideas, applies them to
different characteristics, and considers theoretical as well as practical
consequences of the ideas and findings.

28   Branch, Margaret, and Cash, Aubrey.   Gifted children: recognizing
     and developing exceptional ability.   London: Souvenir Press, 1966.
     222p.
The authors, a psychiatric social worker at a London hospital and a
journalist and film writer, offer a popularized psychology intended to
interest parents, teachers, and the general public in what they consider
to be the latest results of psychological speculation and research in
education of the gifted.

29   Concannon, Sister Josephina.   "Assessing human potential."   Gifted
     Child Q   10(1):   17-22, Spring, 1966.   (17 References)
The author defines the gifted child, reviews some of the early scientific
studies of giftedness, and cites research related to the reading abilities of the gifted.   She concludes with a set of objectives in the education of the gifted from the composite accepted by educators.

30   Copley, Frank O.   The American high school and the talented student.
     Ann Arbor: The University of Michigan Press, 1961.   92p.
     (Bibliography)
This practical book for teachers covers identification of the gifted, enrichment or acceleration,ability, advice on starting and maintaining a
program of advanced placement, teacher selection,course organization,
utilization of resources, etc.   It warns of pitfalls and discusses advantages and disadvantages of programs.

31   DeHaan, Robert F., and Havighurst, Robert J.   Educating gifted chil-
     dren.   2nd ed.   Chicago: University of Chicago Press, 1961.   362p.
     (Bibliography)
This is a systematic and integrated presentation of the problems of educating gifted children.   The book contains a thorough analysis of community factors that influence the education of the gifted, as well as a
chapter on the home influences.

32   Denbury, Marvin L., ed.   Readings for the psychology of the excep-
     tional child: emphasis on learning disabilities.   New York: MSS
     Information Corporation, 1972.   296p.   (Bibliography)
Section III of this collection of monographs contains five articles of
interest to educators of the gifted.   These include "Intellectually
Gifted Children: Their Characteristics and Problems," "The Cognitive and
Affective Stimulation of Gifted Children," and "The Rate of Reading
Development and its Relation to Age of Learning to Read, Sex, and Intel-
ligence."

33   Dissinger, Jean K., and Arnold, Carole R., eds.   Studies in the
     psychological foundations of exceptionality.   Monterey, California:
     Brooks/Cole, 1975.   316p.
Presents an anthology of articles designed for use as a psychology, education, and child development textbook, including studies on giftedness
and mental retardation, physical handicaps, cultural and social differences, and communication disorders.

34   Durr, William K.   The gifted student.   New York: Oxford University
     Press, 1964.   296p.   (Bibliography)
This book deals with a variety of ways in which education of gifted
students can be intensified and broadened.   Specific suggestions for
teachers are intended to be guides and are not prescriptive.   Theoretical
and research-based frameworks are provided as background.

35   Freehill, Maurice F.   Gifted children, their psychology and education.
     New York: Macmillan, 1961.   412p.
Written at a period of crucial concern for maximum development of intellectual talent, this volume contains fifteen chapters treating attitudes,
identification, nature of intelligence, programming, methodology, vocational planning, and affective development.

36   Frierson, Edward C.   "The gifted."   In: Johnson, G. Orville, and
     Blank, Harriett, D., eds.   Exceptional children research review.
     Washington, D.C.:   Council for Exceptional Children, 1968.   3-37.
     (Bibliography)
This review was undertaken within the context of the "creativity research
explosion."   It summarizes studies on creativity and its enhancement among
the gifted, educating the gifted for improved modes of thinking, race,
class and giftedness, and early admission policies and underachievement.

37   ————. "The gifted." Rev Educ Res 39(1):   25-37, February, 1969.
        (58 References)
Surveys the trends of the expanding body of literature on the gifted during the period 1965-1968. Notes the marked shift from studies of gifted
children to studies of creativity and cognitive factors, and explains
the social influences behind this phenomenon.

38   Gallagher, James J. "Gifted children." In: Encyclopedia of
        educational research. 4th ed. New York: Macmillan, 1969.   537-44.
        (85 References)
Covers developments in the area of the gifted during the late 50's and
early 60's. Studies cited show concern for the role of the gifted in
the classroom, interest in the nature of gifted programs, concern for the
gifted underachiever of low socio-economic status, and a great interest
in the multi-dimensional nature of talent.

39   Gallagher, James J., and Rogge, William. "The gifted." Rev Educ
        Res 36(1):   37-55, February, 1966. (75 References)
Surveys significant research on the gifted during the 1962-1965 period.
The authors noted a trend toward exploring the nature of creative thinking and the possibility of expanding the concept of superior intellectual
ability itself.

40   Garrison, Karl C., and Force, Dewey G. The psychology of exceptional
        children. 4th ed. New York: Ronald, 1965. 571p. (Bibliography)
Two of the nineteen chapters in this textbook focus on the gifted.
Chapter 5 gives a general overview on identification and characteristics
of the gifted, and Chapter 6 deals with educational provisions and
guidance for the gifted.

41   Getzels, Jacob W., and Jackson, Philip W. "The meaning of gifted-
        ness." Education 82(8):   460-64, April, 1962. (0 References)
Purpose of this paper is to examine the transformations the concept of
giftedness is presently undergoing, and to suggest some additional modi-
fications in its application.

42   Gold, Milton J. Education of the intellectually gifted. Columbus,
        Ohio: Charles E. Merrill, 1965. 472p. (Bibliography)
Attempts to relate theoretical research and demonstration of practices
in actual situations to problems in education of the gifted. Gold utilized nearly 500 studies in preparation of the volume. His brief description should encourage readers to seek the primary source material.

43   Gold, Marvin J. "Exceptional children abstracts: the gifted."
        Except Child 32(5):   329-31, January, 1966.
Includes nineteen abstracts on gifted and creative which include building a program for superior and talented, teaching the gifted, adolescent
attitudes toward academic brilliance, and imagination.

44   Goldberg, Miriam L. Research on the talented. New York: Bureau
        of Publications, Teachers College, Columbia University, 1965. 72p.
        (Bibliography)
A brief compilation of research on the gifted, including characteristics,
identification, motivational factors, discrepancy between prediction and
achievement, administrative and guidance provisions, course content and
method, current trends and concerns for schools.

45 Gowan, John C. The guidance and measurement of intelligence, devel-
    opment, and creativity: a book of readings drawn from the collected
    papers of John Curtis Gowan. Northridge, California: 1972. 235p.
A book of readings covering guidance and measurement of intelligence,
development, and creativity.

46 Gowan, John C., and Demos, George D. The education and guidance of
    the ablest. Springfield, Illinois: Thomas, 1964. 511p. (Biblio-
    graphy)
Provides extensive coverage of issues in education of the gifted, including philosophy, creativity, acceleration, and grouping. Curriculum in
the humanities and sciences are treated, as are college programs and
teacher training.

47 Gowan, John C., and Torrance, E. Paul, eds. Educating the ablest:
    a book of readings on the education of gifted children. Itasca,
    Illinois: Peacock, 1971. 295p. (Bibliography)
All of the articles in this book are taken from issues of The Gifted
Child Quarterly. It touches on those areas of current concern in the
education of the gifted, including programs, guidance, curriculum,
evaluation, teachers, parents, creativity, the disadvantaged, and mental
health.

48 Guilford, J. P. The nature of human intelligence. New York: McGraw-
    Hill, 1967. 538p. (Bibliography)
A very thorough discussion and explanation of the basic factors in intelligence are presented in this volume. Most useful to all those involved
in identification and program development for the gifted.

49 Hewett, Frank M., and Fornass, Steven R. Education of exceptional
    learners. Boston: Allyn and Bacon, 1974. 464p. (Bibliography)
This introductory text is concerned with children who fall into nine
separate categories of exceptionality. The author utilizes a convenient
index-band system on page margins to identify a particular category of
exceptionality, as all types are combined for much of the discussion.
Chapters treating contemporary practices in special education, flexibility, and intelligence and individualization give special attention to
the gifted.

50 Holcomb, J. David, "The gifted: are they being slighted?" Peabody
    J Educ 48(3): 238-43, April, 1971. (11 References)
Provides a brief history of programs for the gifted, examines alternative
procedures, and explains the reasons for widespread neglect of talented
students in most school systems.

51 Horwitz, Elinor L. "Gifted children." Child Today 2(1): 27-30,
    January/February, 1973.
Traces the history of special programs for the gifted, explains the new
definition of giftedness, and describes special facilities in New York,
California and Connecticut which have been successful in challenging
the gifted.

52 Hughes, Herbert H., and Converse, Harold D. "Characteristics of
    the gifted: a case for a sequel to Terman's study." Except Child
    29(4): 179-83, December, 1962.
Discusses Terman's study and recommends a new investigation to overcome
its shortcomings. Includes outline for new study.

53   Jones, Reginald L., ed. Problems and issues in the education of
      exceptional children. Boston: Houghton Mifflin, 1971. 424p.
      (Bibliography)
The six articles in Chapter 1 on the gifted discuss identification,
creativity and giftedness, research on ability grouping, educational
acceleration, and programs for the gifted. Authors include Martinson,
Yamamoto, and Passow.

54   Jordan, Thomas E. The exceptional child. Columbus, Ohio: Charles
      E. Merrill, 1962. 352p. (Bibliography)
Addressed to present and prospective teachers, this book serves as a
valuable resource to parents as well. It concerns the instruction of
"different" children whose personal characteristics make special educational services essential. Chapter 11, "Understanding Giftedness," and
Chapter 12, "Educating Gifted Children," provide an overview for those
concerned with the gifted.

55   Jordan, Thomas E., and Cegelka, Walter J. Exceptional children.
      New York: MSS Information Corporation, 1972.
This custom-made book of readings contains articles on various aspects
of exceptionality. Section II contains four articles on the gifted
child by Roe, Torrance, Jordan and Keith.

56   Kannan, Jacquelyn P., and Kannan, Michael M. "Education and the
      gifted child." Va Med Mon 101(3): 189-92, March, 1974. (0 Ref-
      erences)
This practical article presents a general review of trends in definition
and education of the gifted child in the U.S.A. Most of the important
researchers of the 60's and 70's are cited and their findings and recommendations are discussed.

57   Kirk, Samuel A. Educating exceptional children. 2nd ed. Boston:
      Houghton Mifflin, 1972. 478p. (Bibliography)
This text covers all areas of exceptionality. Chapter 4 treats the
intellectually gifted child and includes such topics as characteristics
and identification, curriculum planning and instructional procedures.
Useful case studies are presented.

58   Kirk, Samuel A., and Lord, Francis E., eds. Exceptional children:
      educational resources and perspectives. Boston: Houghton Mifflin,
      1974. 503p. (Bibliography)
Included in Chapter 5 are current articles treating topics such as policy
statement on education for the gifted, family influences on creativity,
opinions of gifted students regarding secondary school programs and an
article on broadening concepts of giftedness in the 70's.

59   Kreuter, G. "Vanishing genius: Lewis Terman and the Stanford
      study." Hist Educ Q 2(1): 6-18, March, 1962.
A recapitualation of Terman and his investigation into genius.

60   Laird, Albert W. "Are we really educating the gifted child?"
      Gifted Child Q 12(4): 205-14, Winter, 1968. (30 References)
Laird describes the gifted child as the most neglected pupil in the average public school classroom, and cites examples from various states to
prove it. Many examples are given of precocious behavior of gifted
students and suggestions are made for better identification of these
pupils.

61 Love, Harold D. Exceptional children in a modern society. Dubuque,
    Iowa: William C. Brown, 1967. 171p.
This general textbook for undergraduate and beginning graduate students
contains eleven chapters covering the most common forms of exceptionality.
Chapter III, "The Gifted," treats identification, education, trends,
issues, and influences, and concludes with a short selected bibliography.

62 Martinson, Ruth A. "Children with superior cognitive abilities."
    In: Dunn, Lloyd M., ed. Exceptional children in the schools:
    special education in transition. 2nd ed. New York: Holt, Rinehart
    and Winston, 1973. 189-241. (Bibliography)
Dr. Martinson, who has been prominent in California's program for gifted
students, has written a comprehensive summary of current professional
thinking about the gifted. Topics covered include identification, characteristics, educational planning and procedures, and future developments
for the gifted, talented and creative.

63 Mordock, John B.   The other children: an introduction to excep-
    tionality. New York: Harper and Row, 1975. 734p. (Bibliography)
This text was written by a practicing school psychologist who has had
practical experience with all types of atypical development. In Part
V, "The Intellectual Extremes," he devotes fifty-eight pages to the
gifted, citing nearly 200 references to the literature, and recounting
case histories from his own wide experience.

64 Murphy, Mary K. "Finding and teaching the gifted and talented."
    Scholastic Teach 8-10, December, 1973.
Describes some innovative programs now being implemented in North Carolina,
Connecticut, and Nebraska. Covers finding talent, developing talent, and
the efforts in behalf of the gifted at federal, state and local levels.

65 Newland, T. Ernest. The gifted in socio-educational perspective.
    Englewood Cliffs, New Jersey: Prentice-Hall, 1976. 406p.
Discusses the plight of the gifted child, covering the social, psychological, and philosophical considerations involved. Special attention
given to the situation of the gifted in rural areas and to research on
the gifted and their educational needs.

66 Nichols, Robert C. "The origin and development of talent." Natl
    Merit Scholarsh Corp Res Rep 0(10): 1 20, 1966.
The results of past and current studies conducted by NMSC are discussed
in terms of their implications for three broad questions about talent:
(1) What are the characteristics of talented students? (2) How can
we foster the development of talent once it is identified? (3) What
is the origin of talent?

67 Nissen, Myra H. "Flight from mediocrity." Natl Elem Princ 51(5):
    81-88, February, 1972. (20 References)
Reviews efforts made throughout the country in behalf of gifted children.
Innovative and effective programs are described in California, Georgia,
Illinois, Connecticut, Ohio, New York, and Maryland. Identification
procedures, teacher selection and pupil achievement are discussed.

68 Passow, A. Harry, and Goldberg, Miriam L. "The gifted." In: Kirk,
    Samuel A., and Weiner, Bluma B., eds. Behavioral research on
    exceptional children. Washington, D.C.: The Council for

Exceptional Children, N.E.A., 1963.   3-53.
The reviewers limit their citations to the areas of intellectual, creative, and scientific talent.   Their selections are organized under the
following topics: (1) Characteristics of the gifted, (2) Identification of the gifted, (3) Achievement, motivation, and underachievement,
(4) Educational programs.

69   Reynolds, Maynard C.   "Some research-related thoughts on education
       of the gifted."   Except Child   30(1):   6-12, September, 1963.   (24
       References)
Discusses structure of intellectual abilities, decision theory, personal
and social characteristics of the gifted, the study of cognitive processes, and the issue of general versus specialized education.

70   Rice, Joseph P.   The gifted: developing total talent.   Springfield,
       Illinois: Thomas, 1970.   339p.   (Bibliography)
The former co-director of California's Project Talent has written this
book which summarizes the basic elements of educational program development for the talented.   Program goals and student identification procedures are linked to evaluation processes, and studies of actual student
opinions and needs are related to curriculum planning.   Several developmental models for understanding and educating the gifted child are
presented.

71   Shields, James B.   Gifted child.   Atlantic Highlands, New Jersey:
       Humanities Press, 1968.   96p.   (Bibliography)
Deals with the problems and definitions of giftedness and the research
on the ability, personality and achievement of gifted children.   Includes
chapters on creativity and logical thinking, and concludes with educating
the gifted.

72   Stephens, Thomas M., and Gibson, Arthur R., eds.   Pathways to
       progress: a research monograph from Ohio's programs for the gifted
       child.   Columbus, Ohio: Superintendent of Public Instruction, 1963.
       156p.
This research monograph presents information on ten projects and studies
conducted by Ohio for the gifted child.   Teacher attitudes, peer relations, family dynamics, underachievement and effectiveness of individual
and group intelligence tests are some of the topics treated.

73   Telford, Charles W., and Sawrey, James M.   The exceptional individual.
       2nd ed.   Englewood Cliffs, New Jersey: Prentice-Hall, 1972.   562p.
       (Bibliography)
Emphasizes the humanistic viewpoint in dealing with deviant people.
Examination of intellectual exceptionality covers the intellectually
superior, creativity, mild and severe retardation, and learning disabilities.

74   Tempest, N. R.   Teaching clever children, 7-11.   London: Routledge
       and Kegan Paul, 1974.   111p.
Contains a preface, several chapters on observation, inquiry, problem
solving, imaginative work, and further reading.   Covers projects, curriculum and method, divergent thinking, and creativity.

75   Torrance, E. Paul.   Education and the creative potential.
       Minneapolis: University of Minnesota Press, 1963.   167p.   (Biblio-
       graphy)

A collection of seven papers and six experimental studies; includes
chapters on creative teacher-pupil relationship, factors that facilitate
or inhibit creativity, explores the nature of mental health problems of
the highly creative, religious education and creative thinking.

76 ———. "Psychology of gifted children and youth." In:
    Cruickshank, William M., ed. Psychology of exceptional children
    and youth. 3rd ed. Englewood Cliffs, New Jersey: Prentice-Hall,
    1971. 528-64. (Bibliography)
Author states that the acceptance of a more complex concept of giftedness creates many new problems and calls for a reexamination of much of
the research and development of the past. Offers hope for a more humane
and liberating approach to their problems and education.

77 Trapp, E. Philip, and Himelstein, Philip, eds. Readings on the
    exceptional child. New York: Appleton-Century-Crofts, 1972. 674p.
    (Bibliography)
The second edition of this book of readings emphasizes research developments since the publication of the first edition in 1962. The format
remains basically unchanged: the reader will encounter the classics in
the field, along with the trend-forming studies of the present. Section
II, "Exceptional Intellectual Processes," contains three readings on the
gifted, by Terman and Oden, Torrance, and Newland.

78 White, William F., and Williams, R. E. "Identification of creativity
    and the criterion problem." J Second Educ 40(6): 275-81, October,
    1965. (0 References)
The writers give a brief overview of the literature developed since the
early part of the twentieth century which focus on theory and research,
on the query of what is creativity, in what situations can it be found,
and in whom does it exist.

79 Witty, Paul A. "The gifted child in 1967." Gifted Child Q 11(4):
    255-61, Winter, 1967. (22 References)
Deals with publications on the gifted. Touches on neglect of the gifted,
terminology, increased interest, special provision for the gifted, help
in the regular classroom for the gifted, creativity, and scholarship.

80 Ziv, A. T. "The need to foster gifted children." HaHinukh 42(5):
    333 39, June, 1970. (25 References)
Contains a review of the literature on the gifted, and also covers personality processes, and techniques of measurement of educational achievement.

II

Causal Factors

A. Genetic Studies

81 Adler, Manfred. "Reported incidence of giftedness among ethnic
    groups." Except Child 34(2): 101-5, October, 1967. (23 Refer-
    ences)
Purpose of this study was to review some of the major studies of giftedness, as well as studies of the intelligence testing of ethnic groups,
to ascertain if certain groups appear more frequently than others and,
if so, which ones are reported and how consistently they are found.

82 ———. "A study of the effects of ethnic origin on giftedness."
    Gifted Child Q 7(3): 98-101, Autumn, 1963. (19 References)
Presents the information gathered for the author's doctoral dissertation
on ethnic origins of high I.Q. pupils in the Cleveland, Ohio Major Works
Program. Some groups are over-represented in the program, while others
are rarely found in "gifted" classes.

83 ———. "A study of the identification and development of gifted-
    ness in two ethnic groups." For a summary see: Diss Abstr Int
    27A(1): 44, July, 1966. (0 References)

84 Burt, Cyril L. "The gifted child." Br J Stat Psychol 14(2): 123-
    39, 1961. (19 References)
Written to refute environmentalists claims that genetic inheritance is
not responsible for the ability of gifted persons. Gives many case
histories of eminent people whose early environments were negative and
harmful. Also includes an estimate of the relative frequency of gifted
children in the various socio-economic classes of Britain and suggests
ways of improving the method of selection of high ability children.

85 ———. The gifted child. New York: Halsted, 1975. 214p.
    (Bibliography)
The eminent British educational psychologist gives an historical and
reflective introduction to the problem of giftedness for the gifted individual and for society. This is followed by a perceptive commentary
on associated educational and philosophical concepts and a full account
of the mechanism of inheritance and its implications for intelligence.

86 ———. "Is intelligence distributed normally?" Br J Stat Psychol
    16(2): 175-90, November, 1963.
After giving intelligence tests to large samples of British school children, the author concludes that the distributions have larger tails than
the normal curve would provide. Thus, the number of highly gifted children had been underestimated.

87 Cancro, Robert, ed. Intelligence: genetic and environmental in-
     fluences. New York: Grune and Stratton, 1971. 312p. (Bibliography)
This book is the product of a conference on intelligence held at the
University of Illinois. Papers in the first section address themselves
to the different definitions of intelligence and to the variety of ways
of operationalizing these concepts. The second section discusses genetic
contributions to intelligence, both at an individual and population level.
The final section discusses environmental contributions.

88 Dale, M. H. "Intelligent children and early births." Practitioner
     198(1188): 838-41, June, 1967.
The author undertook the present investigation to see if, in a group of
children of known superior intelligence, there was a greater frequency
of early births than occurred in the whole population. He found that
fifty-three of his eighty-five bright subjects were premature births.

89 Erlenmeyer-Kimling, L., and Jarvik, Lissy F. "Genetics and intel-
     ligence: a review." Science 142(3598): 1477-79, December, 1963.
     (8 References)
A survey of the literature of the past fifty years reveals remarkable
consistency in the accumulated data relating mental functioning to genetic
potentials. Intragroup resemblance in intellectual abilities increases
in proportion to the degree of genetic relationship.

90 Groth, Norma J. "Mothers of gifted." Gifted Child Q 19(3): 217-
     22, Fall, 1975. (5 References)
Reports responses to mail questionnaires by mothers of gifted children
in the Greater Los Angeles area. As a group, these women displayed good
mental health and impressive achievements in formal education and careers.

91 Hayes, Keith J. "Genes, drive and intellect." Psychol Rep 10(2):
     299-342, April, 1962. (155 References)
Integrates developments which have occurred recently in behavioral
genetics, motivation and theory of intelligence.

92 Jensen, Arthur R. Genetics and education. London: Methuen, 1972.
     379p. (Bibliography)
Contains Jensen's controversial chapter, "How Much Can We Boost I.Q. and
Scholastic Achievement?" which appeared in Harvard Educational Review.
Mention is made of studies by Terman and Jensen comparing the gifted
with normal and/or retarded.

93 Karowe, Harris E. "Giftedness and creativity." Gifted Child Q
     7(4): 165-75, Winter, 1963. (15 References)
An M.D. discusses the incidence of giftedness and creativity and finds
them closely related. He also considers giftedness a hereditary characteristic, stimulated or augmented by favorable environmental factors.

94 Keating, Daniel P. "Possible sampling bias in genetic studies of
     genius." Educ Psychol Meas 35(3): 657-62, Autumn, 1975. (12
     References)
Data from Terman's Genetic Studies of Genius (1925-1959) relating to
sample size, mean I.Q., and variance of I.Q. scores were analyzed in
terms of their conformation to the theoretically projected statistics
derived from a consideration of the normal curve.

95   Meade, James E., and Parkes, A. S. Genetic and environmental
     factors in human ability. New York: Plenum, 1966. 242p.
Contains the papers presented at the second symposium of Britain's
Eugenics Society. Topics are the nature of intelligence tests, selec-
tion for higher education, and differential fertility and intelligence.
Several studies are cited showing a positive correlation between high
intelligence and high fertility.

96   Nichols, Robert C. "The resemblance of twins in personality and
     interests." Natl Merit Scholarsh Corp Res Rep 2(8): 1-23, 1966.
     (13 References)
The California Psychological Inventory, the Vocational Preference Inventory, and the Objective Behavior Inventory were administered to 498 sets
of MZ twins and 319 sets of DZ twins who were participants in the 1962
National Merit Scholarship Qualifying Test. Intraclass correlations
computed separately by sex showed significantly greater similarity between MZ twins than between DZ twins for most of the inventory scales
and for about half of the individual items.

97   Pauls, David L. "A genetic analysis of mental retardation and high
     intelligence." For a summary see: Diss Abstr Int 33B(5): 1948,
     November, 1972. (0 References)

98   Shouksmith, George A. Intelligence, creativity and cognitive style.
     New York: Wiley-Interscience, 1970. 240p. (Bibliography)
The author avoids the traditional narrowness of such concepts as cognition, thinking-as-problem-solving, creativity and intelligence, and
emphasizes the fluidity and interaction of such processes with one
another and with effect and motivation. He recognizes that high intelligence is necessary, though not sufficient, for creative acts, and
stresses the intimacy of the relationship between genetic and environmental factors in all psychological processes.

B. Environmental Influences

99   Boyer, William H., and Walsh, Paul. "Are children born unequal?"
     Saturday Rev 51, 61-63+, October, 1968.
Challenges the common assumption of contemporary American education,
that people are innately unequal in intellectual capacity and, therefore,
unequal in capacity to learn. Explains the general constancy of most
I.Q. scores as the expected result of limited mobility between social
class and the resultant constancy of subcultural experiences.

100 Curry, Robert L. "Effect of socioeconomic status on the scholastic
     achievement of sixth grade children." Br J Educ Psychol 32(1):
     46-49, February, 1962. (9 References)
Investigation shows that when a child has above average intellectual
ability he will probably overcome the effects of a deprived home environment. However, as the intellectual ability decreases, deprivation
begins to have a more serious effect on scholastic achievement.

101 Deutsch, Martin, and Brown, Bert. "Social influences in Negro-
     white intelligence differences." J Soc Issues 20(2): 24-35,
     April, 1964. (17 References)
This paper reports on some aspects of experience that influence the
development of intellective functions in children. Attention is given
to social environmental and developmental dimensions.

102 Gowan, John C. "Why some gifted children become creative." Gifted
     Child Q 15(1): 13-18, Spring, 1971. (12 References)
The influence of the family environment on the development of creative
propensities in children is explored.

103 Groth, Norma J. "Differences in parental environment needed for
     degree achievement for gifted men and women." Gifted Child Q 15(4):
     256-61, Winter, 1971. (11 References)
Tested the hypothesis that a "warm" opposite sex parent during first
seven years is a positive contributing factor toward achievement of
academic degrees. Results indicate that hypothesis holds true for males.
For females, warmth from both parents is needed.

104 Hansen, Zona S. "The effects of training on the cognitive develop-
     ment of nursery school children." For a summary see: Diss Abstr
     Int 31A(5): 2181, November, 1970. (0 References)

105 Hunt, J. McVickers. "Environment, development, and scholastic
     achievement." In: Deutsch, M.; Katz, T.; Jensen, A. R., eds.
     Social class, race, and psychological development. New York: Holt,
     Rinehart and Winston, 1968. 293-336. (Bibliography)
Hunt states six major beliefs about intelligence that the geneticists
promulgated, and then gives the reasons behind the beliefs, and the
environmentalist theory that has caused changes in these beliefs.

106 ———. Intelligence and experience. New York: Ronald, 1961.
     416p. (Bibliography)
Examines the historical roots of the assumptions of fixed intelligence
and of predetermined development and the evidence that was interpreted
to support them. Cites evidence from many sources which has forced a
recognition of central processes in intelligence and of the crucial role
of life experience in the development of these central processes. Treats
the challenge for education presented by this transformation in the conception of intelligence.

107 Hurley, John R. "Parental acceptance--rejection and children's
     intelligence." Merrill-Palmer Q 11(1): 19-31, January, 1965.
     (38 References)
In this study all third graders in a rural New York county were given
I.Q. tests, and their parents were surveyed and interviewed on child-
rearing practices. Findings clearly indicate that rejectant parental
behaviors have a substantial and damaging impact upon childrens intellectual development. Data suggest that maternal rejection is especially
detrimental to their daughters' I.Q. scores.

108 Husén, Torsten. Talent, equality and meritocracy: availability
     and utilization of talent. The Hague: Martinus Nighoff, 1974.
     157p. (Bibliography)
The author explores conditions under which scholastic talent is developed
and not developed in a group of twenty-year-old youths registered for
military service in Sweden.

109 Ketcham, Warren A. "Learning patterns among the gifted." Sch Soc
     91(2220): 30, January 26, 1963. (0 References)
The writer asserts that the gifted child finds opportunities to learn
even when his environment seems totally against him.

110   Miller, Theresa M.   "A search for talent in economically distressed
      areas." Gifted Child Q 8(4): 179-80, Winter, 1964. (4 References)
In a study covering the entire population of five elementary schools in
Pittsburgh, gifted (116+ I.Q.) children ranged from 1.4 percent to 3.3
percent of total enrollment. Article suggests reasons why incidence is
so much lower than national 16 percent.

111   Pettigrew, Thomas E.   "Negro-American intelligence: a new look at
      an old controversy." J Negro Educ 33(1): 6-25, Winter, 1964.
Intended to refute the geneticists claim that intelligence is inherited,
this article cites numerous studies of black versus white intelligence
and points out flaws in methodology or choice of subjects. Describes
areas where improved environmental conditions improved Negro I.Q. and
achievement scores.

112   Smith, David W.   "A broader concept of giftedness." Education
      82(5): 295-98, January, 1962. (5 References)
Heredity, environment, personal factors, and social factors are analyzed
here, and a two-fold approach is suggested.

113   Weisberg, Paul S., and Springer, Kyla J.   "Environmental factors
      in creative functions: a study of gifted children." Arch Gen
      Psychiatry 5: 554-64, 1961. (16 References)
Thirty-two fourth graders with high I.Q.'s were tested on several variables of creativity. The optimal family pattern is described. Environmental factors are judged essential in the development of creativity.

114   White, Burton L., and Watts, Jean C.   Experience and environment:
      major influences on the development of the young child. Englewood
      Cliffs, New Jersey: Prentice-Hall, 1973. 552p.
Reports data from the first two years of the Harvard Preschool Project,
a longitudinal study of the psychological development of thirty-one preschool aged children. Contrasts the development of the A (bright) children with that of the C (dull) children in respect to child-rearing
techniques.

III

Characteristics of the Gifted

A. Dimensions of Talent

1. Academic

115 Aiken, Lewis R., Jr. "Ability and creativity in mathematics." Rev
     Educ Res 43(4): 405-32, Fall, 1973. (129 References)
This paper considers how cognitive variables and affective attitudes and
personality aspects combine to produce mathematical creativity. It also
contains practical suggestions for teachers who would be creative in
teaching math.

116 Anastasi, Ann. "Commentary on the precocity project." J Spec
     Educ 9(1): 93-103, Spring, 1975. (23 References)
Evaluates four papers on the precocity of seventh and eighth graders in
mathematics and science presented by Stanley, Keating, Fox, and Astin.

117 Astin, Helen S. "Sex differences in mathematical and scientific
     precocity." J Spec Educ 9(1): 79-91, Spring, 1975. (17 Refer-
     ences)
Examined Keating's finding that many more seventh and eighth grade males
than females were precocious in mathematics in terms of available evidence and opinions concerning biological and social causes for reported
sex differences in mathematical ability.

118 Bachtold, Louise M. "Effects of learning environment on verbal
     creativity of gifted students." Psychol Sch 11(2): 226-28,
     April, 1974. (8 References)
The verbal productivity of fifty-eight gifted fifth and sixth grade
pupils enrolled in special class programs, enrichment programs, and
learning center programs was studied by means of the Torrance Tests of
Creative Thinking. No significant differences were found in fluency,
flexibility, or originality in the different learning settings.

119 Blaeuer, David A. "Gifted college and secondary mathematics
     students--process oriented case studies of creativity." For a
     summary see: Diss Abstr Int 34A(5): 2454, November, 1973. (0
     References)

120 Cline, Victor B.; Richards, James M., Jr.; Needham, Walter E.
     "Creativity tests and achievement in high school science." J Appl
     Sci 47(3): 184-89, June, 1963. (12 References)
This study investigated the relative validities of a battery of "crea-

tivity tests" and an I.Q. test for predicting several indices of achievement in high school science. The creativity battery was found to have
considerable predictive validity, especially for boys.

121   Durkin, Dolores. Children who read early. New York: Teachers
        College Press, Columbia University, 1966. 174p.
Describes the results of two longitudinal studies of first grade children
in California and New York who learned to read before entering school.
Although the I.Q. ranges were wide, median I.Q.'s of the early readers
were high (121 in California and 133 in New York).

122   ———. "An early start in reading?" Elem Sch J 63(3):   147-51,
        December, 1962.
A longitudinal study of children who could read when they entered first
grade found that their actual scores in reading in third grade were
greater than would have been predicted for them on the basis of their
intelligence. As to the fifteen early readers with I.Q.'s of 120 or
less, they profited from the early start, and the lower the I.Q., the
greater the advantage of starting early.

123   Dyasi, Hubert M. "An exploratory investigation of certain affec-
        tive behaviors associated with the learning of science." For a
        summary see: Diss Abstr Int 27A(11): 3770, May, 1967. (0
        References)

124   Gallagher, James J., and Lucito, Leonard J. "Intellectual patterns
        of gifted compared with average and retarded." Except Child 27(9):
        479-82, May, 1961. (21 References)
The gifted in this study appear strongest on Verbal Comprehension on the
WISC, while they are poorest in Perceptual Organization. Discusses
implications for education of gifted. Says their curriculum should be
analytical and evaluative.

125   Garrett, Alfred B. The flash of genius. Princeton, New Jersey:
        Van Nostrand, 1963. 249p. (Bibliography)
Offers teachers and students a series of case studies of scientific
geniuses who have made discoveries which changed the way of life for
humankind. Concludes with appendices which list the nationalities of
those men of science and the very early ages at which they made their
great discoveries.

126   Gibson, William C. "The Genesis of new ideas in science." Gifted
        Child Q 6(4): 130-38, Winter, 1962. (19 References)
Discusses contributions of Jenner, Freud, Hickman, Ehrlich, Loewy,
Banting, Mayer, and other great medical science discoverers.

127   Hansen, Richard A., and Neujahr, James L. "A comparison of career
        development between males and females gifted in science." In:
        American Psychological Association, 81st, Montreal, 1973.
        Proceedings. 8(2): 667-68, 1973. (0 References)
High school students enrolled in the Science Honors Program at Columbia
University from 1959-1962 were studied. Their median I.Q. was 135.
Males showed preference for the physical sciences and math, while
females favored biology. Males were also more actively involved in
science, winning more awards, having more science-related hobbies, and
having labs in their homes.

128 Hauck, Barbara B. "Stimulating the development of semantic evaluation abilities of gifted children." For a summary see: Diss Abstr
Int 27A(11): 372-73, May, 1967. (0 References)

129 Holland, John L., and Richards, James M. "Academic and nonacademic
accomplishment: correlated and uncorrelated." J Educ Psychol
56(4): 165-74, August, 1965. (20 References)
Over 7,000 college freshmen attending twenty-four different schools were
rated on academic achievement and extracurricular activities. Results
suggest that these two areas are relatively independent dimensions of
talent. Implications of the findings for the selection of talented persons and the conservation of talent are discussed.

130 Jacobs, Jon C. "Intellectual, academic and personality growth in
young gifted children as a function of cognitive style, conceptual
tempo, sex, and teacher attributes." For a summary see: Diss Abstr
Int 30A(9): 3788, March, 1970. (0 References)

131 Jensen, Julie M. "Do gifted children speak an intellectual
dialect?" Except Child 39(4): 337-38, January, 1973. (0 References)
Recounts a study which compared forty fifth grade students of average
ability with forty superior fifth graders in the areas of casual and
careful oral language fluency, grammatical control, and function. Significant differences occurred on thirty-eight of 147 comparisons.

132 Johnson, Carolyne M. "The creative thinking, verbal intelligence,
and creative writing ability of young gifted children." For a
summary see: Diss Abstr Int 29A(12): 4187, June, 1969. (0 References)

133 Keating, Daniel P. "The study of mathematically precocious youth."
J Spec Educ 9(1): 45-62, Spring, 1975. (19 References)
Describes an outstanding project for the selection and acceleration of
precocious seventh and eighth grade science and mathematics students.
Corollary information on family background and school performance is
examined.

134 ———, ed. Intellectual talent: research and development.
Baltimore: Johns Hopkins University Press, 1976. 346p. (Biblio-
graphy)
Based on the Sixth Annual Hyman Blumberg Symposium on Research in Early
Childhood Education held at Johns Hopkins University in 1974. Contains
abstracts of the seventeen papers presented there, most of which are
from the Study of Mathematically Precocious Youth and the Study of
Verbally Gifted Youth undertaken at Johns Hopkins with the aid of the
Spencer Foundation.

135 Kemeny, John G. "Mathematically talented student." Natl Assoc
Second Sch Princ Bull 47(282): 26-40, April, 1963. (0 References)
Address given at the annual convention of the NASSP by Dr. Kemeny, Chairman of Mathematics Department at Dartmouth College. He describes the
vast amount of latent mathematical talent in the U.S. which is lost at
every level of the educational system.

136   Ketcham, Warren A.   "What do we know about gifted children?"   <u>High</u>
      <u>Sch J</u>   48(2):   82–87, November, 1964.
Discusses academic achievement, learning styles, and personal characteristics of gifted.   Makes recommendations that a well-planned testing
program is necessary, that academic data can be used to improve public
relations, that educational acceleration is of value, and that a more
generous use of independent study would be wise.

137   Krippner, Stanley.   "Characteristics of gifted children."   <u>Education</u>
      88(1):   15–21, September/October, 1967.   (28 References)
Krippner reports the results of recent studies of the characteristics of
gifted children and concludes that in many schools their abilities are
not properly cultivated.

138   Krutetskii, V. A.   <u>The psychology of mathematical abilities in</u>
      <u>schoolchildren</u>.   Chicago: University of Chicago Press, 1976.   417p.
      (Bibliography)
The Russian author presents the results of a twelve-year research program investigating the structure of mathematical abilities in school
children.   Nine case studies of gifted student mathematicians are cited,
and twenty-six sets of experimental problems are included.

139   McNary, Susan; Michael, William B.; Richards, Leo.   "The relation-
      ship of conservation tasks from the concept assessment kit to the
      SRA primary mental abilities battery for a sample of fifty-six
      kindergarten children."   <u>Educ Psychol Meas</u>   33(4):   967–69, Winter,
      1973.   (2 References)
Findings indicate that the tasks from the concept assessment kit tended
to reflect Piaget's construct of conservation were significantly related
to both chronological age and to quantitative ability, but were relatively independent of verbal ability.

140   Maw, Wallace H., and Maw, Ethel W.   "Children's curiosity as an
      aspect of reading comprehension."   <u>Read Teach</u>   15(4):   236–40,
      January, 1962.   (5 References)
Supports the hypothesis that children with high curiosity tend to sense
the meaning of sentences more accurately than do low curiosity children.

141   Miller, Napoleon A., Jr.   "An analysis of selected characteristics
      of gifted children."   For a summary see: <u>Diss Abstr Int</u>   25(3):
      1658–59, September, 1964.   (0 References)

142   Moore, Arthur D.   <u>Invention, discovery, and creativity.</u>   Garden
      City, New York: Doubleday, 1969.   178p.   (Bibliography)
One of the Science Study Series, this book is designed to explain and
stimulate creativity and ingenuity among those gifted in science and
engineering.   Discussed are intelligence versus creativity, failure of
college grades to reward creativity, and divergent and convergent
thinking as needed by scientists and inventors.

143   Namy, Elmer.   "Intellectual and academic characteristics of fourth
      grade gifted and pseudogifted students."   <u>Except Child</u>   34(1):
      15–18, September, 1967.   (13 References)
A group of thirty-two gifted fourth graders with a mean I.Q. of 126 was
compared with a group of the same size which had been misdiagnosed as
gifted by their teachers (I.Q. 110).   The pseudogifted performed as well

as the gifted on WISC coding and arithmetic subtests and showed significantly lower classroom grades only in the subject of English.

144 Nichols, Robert C., and Davis, James A. "Characteristics of
     students of high academic aptitude." Pers Guid J 42(8): 794-800,
     April, 1964. (4 References)
A group of college seniors who had been National Merit semi-finalists at
high school graduation were compared with a group of college seniors who
were selected to be representative of all graduating college seniors in
the United States. The Merit students differed significantly from the
average students on many aspects of personality, attitude, interest,
career plans, and family background.

145 Pearce, Clifford. "Creativity in young science students." Except
     Child 35(2): 121-26, October, 1968. (6 References)
Compared high school eleventh grade science students on personality
inventories with scores of college students and eminent research scientists. Science students differed from the other groups on a majority of
personality factors.

146 Price, Eunice H. "How thirty-seven gifted children learned to
     read." Read Teach 30(1): 44-48, October, 1976. (7 References)
Presents a profile of thirty-seven students in a program for the gifted
in Palm Beach, Florida. Their early reading experiences at home and at
school are described.

147 Schulman, Paul. "The relationship of certain personality factors
     to the quantitative ability of gifted male adolescents." For a
     summary see: Diss Abstr Int 25(4): 2355, October, 1964. (0
     References)

148 Silverblank, Francine. "Sense of responsibility, level of anxiety,
     and sociability in suburban male high school seniors who are
     talented in mathematics and those talented in English." For a
     summary see: Diss Abstr Int 31A(12): 6414, June, 1971. (0
     References)

149 Snyder, William R. "The question-asking behavior of gifted junior
     high school science students and their teachers." For a summary
     see: Diss Abstr Int 27A(11): 2729, May, 1967. (0 References)

150 Stanley, Julian C. "Youths who reason extremely well mathematically:
     SMPY's accelerative approach." Gifted Child Q 20(3): 237-38,
     Fall, 1976. (7 References)
As guest editor of this issue of the journal, Dr. Stanley, Director of
the Study of Mathematically Precocious Youth at Johns Hopkins University,
describes the project and its participants.

151 Strang, Ruth. "Able reader." Instructor 74(7): 83+, March, 1965.
Discusses characteristics of the able reader and stresses that the
teacher must ascertain child's readiness, proficiency and ability, not
bore him with instruction he does not need, and provide him with meaningful and enjoyable reading experiences.

152 Swiss, Thom, and Olsen, Turee. "ERIC/RCS: reading and gifted
     children." Read Teach 29(4): 428-29+, January, 1976.

Reviews the literature in the Educational Resources Information Center
on various aspects of gifted children's reading problems.

153   Taylor, Calvin W., and Barron, Frank. Scientific creativity: its
      recognition and development. New York: Wiley, 1966. 419p.
      (Bibliography)
Papers from conferences on the creative in science. Includes thirty-one
readings on the criterion, characteristics, environmental conditions,
and analyses of process.

154   Torrey, Jane W. "Learning to read without a teacher." Elem Engl
      46(5): 550-56+, May, 1969.
Study of child learning to read. Author believes that reading is learned
not taught. Says the key to learning is asking the right questions of
print. Also believes high verbal ability and high cultural status are
not necessary.

155   Walberg, Herbert J. "A portrait of the artist and scientist as
      young men." Except Child 36(1): 5-11, September, 1969. (16
      References)
Describes "Harvard Project Physics" which chose a sample of 771 students
from physics students in seventy-two classrooms in sixteen states. On
the basis of biographical information, three subgroups were established:
those with superior science achievements, those with similar achievements in the arts, and those with no special achievements. Comparisons
were then made of the three groups.

156   Welsh, George S. "Verbal interests and intelligence: comparison
      of strong VIB, Terman CMT, and D-48 scores of gifted adolescents."
      Educ Psychol Meas 27(2): 349-52, Summer, 1967.
A consistent relationship between verbal interests and intelligence has
been demonstrated in gifted adolescents. Students scoring relatively
high on a verbal as compared with a nonverbal test of intelligence show
higher interest scores on verbal-linguistic scales.

157   Whittaker, Dora. "That rare phenomenon the gifted pupil." Math
      Sch 3(2): 2-5, March, 1974.
A British teacher of mathematics defines students gifted in that discipline as possessing uncanny insight, intuitive grasp, and mathematical
flair. She then describes a scholarly investigation done by a nine-year
old pupil, with his follow-up at the age of eleven. She concludes with
the case of an eleven-year old who taught himself calculus.

2. Artistic

158   Cross, Peter G.; Cattell, Raymond B.; Butcher, H. J. "The person-
      ality pattern of creative artists." Br J Educ Psychol 37(3):
      292-99, November, 1967. (14 References)
In this study, sixty-three visual artists and twenty-eight crafts
students were compared with a matched control group of teacher trainees
in other areas. Significant differences between the artists and controls were found on twelve of the sixteen factors in the personality
test employed. Scores of the crafts students were intermediate between
those of the artists and the controls.

159 Hammer, Emanuel F. "Artistic creativity: giftedness or sickness."
     Art Psychother 2(2): 173-75, 1975.
Artistic creativity is discussed as an ability to tolerate and transform
emotional stress. Prominent figures throughout history are cited to
illustrate the author's viewpoint.

160 Lowenfeld, Viktor, and Brittain, W. Lambert. Creative and mental
     growth. New York: Macmillan, 1968. 412p. (Bibliography)
Uses the area of the fine arts to show how the child's general growth is
tied up with his creative development. Uses many examples of work by
talented art students to illustrate the interdependence between creation
and growth.

161 Lyon, Jean W. "Reincarnation." Art Act 78: 30-31, 1975.
Gives several examples of artistic projects made by gifted art students
from old, "useless" ecological items. The gifted child's exploration of
new and strange materials, with or without the aid of adults, makes his
own creative life and our appreciation of it all the more full.

162 Miller, Vera V. "Creativity and intelligence in the arts."
     Education 82(8): 488-95, April, 1962. (0 References)
Reports data from an Evanston, Illinois study of creative performance of
academically talented fifth, sixth and seventh graders compared to that
of average peers. After evaluating writing, drama, music, symbolic
thinking, and word association, judges found a significant correlation
between intelligence and giftedness in all areas examined.

163 Rossman, Betty B. "Art, creativity, and the elephant: some clues
     to artistic creativity among the gifted." Gifted Child Q 20(4):
     392-401, Winter, 1976. (27 References)
Begins with a review of recent research on creativity. For this study,
data were obtained for 188 undergraduate and graduate students, half of
them majoring in different areas of art and the other half in different
fields of engineering. Results provide some clues to use in identifying
students creative in art according to both judgmental and production
criteria.

164 Salome, Richard A. "Identifying and instructing the gifted in art."
     Art Educ 27(3): 16-19, March, 1974. (14 References)
The author notes that art instruction is often neglected in schools that
stress the academic subjects. He summarizes the results of research
which attempts to distinguish the artistically gifted from the average,
and offers suggestions for teacher initiated activities to help identify
and provide for the gifted in art.

165 Saray, Julia. "How a musical gift modifies the personality of teen-
     agers." Acta Paedopsychiatr 36(5): 123-27, May, 1969. (3
     References)
Presents the results of the author's psychological research in the field
of music comprehension in relation to the personality of fourteen to
sixteen-year old gifted youth studying at a Budapest Conservatory. Psycho-
neurotic symptoms occurred more frequently among these young musicians
than among secondary school pupils of comparable intelligence. Sex differences were striking, with musical boys showing much greater maladjustment than girls.

B.   Familial-Cultural Background

166   Albert, Robert S.   "Cognitive development and parental loss among
      the gifted, the exceptionally gifted and the creative."   Psychol
      Rep   29(1):   19-26, August, 1971.   (21 References)
Describes characteristics of "exceptionally gifted" children (I.Q. 155+)
and contrasts their cognitive development with that of gifted children.
Discusses high rate of parental loss among historically famous, highly
gifted persons and how this might contribute to activate cognitive
giftedness into high level creative behavior.

167   Aldous, Joan.   "Family background factors and originality in chil-
      dren."   Gifted Child Q   17(3):   183-92, Fall, 1973.   (26 References)
Examined were factors of sex, social class, family size, ordinal position,
and school class composition (blue or white collar) on the originality
of third graders.

168   Armstrong, H. G.   "Wastage of ability amongst the intellectually
      gifted."   Br J Educ Psychol   37(2):   257-59, June, 1967.   (4
      References)
In a follow-up of students with 135+ I.Q.'s, more than twice as many from
professional homes entered full time higher education, even though GCE
levels of both the professional and working class homes were not significantly different.

169   Bernal, Ernest M., Jr.   "Gifted Mexican American children: an
      ethnoscientific perspective."   Calif J Educ Res   25(5):   261-73,
      November, 1974.   (27 References)
This research was undertaken to determine if behavioral descriptors used
by adult Mexican-Americans could be used to differentiate gifted Chicano
children from their average peers.   Chicano views on giftedness are summarized, and implications for cross-cultural research and education are
discussed.

170   Besdine, Matthew.   "Mrs. Oedipus has daughters, too."   Psychol Today
      4(10):   62-65, 99, March, 1971.   (0 References)
Besdine says that very intense mothering is "a necessary, though not sufficient, condition for both male and female geniuses to develop."

171   Chambers, Juanita, and Dusseault, Betty.   "Characteristics of
      college-age gifted."   In: American Psychological Association, 80th,
      Honolulu, 1972.   Proceedings.   7(2):   527-28, 1972.   (3 References)
Compared 200 gifted Canadian college students with average college classmates.   Greatest differences were found in socioeconomic status and
parental education.   In educational achievements, gifted were only
slightly higher, with female subjects showing consistent superiority to
males.

172   Chen, Jocelyn, and Goon, Suzanne W.   "Recognition of the gifted
      from among disadvantaged Asian children."   Gifted Child Q   20(2):
      157-64, Summer, 1976.   (11 References)
The authors report a surprisingly high number of gifted oriental students
in seven junior high schools of New York's Chinatown.   Their findings
show that conventional intelligence tests present no barrier to gifted
Asian youth, even though English is not spoken in the home.

173   Cicirelli, Victor G. "Sibling constellation, creativity, I.Q. and
      academic achievement." Child Dev 38(2): 481-90, June, 1967. (17
      References)
Sibling constellation factors were related to measures of creativity.
Family size was found to be unrelated to ability and achievement. So
was birth order in 3+4 child families. However, in a three-child family
where sibling's had two brothers, the I.Q. was poorer than in a home
with at least one sister. In a two-sibling home, verbal creative abilities, reading, and arithmetic achievement were enhanced for siblings
with siblings of like sex close in age.

174   Frierson, Edward C. "A study of selected characteristics of gifted
      children from upper and lower socioeconomic backgrounds." For a
      summary see: Diss Abstr Int 28A(2): 495, August, 1967. (0
      References)

175   ———. "Upper and lower status gifted children: a study of dif-
      ferences." Except Child 32(2): 83-90, October, 1965. (13
      References)
Using students enrolled in the Cleveland Major Work Program, the author
measured interests, activities, personality traits, creativity, stature,
and school achievement. Upper status gifted pupils differed from lower
status gifted pupils in the quantity and quality of their reading, in
their positive attitudes toward school, in their lower preference for
competitive team sports, and in their awareness of parental aspirations
for college attendance.

176   Gallagher, James J. "The disadvantaged gifted." In: Tannenbaum,
      Abraham J., ed. Special education and programs for disadvantaged
      children and youth. Washington, D.C.: Council for Exceptional
      Children, 1968. 42-58.
Discusses human resources in our society and cites many studies of intellectual and academic ability among culturally deprived sub-groups.
Reviews characteristics of disadvantaged talented, and ends with implications of research findings for education.

177   Getzels, Jacob, W., and Jackson, Philip W. "Family environment and
      cognitive style: a study of the sources of highly intelligent and
      of highly creative adolescents." Am Sociol Rev 26(3): 351-59,
      June, 1961. (0 References)
Two groups of adolescents were studied: (a) those exceptionally high
in I.Q., but not concomitantly high in creativity, and (b) those
exceptionally high in creativity, but lower in I.Q. The groups were
found to differ not only in intellective and social behavior, but to
have their source in differing family environments.

178   Johnson, Russell M. "A comparison of gifted adolescents from high
      and low socioeconomic backgrounds on school achievement and person-
      ality traits." For a summary see: Diss Abstr Int 27A(10): 3226-
      27, April, 1967. (0 References)

179   Lesser, Gerald; Fifer, Gordon; Clark, Donald H. Mental abilities
      of children in different social class and cultural groups. Chicago:
      University of Chicago Press, 1965. 115p.
The purpose of this study is to examine the patterns among various mental
abilities in first-grade children from different social class and cultural

backgrounds. The patterns among four ability areas are studied within
four cultural groups in New York City (Puerto Rican, Negro, Chinese, and
Jewish).

180   McGillivray, R. H. "Differences in home background between high-
      achieving and low-achieving gifted children: a study of one hundred
      grade eight pupils in the city of Toronto public schools." Ontario
      J Educ Res 6(2): 99-106, Spring, 1964. (19 References)
This study investigated the differences between the high and low achievers
in eighth grade with I.Q.'s of 130+. More of the high achievers had
dominant mothers, while the low achievers families were father-dominant.
Most important were parents attitudes and assistance in their child's
education.

181   Morrow, William R., and Wilson, Robert C. "Family relations of
      bright high-achieving and underachieving high school boys." Child
      Dev 32(3): 501-10, September, 1961. (20 References)
Results supported the hypothesis that family morale fosters academic
achievement among bright high school boys via fostering positive attitudes
toward teachers, school and interest in intellectual activities. Also
reports on other characteristics of high achievers parents.

182   Nichols, Robert C. "The financial status of able students." Science
      149(3688): September 3, 1965. (7 References)
Author collected data on the family incomes of talented high school
seniors taking the N.M.S.Q.T. Here he is concerned with two questions:
(1) what proportion of able students of college age are from low income
families? and (2) what is the relationship between funds expended for
primary and secondary education and the achievement of students from
low-income families?

183   ————. "Parental attitudes of mothers of intelligent adolescents
      and creativity of their children." Child Dev 35(4): 1041-49,
      December, 1964. (11 References)
Study found that authoritarian child-rearing attitudes of the mother were
negatively related to measures of the creativity and originality of the
child but were positively related to academic performance.

184   Norman, Ralph D. "The interpersonal values of parents of achieving
      and non-achieving gifted children." J Psychol 64(1): 49-57,
      September, 1966. (23 References)
Parents of gifted children who had been categorized as achievers or non-
achievers were given the Gordon Survey. The identification process was
strongly operative. Fathers of achieving boys and mothers of achieving
girls made significantly higher mean scores in independence and lower
scores in conformity than the same sexed parents of non-achievers. Correlations on mother-father pairs of achievers were less variable than
for parents of non-achievers.

185   Ostrom, Gladys. "The self-concept of gifted children grows through
      freedom of choice, freedom of movement and freedom to do what is
      right." Gifted Child Q 17(4): 285-87, Winter, 1974. (0 Refer-
      ences)
Suggests that a gifted child who comes from a school and home environment
providing these three freedoms will be more likely to develop a healthy
self-concept than one whose freedom is greatly restricted.

186   Schaefer, Charles E.   "A psychological study of 10 exceptionally
      creative adolescent girls."   Except Child   36(6):   431-41, February,
      1970.   (17 References)
Examines the family backgrounds, educational backgrounds, self-concepts,
leisure time and school interests, and personality assessments of these
very talented students.

187   Simmons, Ernest R., Jr.   "A sociological study of the top one hun-
      dred eighth-grade students in the state of Iowa, 1964-65 school
      year."   For a summary see: Diss Abstr Int   28A(8):   3042, February,
      1968.   (0 References)

188   Stevens, Frances.   The new inheritors.   London: Hutchinson Educa-
      tional, 1970.   198p.
Subtitled, "Some Questions About the Education of Intelligent 'First-
Generation' Children," this book grew out of the author's concern for
the "new inheritors," academically talented children whose parents had
only limited education.   It contains much information about ability-
grouping, class structure and pupils attitudes toward school in England.

189   Stronck, David R.   "The sociological backgrounds of scientifically
      talented secondary school students throughout the state of Texas."
      J Res Sci Teach   11(1):   31-37, January, 1974.   (4 References)
It was found that larger schools, larger communities, early science
career selection, and a home environment fostering scholarship favored
better achievement by modern science students.

190   Wieder, Herbert.   "Intellectuality: aspects of its development from
      the analysis of a precocious four-and-a-half-year-old boy."
      Psychoanal Study Child   21:   294-323, 1966.   (43 References)
Presents a case study of a gifted pre-schooler who was exposed to prolonged states of tension by inept mothering and fathering.   His intellectuality is viewed as a way of functioning adaptively or defensively,
depending on the changing level of drive tension.

                          C. Behavioral Characteristics

191   Albert, Robert S.   "Toward a behavioral definition of genius."   Am
      Psychol   30(2):   140-51, February, 1975.   (72 References)
Offers data from several studies showing that eminent persons do in fact
evidence an earlier, more continuous productivity than most of their
peers.   The socio-psychological implications of this finding are discussed.

192   Barbe, Walter B., and Frierson, Edward C.   "Approaching a study of
      behavioral patterns."   Education   85(3):   137-42, November, 1964.
      (0 References)
Reports on a project at Kent State University in which a number of gifted
pre-adolescents were given special opportunities to gain insights into
human behavior.

193   Birnbaum, Judith L.   "Life patterns, personality style and self
      esteem in gifted family oriented and career committed women."   For
      a summary see: Diss Abstr Int   32B(3):   1834, September, 1971.
      (0 References)

194   Bruch, Catherine B.   "Children with intellectual superiority."   In:
      Gallagher, James J., ed.   The application of child development
      research to exceptional children.   Reston, Virginia: The Council
      for Exceptional Children, 1975.   245-261.   (Bibliography)
Summarizes the trends reported in the literature on the gifted, and gives
a brief overview of development, socialization, and learning of the
gifted.

195   Bryan, J.   "Who needs computers with mathematical prodigies like
      these?"   Horizon   12(2):   46-47, Spring, 1970.
Describes many youthful prodigies called "eidetics," who were possessed
of fabulously powerful memories.   Of all the precocious examples given
here, only one was a normal man; the rest all had some defect or flaw to
counterbalance their "genius."

196   Burke, Barbara P.   "An exploratory study of the relationships among
      third grade Negro children's self-concept, creativity, and intel-
      ligence, and teachers' perceptions of those relationships."   For a
      summary see: Diss Abstr Int   30A(4):   1327-28, October, 1969.   (0
      References)

197   Drews, Elizabeth M.   The creative intellectual style in gifted
      adolescents: process and product: a reassessment of students and
      programs.   East Lansing: Michigan State University, 1965.   285p.
      (Bibliography)
Studied all gifted students (I.Q. 120+) in grades ten, eleven, and twelve.
Found that intellectual, creative, and ethical dimensions of psychological
growth would be stunted or warped if youths' development toward identity
did not find a responsive and evocative environment.

198   ————.   "Critical evaluation of approaches to the identification
      of gifted students."   In: Traxler, Arthur E., ed.   Measurement and
      research in today's school.   Washington, D.C.:   American Council on
      Education, 1961.   109-21.
Discusses problems gifted have and divides them into categories: the
studious,   social leaders, creative intellectuals, and rebels.   Discusses
characteristics of each.

199   ————.   "The four faces of able adolescents."   Saturday Rev   46:
      68-71, January 19, 1963.   (0 References)
Result of an eight-year study by the author of able adolescents in the
public schools of Lansing, Michigan and Buffalo, New York.   Research included intensive case studies, as well as studies of the records, interests, and creative products of about a thousand gifted children.   Four
distinct categories of able adolescents emerged: the high-achieving
studious, the social leaders, the creative intellectuals, and the rebels.

200   Duncan, Ann D.   "Behavior rates of gifted and regular elementary
      school children."   For a summary see: Diss Abstr Int   29A(10):
      3520, April, 1969.   (0 References)

201   Entwistle, N. J., and Welsh, Jennifer.   "Correlates of school
      attainment at different ability levels."   Br J Educ Psychol   39(1):
      57-63, February, 1969.   (11 References)
Correlations between school attainment and various intellectual, personality and social variables were reported for the top and bottom thirds

of 2538 children. Suggests that secondary school attainment is more difficult to predict in the high ability group. Academic motivation is more closely related to school attainment for the high ability group. Among bright boys, extraversion [sic] is negatively related to attainment, but in the low ability group the relationship is positive.

202 Faunce, Patricia S. "Personality characteristics and vocational
     interests related to the college persistence of academically gifted
     women." J Couns Psychol 15(1): 31-40, January, 1968. (22
     References)
Review of author's dissertation, which revealed that gifted college non-graduates had less insight into personality structures, greater difficulty in interpersonal relationships, more problems with impulse control, and greater inner tensions. Graduates were more insightful, conventional, temperate, modest, self-confident, and relatively free from tension.

203 Feldhusen, John F; Denny, Terry; Condon, Charles F. "Anxiety,
     divergent thinking, and achievement." J Educ Psychol 56(1): 40-
     45, February, 1965. (11 References)
Study found that high anxiety students were lower than low anxiety students on school and college achievement tests and sequential test of educational progress, but difference on divergent thinking scores was not significant.

204 Feldhusen, John F., and Klausmeier, Herbert J. "Anxiety, intelli-
     gence and achievement in children of low, average and high
     intelligence." Child Dev 33: 403-09, 1962. (8 References)
Forty low, forty average and forty high (120+) I.Q. pupils of fifth grade age were compared on scores on the Children's Manifest Anxiety Scale. The low and average I.Q. children showed much greater anxiety than did the high group. The mean anxiety level for girls was significantly higher than for boys.

205 Feldman, David H., and Bratton, Joseph C. "Relativity and gifted-
     ness: implications for equality of educational opportunity."
     Except Child 38(6): 491-92, February, 1972. (0 References)
Eighteen measures of achievement, intelligence and creativity were administered to two fifth grade classes. The top five students on each measure were selected for a hypothetical program for the gifted. Ninety-two percent were selected on one or more criteria, and none on all criteria.

206 Flescher, Irwin. "Anxiety and achievement of intellectually gifted
     and creatively gifted children." J Psychol 56(2): 251-68,
     October, 1963. (16 References)
Study compared effects of exceptional intellectual potential and unusual creative aptitude on academic achievement. Results consistently demonstrated the significant role of intelligence in scholastic performance, while creativity was not determined to be related to academic success.

207 Forehand, Garlie A. "Relationship among response sets and cogni-
     tive behaviors." Educ Psychol Meas 22(2): 287-302, Summer, 1962.
     (23 References)
Presents research on response sets (a tendency causing a person consistently to give different response to test items than he would when the same content is presented in different form), including the tendency to

prefer positively worded alternatives, tendency to gamble, tendency to
strive for speed, preference for middle category, and preference for
extremely worded responses.

208   Frierson, Edward C. "Gifted child with specific learning disabili-
        ties." Except Child 34(6): 387-88, February, 1968.
Preview of paper to be presented at conference uses biographical analysis
of gifted to show some had disabilities, a summary of literature on gifted,
a study of selection practices of the gifted, an educator's interpretation of several exceptional abilities and disabilities as they affect
classroom performance, and a presentation of teaching strategies.

209   Gallagher, James J. "Expressive thought by gifted children in the
        classroom." Elem Engl 42(5): 559-68, May, 1965. (13 References)
The expressive behavior of gifted children at the junior and senior high
level was studied by analyzing class sessions. It seemed to be dependent
on the teacher's style of question asking, the student's sex, the
teacher's goals, class composition, and the attitudes and personalities
of the students. Consistent sex differences suggested that different
patterns of attitudes and cognitive skills underlie expressive behavior
of boys and girls.

210   ———. "Sex differences in expressive thought of gifted children
        in the classroom." Pers Guid J 45(3): 248-53, November, 1966.
        (11 References)
Compared ninety-two high-achieving gifted girls with ninety-two high-
achieving gifted boys on cognitive thinking, classroom expressiveness,
self-concept, and attitudes. The boys were significantly more expressive than the girls on all classroom variables.

211   Gardner, Thomas D., and Barnard, James W. "Intelligence and the
        factorial structure of person perception." Am J Ment Defic 74(2):
        212-17, September, 1969. (9 References)
Investigated the relationship between intelligence and the factorial
structure of person perception. Concluded that intelligence is a deter-
minant of person perception.

212   Gath, Dennis; Tennent, Gavin; Pidduck, Ronald. "Criminological
        characteristics of bright delinquents." Br J Criminol 11(3): 275-
        79, July, 1971. (13 References)
Compared the criminal characteristics of fifty delinquent boys with
superior intelligence to fifty average delinquents. The bright boys made
their first court appearance at a later age. More high I.Q. boys seemed
to commit offenses which were psychologically determined. The bright
boys were treated more leniently by the courts.

213   ———. "Educational characteristics of bright delinquents." Br
        J Educ Psychol 40(2): 216-19, June, 1970. (8 References)
A group of fifty delinquent boys of superior intelligence were found to
be under-functioning educationally, as shown by inappropriate school
placements, poor school attendance, low levels of attainment in public
examinations, and unsatisfactory relationships at school.

214   Gensley, Juliana. "The gifted child in the affective domain."
        Gifted Child Q 19(4): 307-09, Winter, 1975. (6 References)
Briefly discusses the implications of Mager's behavioral objectives as
applied in the affective domain to the gifted child.

215 Gilbert, Valorie S. "Stereotypes of the gifted: an experimental
     analysis." For a summary see: Diss Abstr Int 30B(10): 4776-77,
     April, 1970. (0 References)

216 Gottlieb, David, ed. Youth in contemporary society. Beverly Hills,
     California: Sage Publications, 1971. 384p.
Attempts to identify how different kinds of youth will be reacting to
different aspects of the social system in the years ahead. Essays include
"Black Brainpower: Characteristics of Bright Black Youth" and "Bright
Achievers: Their Characteristics and Some Expected Behavior Patterns."

217 Groth, Norma J. "The relationship of the affective needs of a sample
     of intellectually gifted adults to their age, sex, and perceptions of
     emotional warmth to their parents." For a summary see: Diss Abstr
     Int 35A(1): 286, July, 1974. (0 References)

218 Gunn, John. "A note on the gifted child and early language develop-
     ment." Gifted Child Q 10(4): 180-82, Winter, 1966. (14 Refer-
     ences)
Arguments are often given for a reciprocal cause and effect relationship
between language skill and high or low intelligence. Upon comparison of
an intellectually superior group of nursery school children with an average group on a number of speech skills, the author found the gifted
producing more complex utterances and making fewer errors than their
average peers.

219 Hoepfner, Ralph, and O'Sullivan, Maureen. "Social intelligence and
     I.Q." Educ Psychol Meas 28(2): 339-44, Summer, 1968. (11 Refer-
     ences)
The authors conclude that the concepts of giftedness must be expanded to
include excellence in intellectual areas other than those measured by
I.Q. tests.

220 Holland, John L. "Achievement syndromes among high aptitude stu-
     dents." Psychol Rep 8(3): 384, June, 1961.
A sample of high aptitude students yielded seventy variables which were
intercorrelated and factor analyzed. Eleven factors emerged, allowing
for prediction for future studies and creative performance.

221 Isaacs, Ann F. "Giftedness and leadership." Gifted Child Q 17(2):
     103-12, Summer, 1973. (19 References)
This is essentially a catalog of leadership qualities and deficiencies.
Parents and teachers can motivate the gifted to develop leadership quali-
ties often by their own examples.

222 Kaplan, Martin F., and Lotsof, Erwin, J. "Are the principles of
     behavior of exceptional children exceptional?" Psychol Rep 23(3,
     pt. 2): 1207-13, December, 1968. (27 References)
Presents the thesis that behavioral differences in groups of "exceptional
children" are the consequence of differences in learning capacity and
modified environmental conditions associated with the exceptionality.
Cites many empirical studies dealing with behavior of the gifted which
fail to compare them with control groups of non-gifted.

223 Kelly, Kerry. "A precocious child in analysis." Psychoanal Study
     Child 25: 122-45, 1970. (3 References)

Describes a case study of a child: the interaction between environment
and the child's capacities, the problems, the ways in which the precocity
affected treatment, and the treatment relationship.

224 Kelley, Robert. "Limits to deviant behavior in the gifted." Sch
     Life 47(1): 4-6, October, 1964.
Defines, discusses and guides as to acceptable limits of deviant behavior
in the gifted.

225 Klausmeier, Herbert J., and Laughlin, Leo T. "Behavior during prob-
     lem solving among children of low, average and high intelligence."
     J Educ Psychol 52(3): 148-52, June, 1961. (5 References)
Investigation purposed to ascertain possible differences among low, average and high I.Q. children in efficiency of method, persistance, and mode
of attack while in the actual process of solving arithmetic problems.
Results indicate the high I.Q. children showed a greater incidence in
noting and correcting mistakes independently, verifying solutions, and
using a logical approach. High I.Q. students were also superior in
efficiency of method.

226 Levinson, Boris M. "The inner life of the extremely gifted child,
     as seen from the clinical setting." J Genet Psychol 99(1): 83-88,
     September, 1961.
Defining "extremely gifted child" as one who has an I.Q. of at least 150
and is also creative, the author describes some of the behavioral characteristics of a clinical sample of these children. His observations
do not support the conclusions of Terman, et. al., regarding the very
positive emotional adjustment of highly gifted children.

227 Lichtenstein, Parker E. "Genius as productive neurosis." Psychol
     Rec 21(2): 151-64, Spring, 1971. (28 References)
Considers the anxiety-reduction theory as useful in explaining the high
productivity of many geniuses who have suffered from severe anxieties.
The habit of productive effort seems, in many cases, to relieve anxiety
sufficiently to allow creative effort to proceed with results highly
beneficial to society.

228 McClain, Edwin W., and Andrews, Henry B. "Self-actualization among
     extremely superior students." J Coll Stud Pers 13(6): 505-10,
     November, 1972. (22 References)
Study involved seventy-seven college seniors who were candidates for
Woodrow Wilson Foundation fellowships in four Southern states. Compared
with ordinary University of Tennessee seniors, they appeared to be highly
self-actualized in areas of intellectual and aesthetic experience. However, their excessive independence appeared to be thwarting to another
important area of human fulfillment--living in rewarding interpersonal
relationships.

229 McGuire, Carson; Hindsman, Edwin; King, F. J., et. al. "Dimensions
     of talented behavior." Educ Psychol Meas 21(1): 3-38, Spring,
     1961. (38 References)
Studied data for 1,242 junior high school pupils from four Texas communities. Forty-one variables were used covering cognitive, perceptual
and psychomotor abilities, motivational and personality indices, environmental pressures, and values.

230 Mayer, Pamela S. "Motivational orientation as a learned construct in gifted elementary children." For a summary see: Diss Abstr Int 35A(5): 2811-12, November, 1974. (0 References)

231 Mowsesian, Richard; Heath, Brian; Rothney, John J. "Superior students' occupational preferences and their fathers' occupations." Pers Guid J 45(3): 238-42, November, 1966. (13 References)
Studied relationship between occupational preferences of superior students and their fathers' occupations. Both male and female superior students tended to state vocational preferences at the professional level early in high school and to maintain this preference throughout. Their occupational preferences were generally at a higher level than those of their fathers.

232 Pasternack, Marian, and Silvey, Linda. "Leadership patterns in gifted peer groups." Gifted Child Q 13(2): 126-28, Summer, 1969. (7 References)
To substantiate Hollingworth's hypothesis that "the leader is likely to be more intelligent, but not too much more intelligent, then the average of the group led," the authors studied leadership patterns at a California summer workshop for gifted students. They concluded that the choice of leaders of gifted children is due to social values affected by: (1) the nature of the school; (2) the grouping of the children; and (3) the status of the children as established by the teachers and counselors.

233 Renz, Paul, and Christoplos, Florence. "Toward an operational definition of giftedness." J Creat Behav 2(2): 91-96, Spring, 1968. (4 References)
Argues that task proficiency and innovative behavior, which is based on proficiency, must be differentiated in any operational definition of giftedness. Such a definition must also take cognizance of culturally determined values which serve as determinants of the boundaries of high and low risk for the manifestation of gifted behavior.

234 Renzulli, Joseph S., and Hartman, Robert K. "Scale for rating behavioral characteristics of superior students." Except Child 38(3): 243-48, November, 1971. (50 References)
Presents the rating scale in its entirety and describes conditions for its reproduction and use. It covers four behavioral characteristics: learning, motivation, creativity, and leadership.

235 Rice, Joseph P. "Total talent development." J Second Educ 42(1): 12-16, January, 1967.
Discusses California Project Talent and says that newer classifications for talent must be isolated. Besides academic talent, creative talent and leadership talent, athletic, manipulative, mechanical, and performing arts talented should be identified.

236 Robinson, F. P. "Study skills for superior students in secondary schools." In: Hafner, L. E., ed. Improving Reading in Secondary Schools. New York: Macmillan, 1967. 175-180.
Author points out that even Phi Beta Kappas study inefficiently, discusses what research says about developing effective reading-study skills; how academic skills are like athletic skills and how a special technique is best used to improve comprehension and retention of material.

237   Roeper, Annemarie. "Some observations about gifted preschool chil-
        dren." J Nurs Educ 18: 177–180, April, 1963.
The founder and director of one of America's best-known private nursery
schools for gifted children describes special characteristics of these
youngsters. She cites examples of scientific curiosity, phenomenal
memories, capacity for abstract thinking, and possible emotional problems
from personal experience.

238   Simono, Ronald. "Observed expressions of the achievement needs of
        gifted students." Psychol Sch 4(2): 174–76, April, 1967. (3
        References)
Study identified gifted student behavior (other than academic grades)
which might reflect need for achievement. Students in the high-achieve-
ment group had a set schedule for homework, took a heavy course load,
participated in outside intellectual activities, were interested in improving school programs, wanted to gain post-high school education, and
actively investigated possible vocations.

239   Watley, Donivan J. "Bright black youth: their educational plans and
        career aspirations." Natl Merit Scholarsh Corp Res Rep 7(8): 1–20,
        1971. (11 References)
Reports the career and educational major plans and the degree aspirations
of bright black youth who received National Merit Scholarships. Differences from white scholarship winners are noted.

240   ———. "Characteristics and performance of N.M.S.Q.T. participants."
        Natl Merit Scholarsh Corp Res Rep 7(3): 1–8, 1971. (0 References)
Provides information about the 796,474 eleventh grade students who took
the NMSQT in February, 1967. Tables give data by sex, state of residence,
decile, college choice and career choice.

241   Welsh, George S. "Vocational interests and intelligence in gifted
        adolescents." Educ Psychol Meas 31(1): 155–64, Spring, 1971.
        (8 References)
Reports a study of gifted adolescents who were given the Strong Vocational Interest Blank, Terman's Concept Mastery Test (of verbal intelligence) and the D–48 (of non-verbal intelligence). Correlations were then
analyzed and some trends in regard to scientific and business career
interests were evident.

242   Werts, Charles E. "The many faces of intelligence." J Educ Psychol
        58(4): 198–204, August, 1967. (6 References)
Studied extracurricular achievements of gifted. In the scientific,
literary, leadership, speech, drama, music and art areas, the percentage
of achievers was greater among students with high grades.

243   Whiteside, Marilyn. "What happens to the gifted girl?" PTA Mag
        68(6): 20–21, February, 1974.
Dr. Whiteside discusses how the assignment of certain traits as masculine
or feminine has caused many gifted girls to not develop their talents and
creativity.

244   Willerman, Lee, and Fiedler, Miriam F. "Infant performance and
        intellectual precocity." Child Dev 45(2): 483–86, June, 1974.
        (6 References)
A Boston study identified 100 white children with I.Q.'s of 140 or more

at four years of age who had been administered the Bagley Scales of
Mental and Motor Development at eight months. Results indicate that these
superior children were not greatly advanced as infants and could not have
been distinguished from the total infant population at eight months.
Among these intellectually precocious children, parental education and the
child's I.Q. at four were significantly correlated for boys but not for
girls.

245 Witteck, M. J. "Reflections of the gifted by the gifted on the
     gifted." Gifted Child Q 17(4): 250-53, Winter, 1973. (0 Refer-
     ences)
Witteck designed an open-end questionnaire which was distributed to three
classes of gifted children in the fifth, sixth, and seventh grades in
Queens, New York. The sample indicated that these gifted children were
motivated, recognized and were proud of their special status in the educational system, highly competitive for school honors, and reacted
strongly to parental pressure for high achievement.

D. Personality and Attitudes

246 Anastasiow, Nicholas J. "A report of self-concept of the very
     gifted." Gifted Child Q 8(4): 177-78, Winter, 1964.
In a sample of very highly gifted children, those who were classified as
low reading achievers had significantly lower self-concept scores of
physical ability, social relations, and total self-concept than high
reading achieving very gifted children. These results were not obtained
in comparing high and low arithmetic achievement.

247 Bachtold, Louise M. "Changes in interpersonal values of gifted
     adolescents." Psychol Sch 6(3): 303-06, July, 1969. (10 Refer-
     ences)
Seventy-three gifted, in group discussion, revealed that gifted girls
place greater value on making their own decisions. After the program,
the gifted boys also were higher on independence and lower on conformity
dimensions.

248 ————. "Interpersonal values of gifted junior high school students."
     Psychol Sch 5(4): 368-70, October, 1968. (7 References)
The purpose of this study was to obtain information on differences in
interpersonal values between sexes and differences between gifted and
average children of twelve to fourteen years in order to differentiate
scholastic procedures. Significant differences were found between
sexes and between average and gifted groups.

249 Bachtold, Louise M., and Werner, Emmy E. "Personality profiles of
     gifted women: psychologists." Am Psychol 25(3): 234-43, March,
     1970. (28 References)
Compared the responses to the sixteen PF of 124 highly successful women
psychologists with women in general, college women, and successful academic men to identify personality factors enabling these women to succeed
in spite of powerful sex-role expectations to the contrary. In terms of
test scores, women psychologists were significantly more intelligent than
women in general. Despite similar test profiles of successful academic
men and women, the women scored higher on intelligence, radicalism and
super-ego strength and lower on self-sentiment.

250   Bailey, Roger C., and Bailey, Kent G.   "Self-perceptions of scholas-
      tic ability at four grade levels." J Genet Psychol 124: 197-212,
      June, 1974. (17 References)
A large sample of students at fourth, eighth, twelfth and college grade
levels were given a Self-Rating Scale of Scholastic Ability and an
objective measure of scholastic ability. Results were consistent with
earlier findings on self-concept differences between high school and
college students.

251   Boehm, Leonore. "The development of conscience: a comparison of
      American children of different mental and socioeconomic levels."
      Child Dev 33(3): 575-90, September, 1962. (11 References)
In a study of some aspects of conscience development, academically gifted
children were compared with children of average intelligence, and upper
middle-class children with children of the working class. The gifted and
upper middle-class children were more mature in their moral judgments
than the average and working-class children.

252   ———. "The development of conscience: a comparison of students
      in Catholic parochial schools and in public schools." Child Dev
      33(3): 591-602, September, 1962. (7 References)
In terms of distinguishing between intent and results of an action,
Catholic parochial school children, regardless of socioeconomic status
or intelligence levels, scored higher and at an earlier age than public
school children. Academically gifted upper middle-class children were
superior to average working-class children. The gifted also showed
greater independence from adults.

253   Capretta, Patrick J.; Jones, Reginald L.; Siegel, Lawrence, et.
      al. "Some noncognitive characteristics of honors program candi-
      dates." J Educ Psychol 54(5): 268-76, October, 1963. (12
      References)
University honors students were given three standard personality inventories and two locally devised instruments. They were found to be intellectually oriented toward academic work and quite flexible thinkers.
Non-honors students were more pragmatic in approach and rather restricted
thinkers.

254   Cashdan, Sheldon, and Welsh, G. S. "Personality correlates of
      creative potential in talented high school students." J Pers
      34(3): 445-55, September, 1966.
The high creative adolescent emerged as an independent, nonconforming
individual who seeks change in his environment and whose interpersonal
relationships are open and active. The low creative adolescent, particularly the male, emerged as a somewhat compulsive individual with a
strong desire to achieve.

255   Cox, F. N. "Educational streaming and general test anxiety."
      Child Dev 33: 381-90, March/December, 1962. (17 References)
Results of this study show that, in a sample of middle-class Australian
fourth and fifth graders, those children placed in the inferior educational track obtained consistently higher mean test anxiety scores than
those in the superior subgroup. It was also found that anxiety scores
increased with grade and that girls obtained higher anxiety scores than
boys.

256 Dentler, Robert A., and Mackler, Bernard. "Originality: some
      social and personal determinants." Behav Sci 9(1): 1-7, January,
      1964. (11 References)
One component of creativity is originality. This paper reports on a study
of the effects of interpersonal relationships and personality traits on
the development of original ideas.

257 Durr, William K., and Schmatz, Robert. "Personality differences
      between high-achieving and low-achieving gifted children." Read
      Teach 17(4): 251-54, January, 1964. (4 References)
Study of elementary children clarifies some of the personality characteristics which differentiate gifted children who are reading in line
with potential from reading underachievers.

258 Eysenck, H. J., and White, P. O. "Personality and the measure of
      intelligence." Br J Educ Psychol 34(2): 197-202, June, 1964.
      (22 References)
Early data show that stable children differ from unstable ones with respect to the structure of their intellectual abilities. Authors summarize a number of studies, most of which support the original hypothesis

259 Feinberg, K. "Growing up gifted." Gifted Child Q 14(3): 172-73,
      Autumn, 1970. (0 References)
This personal account by a doctoral candidate in classical languages
describes the isolation she felt as a gifted child in public elementary
and high schools, as well as the self-awareness which college provided.

260 Götz, Karl O., and Götz, Karin. "Color preferences, extraversion,
      and neuroticism of art students." Percept Mot Skills 41(3):
      919-30, December, 1975. (27 References)
Study found that the preferences of a group of highly gifted art students
on a personality inventory were different from those of average and
less gifted students who had little or no artistic practice.

261 ———. "Introversion--extraversion and neuroticism in gifted and
      ungifted art students." Percept Mot Skills 36(2): 675-78, April,
      1973. (8 References)
It was generally assumed that artists are mostly introverted. To find
out if they were also neurotic, two groups of fifty art students,
judged by their art teachers to be gifted or ungifted, were tested with
the Maudly Personality Inventory. Results show a clear tendency toward
introversion and neuroticism for the gifted group. The mean scores of
the ungifted group, however, were in the vicinity of normal.

262 Gottsdanker, Josephine S. "Intellectual interest patterns of
      gifted college students." Educ Psychol Meas 28(2): 361-66,
      Summer, 1968. (6 References)
This study compared seventy-five male and seventy-five female gifted
freshmen at a California state university with an equal number of randomly selected freshmen. Results of the personality inventory given to all
show that gifted women have a different pattern of intellectual interests
than do the men, and they are far more divergent from average students
than are the gifted men.

263 Groth, Norma J. "Student perception of sex-role in creativity."
      Gifted Child Q 20(3): 327-35, Fall, 1976. (7 References)

This article brings out some of the reasons due to misperception by self and others which keep gifted girls from the full realization of their talents.

264   Groth, Norma J., and Holbert, Priscilla. "Hierarchical needs of
          gifted boys and girls in the affective domain." Gifted Child Q
          13(2): 129-33, Summer, 1969.
During a summer program for gifted children, 281 ten to fourteen-year olds wrote down three wishes. Matched controls from a public school did the same. Gifted subjects were more concerned with self-actualization needs than were controls. Most concerned with self-actualization were gifted girls; their male counterparts showed greater concerns for security and self-esteem.

265   Gruber, Joseph J., and Kirkendall, Don R. "Relationships within
          and between the mental and personality domains in disadvantaged
          high school students." Am Correct Ther J 27(5): 136-40,
          September, 1973.
The authors found that both high- and low-achieving gifted high school students from disadvantaged environments displayed more desirable personality scores than others.

266   Halpin, W. Gerald; Payne, David A.; Ellett, Chad D. "Life history
          antecedents of current personality traits of gifted adolescents."
          Meas Eval Guid 8(1): 29-35, April, 1975. (14 References)
Subjects for this study were 341 high school juniors and seniors chosen to participate in the 1972 Georgia Governor's Honors Program. The data serve to validate the sixteen Personality-Factor Questionnaire for use with gifted teenagers. Results should help counselors and teachers to better understand the ways that past experiences are likely to influence the personality development of the gifted.

267   Houlihan, Margaret B. "A comparison of personality and attitudes
          about teachers, classroom peers, and subject matter as found
          between eighth grade gifted high and low achievers." For a summary
          see: Diss Abstr Int 31A(8): 3957, February, 1971. (0 References)

268   Isaacs, Ann F. "Looking at why giftedness is rejected: self-
          identification, self-acceptance, and self-realization." Gifted
          Child Q 13(1): 32-36, Spring, 1969.
The editor of Gifted Child Quarterly examines the self-concept of gifted children and finds them frequently failing to realize their potential for leadership.

269   Jacks, William R. "Attitudes, preferences and perceptions of
          gifted sixth and eighth grade students." For a summary see: Diss
          Abstr Int 32A(8): 4450-51, February, 1972. (0 References)

270   Jacobs, Jon C. "Rorschach studies reveal possible misinterpreta-
          tions of personality traits of the gifted." Gifted Child Q 15(3):
          195-200, Fall, 1971. (8 References)
Study suggests that gifted have personality characteristics of an older child, thus they are subject to misunderstanding. Gifted are more likely to rely less on adults, dispute the concept of absolute goodness and badness, and be more sensitive and self-reliant. This may lead to problems with teachers who may view them negatively because they are dif-

ferent from their classmates and perhaps less likely to do everything the teacher says.

271 Joesting, Joan, and Joesting, Robert. "Differences among self-descriptions of gifted black college students and their less intelligent counterparts." Gifted Child Q 13(3): 175-80, Fall, 1969. (12 References)
This study attempted to determine the self-concepts of Negro college students and to discover if there are significant differences among students of high, above average, average, below average, and low intelligence.

272 Kanner, Leo. "The integrative aspect of ability." Acta Paedopsychiatr 38(5-6): 134-44, May/June, 1971. (0 References)
Among children of high I.Q., the essential hampering agent is lack of inner comfort, due to lack of opportunity to think and plan for themselves. Thus, educators, etc., must find ways to help gifted make natural use of their abilities.

273 Keiser, S. "Superior intelligence: its contribution to neurosogenesis." J Am Psychoanal Assoc 17(2): 452-73, April, 1969.
Precocious intelligence gave patients access to information as children that overwhelmed their immature egos, thus releasing libidinal and aggresive fantasies that burdened their developing egos. Greater sensitivity to stimuli required stronger methods to master the resultant excitation.

274 Kennedy, Ethel A. "Personality needs in the experience, behavior, and life plans of gifted girls." For a summary see: Diss Abstr Int 25(11): 6337-38, May, 1965. (0 References)

275 Kennedy, Wallace A. "MMPI profiles of gifted adolescents." J Clin Psychol 18(2): 148-49, April, 1962. (3 References)
Data indicate that the profile of the gifted adolescent is within normal limits and that when one finds a superior person whose score deviates from the normal, it is a clue to factors other than his high intelligence.

276 Kennedy, Wallace A., and Smith, Alvin H. "Values of future scientists." Percept Mot Skills 10(3). 703-04, June, 1960. (4 References)
A comparison of scores on the Allport-Vernon-Lindzey Study of Values was made for 130 mathematically gifted adolescents and the normative medical school freshman. The former group is more concerned with theoretical values than with religious and social values.

277 Krippner, Stanley, and Blickenstaff, Ralph. "The development of self-concept as part of an arts workshop for the gifted." Gifted Child Q 14(3): 163-66, Fall, 1970. (13 References)
This study was designed to loosen the stereotyped role choices determined by sex which inhibited creative potential. A workshop did weaken the rigidity of role definitions.

278 Lazar, Alfred L.; Gensley, Juliana T.; Orpet, Russel E. "Changing attitudes of young mentally gifted children toward handicapped persons." Except Child 37(8): 600-02, April, 1971. (7 References)

The Attitudes Toward Disabled Persons Scale was used to investigate whether a special instructional program could influence mentally gifted eight-year-olds attitudes toward handicapped persons. Changes toward greater acceptance and understanding were noted.

279   Lazar, Alfred L.; Orpet, Russel E.; Revie, Virgil. "Attitudes of young gifted boys and girls toward handicapped individuals." Except Child 38(6): 489-90, February, 1972. (3 References)
The Attitude Toward Disabled Persons Scale was given to fifteen male and fifteen female eight-year-olds with high I.Q.'s. Female subjects were significantly more tolerant than the males.

280   McIntosh, Dean K. "Correlates of self concept in gifted students." For a summary see: Diss Abstr Int 27A(8): 2403, February, 1967. (0 References)

281   Mason, Evelyn P.; Adams, Henry L.; Blood, Don F. "Further study of personality characteristics of bright college freshmen." Psychol Rep 23(2): 395-400, October, 1968. (9 References)
On the Allport-Vernon-Lindzey Study of Values, bright students tested at a state college were lower in economic values and higher in esthetic values than a local norm group. On the adjective check list they revealed themselves as more independent and less well adjusted than controls.

282   ———. "Personality characteristics of gifted college freshmen." Psychol Sch 3(4): 360-65, October, 1966. (4 References)
Three measures of personality were administered to a group of academically able college freshmen who volunteered for testing. Results indicate that today's gifted college students are less mature or more at odds with society than were those of a generation ago. For gifted students, a more tolerant and flexible academic environment may be needed.

283   Mason, Evelyn P., and Blood, Don F. "Cross-validation study of personality characteristics of gifted college freshmen." In: American Psychological Association, 74th, Washington, D.C., 1966. Proceedings. 1(1): 283-84, 1966.
Compared attitudes of three groups of bright college freshmen, divided on the basis of participation in an honors program and tested in 1965. Results support the finding that bright students were more negative in attitudes toward self than general college norms.

284   Merrifield, Philip R.; Guilford, J. P.; Christensen, P. R.; et. al. "Interrelationships between certain abilities and certain traits of motivation and temperament." J Gen Psychol 65(1): 57-74, July, 1961. (16 References)
This report is concerned with the extent to which measures of certain intellectual factors or primary abilities can possibly be accounted for in terms of factors or primary traits of needs, interests and temperament. The intellectual aptitudes involved are concentrated in the area of thinking abilities, and more particularly, in the factors of fluency, flexibility, and originality. These factors seem to represent the basic abilities most conspicuously involved in creative production.

285 Milgram, Roberta M., and Milgram, Norman A. "Self-concept as a
     function of intelligence and creativity in gifted Israeli children."
     Psychol Sch 13(1): 91-96, January, 1976.
The relationship of creativity and intelligence to self-concept was
examined in Israeli children of superior intelligence across a wide age
range. It was concluded that for children of superior intelligence,
differences in creativity level were more closely related to personal-
social adjustment than to differences in intelligence.

286 Naor, Nehama K. "Configurational analysis of the Strong Vocational
     Interest Blank (SVIB) and concomittant personality correlates."
     For a summary see: Diss Abstr Int 31B(11): 6908-09, May, 1971.
     (0 References)

287 Niemiec, Carl J. "The prediction of value hierarchies identified
     from self-report data of superior students." For a summary see:
     Diss Abstr Int 31A(1): 158-59, July, 1970. (0 References)

288 Norfleet, Mary A. "Personality characteristics of achieving and
     underachieving high ability senior women." Pers Guid J 46(10):
     976-80, June, 1968. (13 References)
Utilized the CPI and the Gough Adjective Check List in an investigation
of the relationship between personality characteristics and academic
achievement in gifted university women.

289 Payne, David A.; Halpin, W. Gerald; Ellet, Chad D.; et. al.
     "General personality correlates of creative personality in academ-
     ically and artistically gifted youth." J Spec Educ 9(1): 105-
     08, Spring, 1975. (7 References)
Studied 312 high school students participating in the Georgia Governor's
Honors Program, an intensive summer program for the academic and
artistically gifted. The general intent of the study was to explore
possible relationships between selected personality factors and the
concept of the "creative personality" (as described by Torrance and
Khatena).

290 Payne, David A.; Halpin, W. Gerald; Ellet, Chad D. "Personality
     trait characteristics of differentially gifted students." Psychol
     Sch 10(2): 189-95, April, 1973. (10 References)
High school students participating in the 1972 Georgia Governor's Honors
Program were given personality inventories. Five scales were found to
discriminate significantly among the eight differentially gifted groups.

291 Porter, Rutherford B. "A comparative investigation of the per-
     sonality of sixth-grade gifted children and a norm group of chil-
     dren." J Educ Res 58(3): 132-34, November, 1964. (3 References)
Study found that gifted children were more likely to be conscientious,
persevering,self-reliant,self-sufficient, resourceful, and secure.
The girls tend to be warm and sociable, kindly and soft hearted and
somewhat adventurous.

292 Rothman, Frances D. "A study in the measurement and an attempted
     modification of attitudes toward academic achievement among
     gifted students in two independent schools." For a summary see:
     Diss Abstr Int 22(5): 1512-13, November, 1961. (0 References)

293   Sanborn, Marshall P., and Niemiec, Carl J.   "Identifying values of
       superior high school students." Sch Couns   18(4): 237-45, March,
       1971. (10 References)
This study attempted to develop a procedure whereby cumulative records
and structured interviews could be used to determine hierarchies of
values thought to be related to choices and achievements of gifted high
school students.

294   Schab, Fred. "The work ethic of the gifted." Gifted Child Q
       20(2): 169-72, Summer, 1976. (2 References)
This report summarizes and compares the responses of over 400 white and
300 black male and female honors students in eleven public high schools
in Georgia. Both groups expressed some idealistic and unrealistic
expectations about their future careers. Competition, working conditions and compensation seemed to preoccupy black students more than
white. Possible reasons are given.

295   Schauer, George H. "Emotional disturbance and giftedness." Gifted
       Child Q 20(4): 470-77, Winter, 1976. (22 References)
Purpose of this study is to present: (1) accurate information about
emotional disturbance and giftedness, (2) the necessity for early
identification of both emotionally disturbed and gifted children, and
(3) the need for schools and communities to establish facilities which
will provide the atmosphere for proper development and treatment of
such children.

296   Silverblank, Francine. "A selection of selected personality
       factors between students talented in English and students talented
       in mathematics." Calif J Educ Res   24(2): 61-65, March, 1973.
       (0 References)
This study concluded that students talented in mathematics or English
do not differ in levels of responsibility or anxiety, but that English
students are considerably more sociable than mathematics students, who
tend toward extremes--unusually secure to severely anxious.

297   Torrance, E. Paul. "Identity: the gifted child's major problem."
       Gifted Child Q 15(3): 147-55, Fall, 1971. (5 References)
Torrance says gifted children resolve their search for identity by
either conformity, rebellion, or creative individuality. He examines
six individuals and concludes that wandering is perfectly normal and
necessary. He finds the most creative individuals studied were more
likely to have attended more colleges, to have held more diverse jobs,
and to have been abroad more.

298   Torrance, E. Paul, and Dauw, Dean C. "Attitude patterns of crea-
       tively gifted high school seniors." Gifted Child Q 10(2): 53-
       57, Summer, 1966. (7 References)
An attempt to extend the understanding of the dynamics of the mental
and personality functioning tapped by the tests of creative thinking
in the direction of attitude patterns and orientations to life.

299   Welsh, George S. "Color preferences of gifted adolescents." Sci
       Art 7(1-2): 55-61, 1970. (15 References)
Participants in a summer program for gifted high school students listed
the colors they liked the most and the least. Blue was most popular
with both boys and girls. Several colors showed marked sex differences

and relationships of color preferences to personality characteristics were found.

300 Werblo, Dorothy, and Torrance, E. Paul. "Experiences in historical research and changes in self evaluations of gifted children." Except Child 33(3): 137-41, November, 1966. (9 References)
The data presented reveals that even gifted high-achieving and socially well adjusted children tend to underevaluate themselves. The evidence also seems to indicate that with only a minimum of instruction these children can apply procedures to attain a more realistic self-evaluation.

301 Werner, Emmy E., and Bachtold, Louise M. "Personality factors of gifted boys and girls in middle childhood and adolescence." Psychol Sch 6(2): 177-82, April, 1969. (12 References)
Study investigated whether there are sex differences in personality factors that differentiate the gifted from the norm, both in middle childhood and adolescence and whether there are significant differences among gifted boys and girls who differed in their special interests. It found that gifted boys differed markedly from the norm, whereas girls did not as much. The gifted boys were more intelligent, more dominant, more venturesome, more individualistic, more self-assured, and more self-disciplined. There were few differences among children with high I.Q.'s and special interests.

302 White, William F., and Anderson, Joy. "Personality differences among female student teachers of relatively high and low mental ability." Percept Mot Skills 41(1): 29-30, August, 1975. (5 References)
Compared thirty female undergraduates in education with low scores on a test of mental maturity with thirty who had high scores. Significant comparisons appeared to be chance effects.

C. Physical Traits

303 Barber, Prudence S., and Rose, Darrell E. "Bone conduction oscillator placement in testing hearing of selected groups of children." Am J Ment Defic 73(4): 666-72, January, 1969. (33 References)
Ten gifted children were compared with ten retardates to find threshold measurements from the mastoid and forehead processes. The forehead position had a less sensitive threshold at all frequencies for both groups. The gifted displayed the smallest amount of variability at the mastoid placement.

304 Copple, Peggy J., and Isom, John B. "Soft signs and scholastic success." Neurology 18(3): 304, March, 1968. (0 References)
The authors report a study performed on a group of gifted children (I.Q. 130+) and a control group of schoolmates of normal intelligence. Complete neurological exams, tests of motor coordination, perception and auditory recall, and EEG's were given to all gifted subjects. Results showed that some children in both groups had "soft signs." The gifted did significantly better in the perception and auditory tests, and there was no significant difference in the performance of the groups on manual dexterity or fine motor coordination tests.

305 Laycock, Frank, and Caylor, John S. "Physiques of gifted children and their less gifted siblings." Child Dev 35(1): 63-74, March, 1964. (12 References)

Study compared eighty-one gifted youngsters to less able siblings on several physical measurements. Results do not support the claim that bright children are larger than ordinary children from the same homes.

IV

Identification Techniques

A. Psychological and Educational Testing

306 Ahr, A. Edward. "The development of a group preschool screening
     test for early school entrance potentiality." Psychol Sch 4(1):
     59-63, January, 1967. (5 References)
Describes the development and evaluation of a group preschool screening
test designed for early admission programs. The data suggest that it is
possible to test preschoolers in a group setting with a reasonable degree
of reliability and validity.

307 Baldwin, Joseph W. "The relationship between teacher-judged gifted-
     ness, a group intelligence test and an individual intelligence test
     with possible gifted kindergarten pupils." Gifted Child Q 6(4):
     153-56, Winter, 1962. (6 References)
Reports the results of screening experiments on 100 children from twenty-
two different California kindergarten classes rated as gifted by experienced teachers. Of those who rated gifted on the Stanford-Binet, only
38 percent were identified by teachers and only 39 percent through use
of group tests. Gives suggestions for improving teachers' performance.

308 Blosser, George H. "Group intelligence tests as screening devices
     in locating gifted and superior students in the ninth grade."
     Except Child 29(6): 282-86, February, 1963.
Blosser used three different tests to identify gifted students. All of
the measures fell far short of complete efficiency and suggested that
any type of screening device will identify as gifted far more youngsters
than would qualify by individual intelligence tests standards.

309 Bruch, Catherine B. "Modification of procedures for identification
     of the disadvantaged gifted." Gifted Child Q 15(4): 267-72,
     Winter, 1971. (8 References)
Demonstrated utility of Meeker's method of interpreting Stanford-Binet
Intelligence Scale results as a means of identifying giftedness among
low-income individuals.

310 Cassel, Russel N. "Eleven great tests that have made major contri-
     butions to measurement theory." Psychology 5(4): 17-22, 1968.
Identifies eleven psychological tests which have had profound influence
on the development of present test theory. All have great utility in
identification and assessment of the gifted.

311 Chauncey, Henry, and Hilton, Thomas L. "Are aptitude tests valid
     for the highly able?" Science 148(3675): 1297-1304, June 4, 1965.
     (30 References)

Predictions of achievement based on test-score differences among high-scoring persons are reviewed. Authors conclude that research on students of high ability demonstrates that quality of performance increases with increasing test scores even at very high levels.

312 Cornish, Robert L. "Parents', teachers', and pupils' perception of the gifted child's ability." Gifted Child Q 12(1): 14-17, Spring, 1968. (8 References)
Four classes of sixth grade pupils were rated for intelligence by teachers, parents, and pupils themselves, and also given group I.Q. tests and achievement tests. Results showed that the best method of identifying a gifted child in the intermediate grades is to use a group I.Q. test score plus teacher judgment.

313 Cox, Joseph A. "Suggested instruments for the identification of the preschool and kindergarten disadvantaged gifted." South J Educ Res 8(5): 198-208, Winter, 1974.
Presents a list of spatial relations, memory, reasoning, classification and aptitude tests which can be used to identify disadvantaged gifted children in preschool and kindergarten classes.

314 Dailey, John T., and Shaycoft, Marion F. Types of tests in Project Talent. Washington: U. S. Department of Health, Education and Welfare, Office of Education, 1961. 62p. (Bibliography)
Discusses the history of objective tests, the purpose of standardized tests, and describes the aptitude and achievement tests used in Project Talent.

315 Damrin, Dora E. "Selection of honors students at the University of Illinois." Super Stud 7: 23-28, March/April, 1965.
This article discusses the selection procedures used for each group eligible for the honors programs at the University of Illinois. Also discusses the validity and reliability of the selection procedures used, supported by statistical data.

316 Dyer, Henry S. "On the assessment of academic achievement." Teach Coll Rec 62(2): 164-72, November, 1960. (11 References)
Dyer discusses many of the faults of tests, gives some examples of good test items, and makes recommendations concerning assessing achievement.

317 Endler, Norman S., and Snyder, Larry S. "Anxiety, aptitude, and academic achievement." Ontario J Educ Res 6(2): 85-91, Spring, 1964. (11 References)
The authors collected data from forty-two male and female first and second year students in a small Canadian liberal arts college. They were given inventories of anxiety and results were compared with their scores on college entrance tests and their high school grade averages. A strong negative relationship between aptitude and anxiety and a lesser relationship between achievement and anxiety resulted.

318 Engin, Ann W. "An analysis of supplementary subtests and their influence on total WISC scores of high achieving students." J Psychol 88(1): 121-25, September, 1974. (6 References)
All twelve subtests of the WISC were individually administered to forty-four high achieving fifth grade subjects. I.Q.'s were then calculated in such a manner that specific comparisons could be made. Results showed

that addition of digit span and mazes in the WISC battery served to
depress the verbal, performance and full-scale I.Q.'s of the high-
achieving subjects.

319   Engin, Ann W.; Geis, Jean; Walbrown, Jane D.   "The influence of sup-
      plementary subtests on WISC I.Q. scores for high achieving students."
      Psychol Sch   13(1):   29-31, January, 1976.
Twenty high-achieving fifth grade pupils were given the WISC to determine the influence of supplementary subtests on their scores.   Findings
showed that the addition of digit span and mazes subtests significantly
lowered the verbal, performance and full-scale I.Q. scores.

320   Eysenck, H. J.   "Intelligence assessment: a theoretical and experi-
      mental approach."   Br J Educ Psychol   37(1):   81-98, February, 1967.
      (57 References)
This paper, which was delivered at a meeting of the British Psychological
Society, reviews the four stages in the development of intelligence tests
and offers suggestions for a fifth stage of intelligence assessment.
This stage would include personality variables in experimental studies
of intellectual functioning, because of their proven value in mediating
predictions and their interaction potential in all types of learning and
performance tasks.

321   Frederiksen, Norman; Evans, Franklin R.; Ward, William C.   "Develop-
      ment of provisional criteria for the study of scientific creativity."
      Gifted Child Q   19(1):   60-65, Spring, 1975.   (0 References)
Describes a test battery being constructed for graduate students in
research psychology to measure creativity.   The tests have sections which
measure students' knowledge of psychological constructs, formulating
research ideas, selecting personnel, analyzing psychological constructs,
evaluating hypotheses, evaluating proposals, ideational fluency in
psychology and scanning speed.

322   Galliani, Cono, and Pennington, Harry.   "Intelligence quotients in
      maladjusted children."   Del Med J   34(17):   178-79, June, 1962.
Recounts a systematic and comprehensive analysis of the 114 children
between the ages of six and seventeen at the Governor Bacon Health
Center.   Although I.Q.'s were generally below average, a range from 44
to 118 among the boys was noted.   Performance scores exceeded verbal
scores for boys and girls and whites and Negroes,

323   Goslin, David A.   The search for ability.   New York: Russell Sage
      Foundation, 1963.   204p.
Written in an effort to provide a basis for a program of research on the
social consequences of testing.   In addition to a survey of past and
current practices in the measurement of intellectual abilities, an
attempt has been made to clear up some of the confusion about testing
and to suggest some of its possible effects on society and its members.

324   Identification of the gifted: tests and measurements: a selective
      bibliography series No. 668.   Reston, Virginia: The Council for
      Exceptional Children, 1975.   12p.
Contains approximately seventy-five abstracts from CEC files and ERIC.
The references included treat aspects such as student evaluation, test
interpretation, test reliability and validity, creativity, predictive
measurement, academic achievement, teacher and parent roles, psychological characteristics, enrichment, program planning, and culture-free tests.

325   Kaltsounis, Bill. "Instruments useful in studying creative behavior and creative talent." J Creat Behav 5(2): 117-26, Second quarter, 1971.
A partial listing of commercially available tests of creativity characteristics. Lists forty-two tests of verbal ability, non-verbal ability and personality. Also lists source addresses.

326   ———. "What Kind of Person Are You and mathematically accelerated students." Psychol Rep 35(1, Part I): 114, August, 1974. (1 Reference)
The intention of the study was to show that reliance on performance on New York Survey (mathematics) and National Educational Development Tests for the purpose of identifying individuals for guidance in mathematics might exclude creatively gifted children.

327   Keating, Daniel P. "Testing those in the top percentiles." Except Child 41(6): 435-36, March, 1975. (2 References)
The author advocates the use of high level tests with gifted youngsters in educational as well as research settings. In-grade tests present two major problems with exceptionally gifted children: (1) they can give no indication of how such students are different from each other, (2) they cannot give an accurate estimate of an individual's ability if his true level is above the ceiling of the test.

328   Kelly, E. F., and Kanthamani, B. K. "A subject's effort toward voluntary control." J Parapsychol 36(3): 185-97, September, 1972. (9 References)
Gifted subject tested with ESP cards, mechanical and electronic devices. Results were highly significant.

329   Lesser, Gerald S.; Davis, Frederick B.; Nahemow, Lucille. "The identification of gifted elementary school children with exceptional scientific talent." Educ Psychol Meas 22(2): 349-64, Summer, 1962. (26 References)
The authors constructed and validated an instrument for the identification of science gifted at the elementary level. Two parallel forms of the Hunter Science Aptitude Test were given. High predictive validity coefficients were obtained.

330   Lovell, K., and Shields, J. B. "Some aspects of a study of the gifted child." Br J Educ Psychol 37(2): 201-08, June, 1967. (18 References)
Study of fifty students deals with personality, mathematical attainment, logical thought, and the relationship between scores on creativity tests, WISC, and tests on logical thinking.

331   Machen, Lorella H. "A validity and reliability study of the Slosson Intelligence Test with an atypical population--gifted children." Diss Abstr Int 33A(7): 3296, January, 1973. (0 References)

332   Malone, Charlotte E. "Early childhood education of gifted children." Gifted Child Q 18(3): 188-90, Fall, 1974. (11 References)
States the need for true intellectual peer groupings and differentiated educational experiences for the gifted as early as kindergarten. The author has developed an inexpensive screening device capable of identi-

fying gifted children at entrace to kindergarten. A San Diego pilot
program utilizing this device has proved successful.

333 Martinson, Ruth A. "Issues in the identification of the gifted."
     Except Child 33(1): 13-16, September, 1966. (8 References)
Martinson found that the need to identify gifted children through careful and complete individual tests and case studies has not been accepted.
She identified categories of concern which inhibit identification procedures: inadequacy of existing measures, variability of intelligence,
cost of identification and fear of establishment of a meritocracy. She
says that identification of gifted children and special programs for
them is necessary for maximizing each child's potential.

334 Martinson, Ruth A., and Seagoe, May V. The abilities of young
     children. Washington, D.C.: The Council for Exceptional Children,
     1967. 66p. (Bibliography)
The authors attempted to differentiate the gifted by evaluating the
creative products of school children. They compared the scores of the
Stanford-Binet Intelligance Scale and the Guilford tests of divergent
thinking with judges ratings of creative products in the areas of science,
writing, social studies, music, and art. The traditional I.Q. proved to
be the better predictor of creative productions.

335 Mauger, Paul A., and Kolmodin, Claire, A. "Long-term predictive
     validity of the Scholastic Aptitude Test." J Educ Psychol 67(6):
     847-51, December, 1975. (8 References)
Results indicate that the SAT-V and SAT-M scores are valid for predicting
student performance in college. They also predict relative level of
achievement for those persisting until graduation, especially if measured
by achievement tests.

336 Maw, Wallace H., and Maw, Ethel W. "Selection of unbalanced and
     unusual designs by children high in curiosity." Child Dev 33:
     917-22, March/December, 1962. (5 References)
Children of high and low curiosity were compared on a test which allowed
them to choose between balanced and unbalanced, or familiar and un-
familiar designs. Differences in favor of the high curiosity groups
were found which were significant at the .02 level. Results indicate
that a test of designs could be developed that could be used to screen
groups of children high in curiosity from those low in curiosity.

337 Mednick, Martha T., and Andrews, Frank M. "Creative thinking and
     level of intelligence." J Creat Behav 1(4): 428-31, Fall, 1967.
     (7 References)
This report analyzes the relationship between creative thinking, defined
as performance on the Remote Associates Test (RAT), and level of intellectual functioning. For the subjects, 1,211 University of Michigan
freshmen, there was a correlation of .43 between RAT and SAT verbal and
of .20 between RAT and SAT math scores.

338 Miner, John B. "On the use of a short vocabulary test to measure
     general intelligence." J Educ Psychol 52(3): 157-60, June, 1961.
     (7 References)
In light of the high correlation between scores of longer vocabulary
measures and general intelligence tests, the author undertook a study of
the validity of a twenty item vocabulary test developed by Thorndike.

With his subjects of superior mental ability, the short test proved to have a correlation nearly as high as longer measures.

339   Orpet, Russel E., and Meyers, C. E.   "Six Structure-of-Intellect hypotheses in six-year-old children."   J Educ Psychol   57(6): 341-46, December, 1966.   (25 References)
A twenty-test battery hypothesizing six Guilford Structure-of-Intellect cells was administered to 100 six-year-old kindergarten children. Suggests that reaction to visual language symbols is still perceptual at age six.

340   Patterson, Henry J.   "A validation and comparison of the pictorial test of intelligence with the Stanford-Binet (L-M)."   For a summary see: Diss Abstr Int   29A(2):   485, August, 1968. (0 References)

341   Pinneau, Samuel R.   Changes in intelligence quotient.   Boston: Houghton Mifflin, 1961.   233p.
Includes new insights from the Berkeley Growth Study with implications for the Stanford-Binet Scales and applications to professional practice.

342   Rader, John R.   "Development and evaluation of a simulation on the identification of the gifted and talented."   Viewpoint   52(2): 33-52, March, 1976.   (21 References)
Describes a simulation program designed to increase awareness of educational needs of gifted and talented through the use of a one-hour group activity.   Objectives are to make participants aware of the inappropriateness of I.Q. as the sole identification criterion, and the need for diverse programs for the gifted and talented.

343   ————.   "Piagetian assessment conservation skills in the gifted first grader."   Gifted Child Q   19(3):   226-29, Fall, 1975.   (17 References)
Upon being administered a Piagetian task, a group of intellectually gifted first graders far out-performed their average peers--most of them reached the ceiling on the test.

344   Rellas, Archie J.   "The use of the Wechsler Preschool and Primary Scale (WPPSI) in the early identification of gifted students." Calif J Educ Res   20(3):   117-19, May, 1969.   (3 References)
Twenty-six five and six-year-olds were tested on the Stanford-Binet and Wechsler Preschool and Primary Scale.   I.Q. scores on the Binet were higher than the WPPSI scores.   The advisability of using the WPPSI for the early identifcation of gifted students is limited by its low ceiling and lack of agreement with the Binet.

345   Rosenberg, Leon A.   "Identifying the gifted child in the culturally deprived population: the need for culture-fair instruments."   Am J Orthopsychiatry   37(2):   342-43, March, 1967.
Describes a culture-fair instrument for assessment of intelligence, the "Johns Hopkins Perceptual Test," developed by the author.   Validated on middle and lower class preschool subjects, the test correlated positively with other intelligence tests.   Its use is advocated in the selection of gifted children for special programs in poverty areas.

346 Ruschival, M. Lena, and Way, John G.   "The WPPSI and the Stanford-
     Binet: a validity and reliability study using gifted preschool
     children."   J Consult Clin Psychol 37(1): 163, August, 1971.
     (2 References)
The WPPSI was given to thirty white male and female four and five-year-
olds with Stanford-Binet I.Q.'s of 120 or more. Only the WPPSI full
scale scores were significantly related to the Stanford-Binet scores.

347 Schmeding, Robert W. "Group intelligence test scores of gifted
     children: degree of consistency and factors related to consistency."
     Pers Guid J 42(10): 991-96, June, 1964. (0 References)
Major finding of this study on group intelligence tests was that students
who scored at or above 120 seldom maintained this level in subsequent
testings. Also, there was little basis for expecting trustworthy
early identification of the gifted.

348 ————. "A study of the degree of consistency and factors related
     to consistency in the group intelligence test scores of gifted
     children in four Ohio schools." For a summary see: Diss Abstr Int
     23(3): 929-30, September, 1962. (0 References)

349 Sheverbush, Robert L., Jr. "An analysis of subtests performance of
     gifted students in the Stanford-Binet intelligence scale (1960 Form
     L-M)." Gifted Child Q 18(2): 97-107, 115, Summer, 1974.
     (6 References)
This study used Stanford-Binet subtests to learn about characteristics
of the gifted. Sheverbush found that a greater percentage of the
gifted group passed a higher number of language and vocabulary subtests.
The successful group had the highest rank on subtests of the reasoning
category, whereas the unsuccessful group had the highest rank in the
verbal category.

350 Silverstein, A. B. "WISC and WPPSI I.Q.'s for the gifted."
     Psychol Rep 22(3, pt. 2): 1168, June, 1968. (4 References)
Wechsler's I.Q. tables for the WISC and Wechsler Preschool and Primary
Scale of Intelligence are extended to the maximum possible sum of
scaled scores so that the I.Q. of gifted children can be determined.

351 Stalnaker, John M. "Recognizing and encouraging talent."
     Am Psychol 16(8): 513-22, August, 1961. (0 References)
A lecture which describes how the problem of discovering and encouraging
talent on an extensive scale was handled by the National Merit Scholarship Corporation.

352 Steel, Joe M.; House, Ernest R.; Kerins, Thomas. "An instrument
     for assessing instructional climate through low-inference student
     judgments." Am Educ Res J 8(3): 447-66, May, 1971. (18 Refer-
     ences)
Authors developed an instrument for assessing both cognitive and affective dimensions of a class and used it to evaluate a statewide gifted
program. A comparison of sixty-two gifted classes with sixty-nine
average classes showed the gifted to be superior on the dimensions of
higher thought processes, classroom focus, and classroom climate.

353 Thompson, Jack M., and Finley, Carmen J. "Abbreviated WISC for use
     with gifted elementary school children." Calif J Educ Res 14(4):

167-77, September, 1963. (10 References)
An abbreviated scale of the WISC for use with gifted was developed and
tested. Authors found that with a correlation of .75 and an error
estimate of approximately four I.Q. points, the shorter test might have
some value.

354   Webb, Roger A. "Concrete and formal operations in very bright 6-11
       year olds." Hum Dev 17(4): 292-300, 1974.
The findings support the reality of Piaget's stage structure but suggest
that the speed with which tasks within a stage are mastered is a function of intelligence in the psychometric sense.

355   Wechsler, David. "Intelligence defined and undefined: a relativ-
       istic appraisal." Am Psychol 30(2): 135-39, February, 1975. (2
       References)
After reviewing assumptions about intelligence, constraints relative to
the concept, and complexities of definition, the author concludes that
intelligence tests measure an important quality--a person's capacity to
understand and to cope with the world.

356   Weise, Phillip, et. al. "PMA factors, sex, and teacher nomination
       in screening kindergarten gifted." Educ Psychol Meas 25(2): 597-
       603, Summer, 1965. (1 Reference)
Concerned with the efficiency of nomination of kindergarten children for
Binet testing. Teachers were accurate on 70 percent. Study devised
tables to predict probable Binet scores with and without teacher nomination on the basis of two Primary Mental Ability subtest scores.

357   Welsh, George S. "Comparison of D-48, Terman CMT, and Art Scale
       scores of gifted adolescents." J Consult Psychol 30(1): 88,
       February, 1966. (8 References)
Although both intelligence tests are significantly correlated with each
other and are uncorrelated with the creativity measure, the D-48 may
possess some advantages over the CMT. In addition to its brevity
and non-verbal content, the nature of the task in the D-48 seems to
possess inherent appeal, even for gifted adolescents.

358   ———. Creativity and intelligence: a personality approach.
       Chapel Hill: University of North Carolina Institute for Research
       in Social Science, 1975. 276p.
Reported is a study of non-cognitive aspects of creativity and intelligence with 1,155 academically or artistically talented adolescents
attending the Governor's School in North Carolina. A battery of intelligence and personality inventories was given them, resulting in the
identification of four distinct groups differing in intelligence and
originality.

359   Wisland, Milton, and Many, Wesley A. "A factorial study of the
       Illinois Test of Psycholinguistic Abilities with children having
       above average intelligence." Educ Psychol Meas 29(2): 367-76,
       Summer, 1969. (15 References)
Intellectually superior preschoolers at an Illinois university lab
school were given the ITPA, since little was known about the effectiveness of this instrument with children in the upper intelligence range.
An attempt was made to isolate the nine factors allegedly tested by the
nine subtests, however, three of these factors accounted for 79 percent

of the total common factor variance of the entire test with these superior children.

360   Yamamoto, Kaoru, and Dizney, H. F. "Effects of three sets of test instructions on scores on an intelligence scale." Educ Psychol Meas 25(1): 87-94, Spring, 1965. (7 References)
Study confirmed that both part and whole performances on cognitive tests are influenced by the direction given to subjects in their general approach to those tasks.

B.   Teacher and Administrative Identification

361   Anastasiow, Nicholas J. "Maximizing identification of the gifted." J Educ Res 57(10): 538-41, July, 1964. (7 References)
Discusses a California district's attempt to identify elementary gifted based on teacher recommendations and testing.

362   Davis, Betty W. "Identifying the gifted child in the average classroom." Peabody J Educ 41(1): 28-32, July, 1963. (14 References)
Article written to help the classroom teacher identify the gifted, deals with appearance, interests, scholarship and classroom behavior of the gifted to stress the importance of recognizing the gifted.

363   Davis, Frederick B. "Intellectually gifted." J Teach Educ 12(4): 497-99, December, 1961. (12 References)
Comments briefly on identification of gifted and encouragement of talents. Contains information for teachers on those topics and on the development of creativity.

364   Haberman, Martin, and Raths, James D. "High, average, low: and what makes teachers think so." Elem Sch J 68(5): 241-45, February, 1968. (0 References)
The findings of this study support the hypothesis that teachers' perceptions of the child who needs remedial help or enrichment are related to the range of achievement in the class to which the child belongs.

365   Jacobs, Jon C. "Are we being misled by fifty years of research on our gifted children?" Gifted Child Q 14(2): 120-23, Summer, 1970. (6 References)
Presents results of a study in which 740 kindergarten children were tested and nineteen identified as gifted. When teachers were later asked to nominate gifted, not one of the nineteen was named.

366   ———. "Effectiveness of teacher and parent identification of gifted children as a function of school level." Psychol Sch 8(2): 140-42, April, 1971. (6 References)
Parents and teachers of kindergarteners were asked to nominate those children they thought were gifted. Sixteen of the twenty-six nominated by parents were gifted, two of the forty-four nominated by teachers were gifted. It is concluded that parents were more conservative than teachers when naming their child as gifted, and were much more accurate.

367   Lessinger, Leon M., and Martinson, Ruth A. "The use of the California Psychological Inventory with gifted pupils." Pers Guid J 39(7): 572-75, March, 1961. (1 Reference)
Scores on the California Psychological Inventory show gifted eighth

graders to be unlike their chronological age peers of average intelligence. When compared with high school gifted students, the similarity is strong. CPI norms for a random population are inappropriate for this gifted group.

368   Minifie, Darrel G. "A study of teachers' ability to identify mentally retarded or gifted children in a self-contained classroom compared with psychological findings." For a summary see: Diss Abstr Int 23(11): 4227-28, May, 1963. (0 References)

369   Pohl, Rudolph G. "Teacher nomination of intellectually gifted children in the primary grades." For a summary see: Diss Abstr Int 31A(5): 2237, November, 1970. (0 References)

370   Renzulli, Joseph S.; Hartman, Robert K.; Callahan, Carolyn M. "Teacher identification of superior students." Except Child 38(3): 211-14, November, 1971. (7 References)
Presents data on the teacher-administered Scale for Rating Behavioral Characteristics of Superior Students. The instrument may prove useful in planning curricula experiences which capitalize on individual strengths.

371   Scharff, Charles E. "A study of the ability of verbally creative teachers to identify verbally creative students." For a summary see: Diss Abstr Int 33A(12, pt. 1): 6739-40, June, 1973. (0 References)

372   Wilson, Carroll D. "Using test results and teacher evaluation in identifying gifted pupils." Pers Guid J 41(8): 720-21, April, 1963. (0 References)
Discussed teacher identification of gifted. Found that a combination of I.Q. scores and achievement scores is probably best locater. Also good are honor roll grades. Even after training, teachers were not accurate enough in identifying all the gifted.

373   Worms, Peter F. "An investigation of elementary school teachers' ability to identify gifted and slow learning pupils." For a summary see: Diss Abstr Int 27A(2): 402-3, August, 1966.

C. General Methods

374   Barbe, Walter B. "Identification of gifted children." Education 88(1): 11-14, September/October, 1967. (5 References)
The author discusses various important factors which should be taken into account in identifying gifted children. He believes that sensitivity is the trait most characteristic of gifted children.

375   Bernal, Ernest M., Jr. "Gifted programs for the culturally different." Educ Dig 41(9): 28-31, May, 1976. (0 References)
Bernal points out drawbacks of the traditional identification measures of the gifted, which select only the most acculturated members of some ethnic minority groups. Suggests use of experts to judge students work, use of peers to identify other gifted, checklists, case studies and related techniques.

376   Doob, Heather S. Gifted students: identification techniques and program organization. Washington, D.C.: Educational Research

Service, April, 1975. 61p.
Provides an overview of identification procedures and types of programs found in the literature and in local school systems. Description of eight methods of identifying the gifted and of ten programs in use in a variety of school districts are outlined.

377 Ellison, Odia. "Identifying racial minority second grade gifted students." For a summary see: Diss Abstr Int 32A(7): 3783-84, January, 1972. (0 References)

378 Fitz-Gibbon, Carol T. "The identification of mentally gifted, 'disadvantaged' students at the eighth grade level." J Negro Educ 43(1): 53-66, Winter, 1974. (0 References)
Since few "disadvantaged" students qualify for gifted programs on the basis of full-scale I.Q. scores of 130+, California changed its code to allow 2 percent of the "disadvantaged" in a school district to be designated as gifted under separate criteria allowing lower test scores. The author describes initial screening by group testing and final selection of eight "gifted" minority students out of 400 disadvantaged eighth graders.

379 Gallegos, Arnold M. "The gifted poor." Educ Leadersh 30(8): 749-53, May, 1973. (7 References)
Presents available data on poor children and explains the factors causing their low performance on all measures of academic achievement. Identifies promising developments in construction of new instruments to assess the disadvantaged without cultural bias.

380 Garlock, Jerry C. "A multiple criterion for including pupils in a gifted program based on trivariate distribution." Calif J Educ Res 19(2): 87-94, March, 1968. (4 References)
Examines the California administrative code as a basis for including pupils in a gifted program. It selects 1 percent of the population as gifted.

381 Gonzalez, Gustavo. "Language, culture, and exceptional children." Except Child 40(8): 565-70, May, 1974. (7 References)
The role of linguistics in the educational assessment of culturally different children is emphasized. The linguistic and cultural biases of I.Q. tests, as well as the role of adaptive behavior and community acceptance in minority groups are discussed. Note is made of the difficulty of identifying gifted children who are culturally different.

382 Grant, Thomas E. "Instrument development and construct validation of an alternative means for the identification of exceptional achievement potential among ethnic minorities." For a summary see: Diss Abstr Int 33A(6): 2788-89, December, 1972. (0 References)

383 Grant, Thomas E., and Renzulli, Joseph S. "Identifying achievement potential in minority group students." Except Child 41(4): 255-59, January, 1975. (8 References)
An inventory was developed to identify potentially successful college students who are from minority cultures and, therefore, might be missed by traditional screening procedures. An initial pool of 145 items was developed and field tested. The final instrument, entitled Relevant Aspects of Potential, consists of thirty items and is intended to supplement other methods for evaluating student performance.

384   ————. Relevant aspects of potential. Marlborough, Connecticut:
       1974, 22p.
This instrument which originally consisted of 145 items is designed for
self-identification by disadvantaged minority group youth. It can be
used to supplement teacher judgment and test results in placement of able
Black students.

385   Granzin, Kent L., and Granzin, Wilma J. "Peer group choice as a
       device for screening intellectually gifted children." Gifted
       Child Q 13(3): 189-94, Fall, 1969. (7 References)
Fourth-graders were asked to distinguish between fifteen traits pertaining to children in general and fifteen traits pertaining primarily to
gifted children. They were later asked to name those of their peers
possessing the fifteen gifted traits. Results showed both gifted and
non-gifted pupils able to judge traits of giftedness; in addition, peer-
group choice of gifted pupils agreed significantly with teacher rankings.

386   Harrison, A.; Netchine, S.; Rouzieres, J. "An EEG study of the
       child with superior intelligence." Electroencephalogr Clin Neuro-
       physiol 26(6): 638-39, June, 1969. (0 References)
Two groups of thirty-nine children between six and twleve years of age
were classified as of high I.Q. (120+) and matched for mental level,
SES, and C.A. One of the groups consisted of normal subjects and the
other of neuropsychiatric patients. Fifteen aspects of the subjects
EEG exams were compared, and it was found that the patients differed
significantly from the normal subjects in six of the variables.

387   Kaufman, Shirley H. "A comparison of alternate methods for iden-
       tifying kindergarten pupils for mentally gifted minor programs."
       For a summary see: Diss Abstr Int 34A(6): 3142, December, 1973.
       (0 References)

388   Khatena, Joe. "Something about myself: a brief screening device
       for identifying creatively gifted children and adults." Gifted
       Child Q 15(4): 262-66, Winter, 1971. (19 References)
Describes an autobiographical instrument useful as a screening device
for locating the highly gifted. Administration, scoring, reliability
and validity are discussed.

389   ————. "Vividness of imagery and creative self perceptions."
       Gifted Child Q 19(1): 33-37, Spring, 1975. (9 References)
After testing college students by means of three instruments, the author
concludes that vividness of imagery has significant relationship with
creative self perceptions, especially relative to seeing, hearing and
touching.

390   Kirk, Winnifred D. "A tentative screening procedure for selecting
       bright and slow children in kindergarten." Except Child 33(4):
       235-41, December, 1966. (0 References)
A screening device for selecting bright and slow kindergarten children.
It shows that an acceptable level of efficacy may be reached in identifying slow children by the present device, but the technique is of
marginal effectiveness in identifying bright children.

391   Malone, Charlotte E. "Identification of educationally deprived
       gifted kindergarten children." For a summary see: Diss Abstr Int
       35A(3): 1533, September, 1974. (0 References)

392 ———. "Potential abilities: to preserve and to enhance." Gifted
    Child Q 19(2): 161-63, Summer, 1975. (0 References)
Describes a method of identifying non-white young gifted children through
behavioral indices (the Behavioral Identification of Gifted--BIG).

393 Malone, Charlotte E., and Moonan, William J. "Behavioral identifi-
    cation of gifted children." Gifted Child Q 19(4): 301-6, Winter,
    1975. (22 References)
Indicators of advanced development of gifted persons can be found at
very early ages. Though numerous studies have confirmed the general
superiority of the gifted on both growth and development, there are
still problems associated with giftedness which have direct bearing on
emotional and intellectual development.

394 Martinson, Ruth A., and Lessinger, Leon M. "Problems in the iden-
    tification of intellectually gifted pupils." Except Child 26(5):
    227-31, January, 1960. (0 References)
Discusses the California State Study Program for Gifted Pupils and its
methods of assessing student potential. Suggests preliminary screening
plus the use of multiple measures such as achievement tests, group intelligence tests and teacher judgments. Early identification and continuous
assessment is recommended.

395 Meeker, Mary N. "Identifying potential giftedness." Natl Assoc
    Second Sch Princ Bull 55(359): 92-95, December, 1971.
Raising a strong objection to the notion that I.Q. scores are the only
means for identifying giftedness in children, the author suggests that
correlated characteristics of giftedness be watched for in environ-
mentally deprived youngsters as possible signs of undeveloped gifts.
She goes on to make a case for the school's responsibility for nurturing
types of giftedness other than verbal or semantic.

396 ———. "The prophecy of giftedness." Gifted Child Q 20(1):
    100-104+, Spring, 1976. (8 References)
A paradigm for the identification and development of giftedness is
offered. The paradigm is illustrated and shown to involve three major
areas of functioning: academic, social-emotional, and physiological.

397 ———. "Understanding the evaluation of gifted: a new method."
    Gifted Child Q 13(4): 220-26, Winter, 1969
Contains a sample evaluation form used by a California school district.
It is divided into four parts. The first part is subject-matter oriented
and is closely tied to grade level expectations. Part II covers skills
in which gifted children need competency. Part III assesses social,
attitudinal and emotional growth, and Part IV covers motivation and
interest.

398 Payne, David A., and Farquhar, William H. "The dimensions of an
    objective measure of academic self-concept." J Educ Psychol 53(4):
    187-92, August, 1962. (9 References)
Study developed an instrument to measure academic self-concepts. Found
theory-derived items which discriminated the motivated.

399 Pielstick, N. L. "Perception of mentally superior children by
    their classmates." Percept Mot Skills 17(1): 47-53, August,
    1963. (12 References)

Classmates of high superior (140+) and low superior (130-140) students successfully identified the high superiors and indicated that they would like to emulate the gifted.

400   Plowman, Paul D. "What can be done for rural gifted children and
      youth?" Gifted Child Q 12(3): 160-74, Fall, 1968. (7 References)
Gifted child education in sparsely populated areas is a matter of identifying and placing children in appropriate learning situations. The
key words are "identification," "placement," "access," "involvement,"
"motivation," "acquiring higher aspirations," and "receiving individualized instruction and opportunities for independent learning."

401   Pysh, F. "Are the gifted the new disadvantaged?" Kootenay Cent
      Gifted J 1(1): 8-10, June, 1973.
The gifted are neglected in many school systems. Suggestions are given
here for identifying the gifted, and establishing educational programs
that will meet their special academic needs.

402   Renzulli, Joseph S. "Talent potential in minority group students."
      Except Child 39(6): 437-44, March, 1973. (38 References)
Pointing out the nature and scope of talent loss among low socio-economic
and minority group members, the author identifies and explores some of
the issues in the retrieval of talent potential.

403   Schena, Richard A. "Search for talented pupils." J Exp Educ
      32(1): 27-41, Fall, 1963. (10 References)
Describes the procedure utilized by the Haverhill School officials in
screening probable candidates for placement into advanced classes. Provides statistical data.

404   Solomon, R. "The gifted child--a problem of recognition." Nurs
      Times 71(24): 940-41, June 12, 1975.
A British educational psychologist notes many cases of failure to recognize highly gifted youngsters. This leads not only to personal and
family maladjustment, but also to wastage of talent so badly needed by
the nation.

405   Sullivan, Allen R. "The identification of gifted and academically
      talented black students: a hidden exceptionality." J Spec Educ
      7(4): 373-79, Winter, 1973. (19 References)
Cites many studies confirming the bias and irrelevance of most stand-
ardized instruments in assessing the intelligence of black youth.
Suggests alternative ways of locating talent in the black community.

406   Taylor, Calvin W. "The highest talent potentials of man." Gifted
      Child Q 13(1): 9-30, Spring, 1969. (15 References)
The author bases his discussion on Guilford's "Structure of Intellect,"
with its 120 high-level talents. In educators' search for talent and
ability in heretofore neglected student populations, it is suggested
that they seek to assess the eighty talents that can now be measured,
instead of concentrating narrowly on the seven or eight abilities
measured by the present I.Q. tests.

407   Thomas, George I., and Crescimbeni, Joseph. Guiding the gifted
      child. New York: Random House, 1966. 206p. (Bibliography)
This book suggests a variety of identification techniques other than

intelligence tests to use in recognizing the gifted student. Alternate
methods of meeting the needs of the gifted are examined such as special
classes, acceleration, enrichment and special programs and activities.

408 Torrance, E. Paul. "Broadening concepts of giftedness in the 70's."
     Gifted Child Q 14(4): 199-208, Winter, 1970. (10 References)
Discussion of multi-faceted definition of giftedness to include many
students who are creative thinkers but do not score in the top percentiles
on intelligence tests.

409 ————. "Differences are not deficits." Teach Coll Rec 75(4):
     471-87, May, 1974.
Discusses issues in the identification and provision of special services
to culturally different gifted children.

410 Torrance, E. Paul, and Khatena, Joe. "What Kind of Person Are You?"
     Gifted Child Q 14(2): 71-75, Summer, 1970. (9 References)
Describes a brief screening device produced by the senior author for the
purpose of identifying creatively gifted adolescents and adults and for
use in teaching and experimental grouping situations. The instrument has
been found to identify persons interested in creative fields of endeavor
and to correlate with other tests that purport to identify creative
persons.

411 Wing, Cliff W. "Student selection, the educational environment, and
     the cultivation of talent." Daedalus 94(3): 632-41, Summer, 1965.
A thoughtful appraisal of selection of the talented which presents a
selection model.

412 Wolfle, Dael L., ed. The discovery of talent. Cambridge,
     Massachusetts: Harvard University Press, 1969. 316p.
The eleven Bingham lectures on the Development of Exceptional Abilities
and Capacities presented in this volume illustrate the thinking of educational psychologists about the problem of early identification of exceptional talent during the 50's and early 60's. This collection documents
the concern and energy shown by psychologists and psychometricians in
finding ways to identify talented individuals.

V

Programming for the Gifted

A. Educational Provisions

1. Grouping

413 Alam, Sami J. "A comparative study of gifted students enrolled in separate and regular curriculums." For a summary see: <u>Diss Abstr Int</u> 29A(10): 3354, April, 1979. (0 References)

414 Allen, Arthur T. "Leadership for the gifted in Catholic elementary schools." <u>Cathol Educ Rev</u> 65(3): 195-204, March, 1967. (0 References)
This article describes the practicum conducted during the second summer and shows how other Catholic colleges and universities may sponsor similar programs for the education of the gifted.

415 Austin, C. Grey. "Honors learning in the seventies." <u>Educ Rec</u> 56(3): 160-69, Summer, 1975. (0 References)
Proposes that secondary schools and colleges promote honors programs, a step toward educational quality.

416 Axford, Lavonne B. <u>A directory of educational programs for the gifted</u>. Metuchen, New Jersey: Scarecrow, 1971. 282p.
This is a listing of public and private schools in alphabetical order by state. Information provided includes name and address, entrance requirements, and number of titles in the library. A section at the end of each state gives summer-only programs.

417 Balcerak, Carl. "Educating the gifted disadvantaged: Msgr. Kelly Junior High School, New York." <u>Cathol Sch J</u> 68(9): 15-18, November, 1968.
Gifted students from the ghetto are challenged and respond with openness and spontaneity. Teachers guide and motivate students to pursue their education with greatest possible freedom. The program prevents dropouts.

418 Balow, Bruce, and Curtin, James. "Ability grouping of bright pupils." <u>Elem Sch J</u> 66(6): 321-26, March, 1966.
The present study was designed to investigate the effect of grouping by intelligence quotient on the distribution of basic school skills among bright third-grade pupils. Neither of the findings offers any support for ability grouping.

419 Becker, Leonard J. "An analysis of the science and mathematics achievement of gifted sixth grade children enrolled in segregated,

partially segregated and non-segregated classes." For a summary
see: Diss Abstr Int   24(4): 1446, October, 1963. (0 References)

420 Bennett, Frances, et. al. "Potentially gifted and talented high
     school youth benefit from independent study." Gifted Child Q 15(2):
     96-108, Summer, 1971. (22 References)
Deals with the philosophy, characteristics, selection and examples of
projects in an independent study program for the gifted implemented by
the author in a Connecticut school district.

421 Berk, Ron. "The perception of divergency in highly gifted and
     heterogeneous preadolescents." Gifted Child Q 10(2): 58-61,
     Summer, 1966. (3 References)
It was safe to conclude that homogeneously grouped gifted students will
perceive less pressure to conform and will tend to evaluate divergency
in a more neutral or positive manner than will those heterogeneously
grouped.

422 Bettelheim, Bruno, and Mott, Kenneth. "Grouping the gifted:
     opinions differ." NEAJ 54(3): 8-11, March, 1965.
Bettelheim argues that the gifted benefit and develop constructively
when they are not ability grouped; Mott argues for ability grouping.

423 Borg, Walter R. An evaluation of ability grouping. U.S. Depart-
     ment of Health, Education, and Welfare, Office of Education,
     Cooperative Research Project No. 577. Logan: Utah State Univer-
     sity, 1964. 441p.
A definitive study of the ramifications of ability grouping. The study
should prove useful to administrators considering special provisions for
the gifted.

424 Briscoe, Delphina. "A rationale, design and assessment for a program
     for intellectually gifted minority children." For a summary see:
     Diss Abstr Int 37A(2): 792-93, August, 1976. (0 References)

425 Burch, Joyce A., and Calovini, Charles R. "A day with the gifted."
     Natl Elem Princ 52(2): 82-84, October, 1972. (0 References)
Recounts the author's visit to one of the nine Major Work centers for the
gifted in the Cleveland Public Schools. They discuss the approach to
reading, performance in foreign languages, experience in research, and
the discovery method used in science and mathematics in the second to
sixth grade classes they observed.

426 Cantrell, Robert P., and Cantrell, Mary L. "Preventive mainstream-
     ing: impact of a supportive service program on pupils." Except
     Child 42(7): 381-86, April, 1976.
Evaluated the effects of a support-teacher program in maintaining exceptional and potentially exceptional children within the regular school
program. Included were almost 400 high I.Q. subjects.

427 Carson, Kenneth O. "An evaluation of the objectives and achieve-
     ment of special classes for gifted children in the Kingston public
     schools." Ontario J Educ Res 6(1): 23-36, Autumn, 1963.
     (18 References)
Discusses the aims and objectives of a special class for gifted children
in Canada which extends from fifth to eighth grade and involves twenty-

five to thirty pupils chosen from the school population of 600 fourth
graders in Kingston.

428   Chidley, Nadine. "Education for the exceptional child." Pediatr
      Clin North Am 12(4): 1099-1107, November, 1965. (12 References)
The author, director of special education in Winnipeg, Canada, describes
in detail her school district's comprehensive and forward-looking program
for exceptional children. The Major Work Program for gifted students
(I.Q. 125+) begins in grade four and continues through grade nine. At
the senior high level, an honors program has been developed for these
pupils. Follow-up studies are being conducted of M. W. graduates now at
Canadian universities.

429   Cluff, James E. "The effect of experimentation and class reorganiza-
      tion on the scholastic achievement of selected gifted sixth grade
      pupils in Wichita, Kansas." For a summary see: Diss Abstr Int
      25(3): 1676-77, September, 1964. (0 References)

430   Daniels, J. C. "The effects of streaming in the primary school: a
      comparison of streamed and unstreamed schools." Br J Educ Psychol
      31(Part I): 69-78, February, 1961; (Part II): 119-127, June, 1961.
      (22 References)
Reports the results of a questionnaire designed to determine the views of
English primary school teachers on streaming. The second paper reports
on the results of streaming. Researchers found that non-streaming was
more beneficial.

431   Drews, Elizabeth M. Student abilities, grouping patterns, and class-
      room interaction. East Lansing: Michigan State University, 1963.
      246p.
This is the final report of a cooperative research project done under the
auspices of the Office of Education, U. S. Department of Health, Education
and Welfare. Entitled "The Effectiveness of Homogeneous and Heterogeneous
Ability Grouping in Ninth Grade English Classes with Slow, Average, and
Superior Students," the project differentiated learning situations by
varying patterns of grouping and teaching. This report is divided into
Part I: Background, Part II: Research Procedures, and Part III: Findings and Interpretations.

432   George, John C. "Language arts for the gifted." Elem Engl 49(4):
      582-84, April, 1972. (0 References)
Describes the author's language arts class of thirty upper elementary
school pupils who read at advanced levels. He combines an individualized
reading program with weekly compositions, skill work, vocabulary development, daily oral selections from adult and teenage literature, and
exposure to the great art and music of Western society.

433   Goldberg, Miriam L., and Passow, A. Harry. "The effects of ability
      grouping." Education 82(8): 482-87, April, 1962. (0 References)
The authors discuss the Columbia University Talented Youth Project's
research on the effects of ability grouping on the academic, social and
personal growth of intermediate grade children. They conclude that in
the absence of specific plans for changing the content and methods of
teaching to suit each group of pupils, ability grouping does not seem to
make any appreciable difference.

434 Goldberg, Miriam L.; Passow, A. Harry; Justman, Joseph. The effects
     of ability grouping. New York: Bureau of Publications, Teachers
     College, Columbia University, 1965.
This large-scale formal educational experiment found that ability grouping
of itself has no important effect on the academic achievement of students.
However, ability grouping may be used effectively when it grows out of
the needs of the curriculum and when it is varied and flexible.

435 Handler, Harry. "An analysis of the selection criteria for assign-
     ment of students to advanced placement classes in the Los Angeles
     Unified School District." For a summary see: Diss Abstr Int 28A(8):
     3025, February, 1968. (0 References)

436 Hermanson, David P., and Wright, David C. "Perceptual change of
     student and staff toward learning by participation in a seminar
     program for the gifted learner." For a summary see: Diss Abstr
     Int 30A(7): 2905-6, January, 1970. (0 References)

437 Hofset, Arnold. "Gifted pupils as sources of inspiration in the
     class." Pedagog Forsk 15(3): 137-48, 1971. (10 References)
This study tested the reality of the statement that gifted pupils are a
source of inspiration in elementary school classes. No significant
achievement differences were found in classes with four or more gifted
pupils, and attitudes toward school were about equal in all classes,
regardless of gifted students.

438 Hogan, Ralph E. "Georgia's GHP." Today's Educ 62(5): 34-35,
     May, 1973. (0 References)
The director of Georgia's Governor's Honors Program discusses the
details of this state's ten-year old summer program for gifted junior
and senior high school students.

439 Jackman, William D., and Bachtold, Louise M. "Evaluation of a
     seminar for gifted junior high students." Gifted Child Q 13(3):
     163-68, Fall, 1969.
A report of the Seminar Program, a regularly scheduled series of small
group discussions led by school counselors during the school day. It was
appraised by both students and teachers as a valuable learning experience.

440 Jannon, Vorna C., and Gallagher, James J. "The social choices of
     students in racially integrated classes for the culturally dis-
     advantaged talented." Except Child 33(4): 221-26, December,
     1966. (9 References)
Study investigated sociometric choices of 100 able disadvantaged pupils
in intermediate classrooms. There were substantial cross-racial choices
within the group, with many factors such as sex and racial proportion
influencing the nature and kind of choice.

441 Kelly, Robert E. "An appraisal of the influence of special honors
     programs on selected experiences of intellectually gifted students."
     For a summary see: Diss Abstr Int 26(12): 7128-29, June, 1966.
     (0 References)

442 Lamb, Ronald D. "An evaluation of a differential education program
     for able and gifted high school students in southwestern Oregon."
     For a summary see: Diss Abstr Int 31A(4): 1650-51, October,
     1970. (0 References)

443   Lee, J. Murray. "Demonstration centers for gifted elementary pupils."
      Ill J Educ 56(6): 10-14, October, 1965. (0 References)
Presents a brief discussion of pupil selection, curricular innovations,
newer teaching methods, parental involvement, organizational patterns,
cooperative work by teachers and in-service training at Illinois demonstration centers for gifted pupils.

444   Ling, Barbara, and Simonson, E. H. The challenge of the highly
      gifted. Columbus, Ohio: State of Ohio Department of Education,
      1965. 99p.
This publication describes how the challenge in the title was met in
Ohio's Summit County Schools where a two-year demonstration project for
highly gifted fifth graders was conducted from 1962-1964.

445   Lynn, Bob. "Disadvantaged gifted progress in a new residential
      school." Gifted Child Q 12(1): 18-22, Spring, 1968.
Describes the first year of operation of The Lincoln School, a revolu-
tionary college-preparatory school for Kentucky teenagers from economically disadvantaged families. Its main objective is to prepare its
integrated student body of high I.Q. youngsters to meet admission standards of the most selective colleges and universities.

446   Maaia, Linda J. "Rhode Island's Tri-City Project Gifted." Todays
      Educ 62(5): 36-37, May, 1973.
Project Gifted takes place in three Rhode Island cities and involves
students in grades four, five and six. Techniques discussed could provide
stimulation for other communities interested in developing programs for
their gifted.

447   Mahler, Fred L. "A study of achievement differences in selected
      junior high school gifted students heterogeneously or homogeneously
      grouped." For a summary see: Diss Abstr Int 22(7): 2267, January,
      1962. (0 References)

448   Marland, Sidney P. "Advanced Placement." Todays Educ 65(1): 43-
      44, January/February, 1976. (0 References)
As president of the College Entrance Examination Board, Dr. Marland reviews the success of its Advanced Placement Program, which enables
talented high school students to study college-level courses while still
in school. In spite of its proven effectiveness, the option is still
under-utilized, and some reasons for this fact are offered.

449   Maybury, Margaret W., and Lesser, Gerald S. "Program for gifted
      children." Elem Sch J 64(2): 94-101, November, 1963. (2 Refer-
      ences)
Focused on an experimental teaching program for first graders. Found
that children selected as gifted in a given area of mental ability benefit more from special instruction in that area than do children selected
for giftedness in other areas.

450   Pace, Warren J. "The academic effects of assigning gifted students
      to special centers in the Fairfax County Schools." For a summary
      see: Diss Abstr Int 31A(3): 936, September, 1970. (0 References)

451   Pearlman, Lauree A. "A comparison of selected characteristics of
      gifted children enrolled in Major Work and regular curriculums." For

a summary see: Diss Abstr Int 32A(9): 4846, March, 1972.
(0 References)

452 Powell, Wilma R., and Munsey, Cecil. "San Diego's program for the
     gifted." Today's Educ 62(5): 38-39, May, 1973.
This article presents a capsule view of San Diego's programs for the
gifted which began in 1949. Some of the techniques for educating the
gifted include seminar groups, independent study, resource people in the
community, and joint retreats and study groups between students and
parents and teachers.

453 Press, Billie K. "Education of the gifted in the USSR." Except
     Child 30(6): 241-44, February, 1964. (9 References)
Describes the equalitarian system of elementary education in the USSR
which refuses to recognize individual differences in ability. The talents
of academically gifted children (the top five to ten percent) are developed by means of diverse programs offered after school at the Young
Pioneer Palaces. Most of these students are later admitted to the university where they receive many privileges.

454 Raspberry, William. "What about elitist high schools?" Today's
     Educ 65(1): 36-39, January/February, 1976. (0 References)
The Public Affairs Columnist for the Washington Post makes a very con-
vincing plea for special high schools for the academically talented, on
the order of Brooklyn Tech and Boston Latin School. He cites Washington,
D.C.'s Dunbar High School, which produced many outstanding black leaders,
as an example of the intellectual atmosphere needed for rigorous academic
work.

455 Tisdall, William J. "Disadvantaged gifted child, Lincoln School,
     Lexington." Except Child 34(6): 389, February, 1968.
Describes the program of a University of Kentucky laboratory school for
gifted from economically and culturally disadvantaged backgrounds.
Curriculum is determined by students' needs and abilities with an ongoing research program.

2. Acceleration

456 Adler, Marilynne J.; Pass, Lawrence E.; Wright, E.N. " A study of
     the effects of an acceleration programme in Toronto secondary
     schools." Ontario J Educ Res 6(1): 1-22, Autumn, 1963.
Evaluates the results of accelerated programs in eleven Toronto secondary
schools (nine academic, one commercial, and one technical) for students
of high I.Q. (125+) who had not previously been accelerated during public
school.

457 Barnickle, Donald W., and Lindberg, Ruth T. "Unwilling accelerate:
     a problem of the non-graded school." Elem Sch J 67(2): 84-87,
     November, 1966. (1 Reference)
Presents case study problems that could only exist in a non-graded
school--those of boys whose parents did not want them accelerated.

458 Birch, Jack W.; Barney, David; Tisdall, William J. "Early admission
     of able children to school." Sch Life 46(7): 7-9, June, 1964.
Results supply evidence that able children, properly selected, can successfully enter school at an age earlier than that of usual admission.

459   Braga, Joseph L. "Analysis and evaluation of early admission to
      school for mentally advanced children." J Educ Res 63(3): 103-6,
      November, 1969. (7 References)
A study of the effect of early admission on children in the first, third,
fifth and seventh grades in terms of academic and non-academic achievement, social, and emotional development. No significant differences were
found between early admission pupils and their peers.

460   ————. "Early admission: opinion versus evidence." Elem Sch J
      72(1): 35-46, October, 1971. (47 References)
A comprehensive review of research related to early admission to school
of mentally advanced children. Covers criteria for admission, effect on
achievement, social and emotional adjustment, future occupational adjustment, and teacher attitudes toward acceleration.

461   Fox, Gudelia A. "The accelerated adults view acceleration." Gifted
      Child Q 10(1): 15-16, Spring, 1966. (7 References)
Reviews a study of a small sample of talented adults (teachers), all of
whom had been accelerated while in elementary school. Questionnaire data
indicated that for the subjects more disadvantages than advantages were
attributed to acceleration.

462   Gustav, Alice, and Crosman, Arthur M. "College grades of underage
      students." Sch Soc 90(2212): 298-99, September 22, 1962. (0
      References)
In a study of underage college students, results showed they were doing
less well than the general population. Girls were doing better than boys.
However, those underage students doing best matched the top percentage
of the normal age population, thus acceleration can be beneficial.

463   Hobson, James R. "High school performance of underage pupils
      initially admitted to kindergarten on the basis of physical and
      psychological examinations." Educ Psychol Meas 23(1): 159-70,
      Spring, 1963. (37 References)
Draws the following conclusions: (1) the underage scholars continue to
be superior through high school, (2) they engaged in a larger number of
extracurricular activities, (3) the underage scholars got twice as many
awards, (4) a larger percentage of underage entered college, and (5)
thus, underage scholars should be admitted to school programs.

464   Keating, Daniel P., and Stanley, Julian C. "Extreme measures for
      the exceptionally gifted in mathematics and science." Educ Res (U.S.)
      1(9): 3-7, September, 1972.
Results of a search for junior high school students with precocious mathematical and scientific ability indicated that many had already mastered
senior high science and mathematics material. Measures of acceleration
for these students are discussed.

465   King, Fred M. "Student attitudes toward acceleration." Education
      88(1): 73-77, September/October, 1967. (0 References)
Reports on an investigation of nearly 600 secondary school students
accelerated in science, mathematics and English. A great majority indicated that acceleration met their needs for a more demanding and challenging program.

466 Klausmeier, Herbert J. "Effects of accelerating bright older ele-
     mentary pupils: a follow-up." J Educ Psychol 54(3): 165-71,
     June, 1963. (15 References)
Reports on twenty pupils finishing fifth grade who had been "skipped"
from second to fourth grade. They showed no unfavorable academic, social,
emotional, or physical consequences in comparison with four kinds of
control groups.

467 Klausmeier, Herbert J.; Goodwin, William L.; Ronda, Teckla.
     "Effects of accelerating bright, older elementary pupils: a second
     follow-up." J Educ Psychol 59(1): 53-58, February, 1968. (2
     References)
Bright older children accelerated in lower elementary grades were compared with non-accelerants toward end of ninth grade. On tests, both
accelerant groups were equal to or higher than the other groups. The
non-accelerated older bright children surpassed the accelerated of one
group in some tests. Both groups participated in school activities,
advanced classes and athletics at about the same rate.

468 Kraus, Philip E. "The accelerated." Gifted Child Q 17(1): 36-47,
     Spring, 1973. (7 References)
Acceleration is discussed as one method of educating elementary age
gifted children in New York City's special progress classes. Follow-up
studies are cited.

469 Meskill, Victor P., and Lauper, Russell T. "Breaking the lockstep
     for the gifted." Natl Assoc Second Sch Princ Bull 57(370): 58-
     62, February, 1973.
This article describes a program that offers freshman college courses
taught by college professors to qualified high school seniors in place
of the normal senior year curriculum.

470 Porter, Rutherford B. "A reporting procedure for early school
     admission for mentally advanced children." J Sch Psychol 9(2):
     127-30, 1971. (12 References)
A short developmental technique for reporting a prediction of school
success for children being investigated for possible early entrance into
school. Emphasis is on communication with the parent. A sample parental
explanation form is included.

471 Pressey, Sidney, L. "Educational acceleration: occasional proce-
     dure or major issue?" Pers Guid J 41(1): 12-17, September, 1962.
     (15 References)
Presents considerations arguing that acceleration is the most advanta-
geous method of dealing with talented pupils, that the top fifth of all
students might well benefit from it, and that it may occur desirably any-
where from kindergarten to professional school.

472 ————. "Education's (and psychology's) disgrace: and a double-
     dare." Psychol Sch 6(4): 353-58, October, 1969. (15 References)
Pressey deplores the rigid and time-consuming academic requirements
imposed on the talented student, as well as on his average classmate.
He suggests pre-tests, with credit given and basic courses skipped for
the able students who can then finish courses in half the usual time,
thus saving themselves and the colleges untold expense.

473 ————. "Two basic neglected psychoeducational problems." Am
     Psychol 20(6): 391-95, June, 1965. (17 References)
This paper, read by the author at the ceremony presenting him with the
Thorndike Award for distinguished psychological contributions to education, is concerned with increasing educational efficiency by shortening
overlong programs. Research is cited showing that bright children, when
accelerated, were well adjusted and more successful academically than
those progressing at the usual rate. Pressey advocates acceleration as
a way of permitting the talented to begin their professional careers
earlier and thus save society much time and money.

474 Reynolds, Maynard C., ed. Early school admission for mentally
     advanced children. Washington, D.C.: The Council for Exceptional
     Children, NEA, 1962. 56p. (Bibliography)
A thorough discussion of the issue of early admission, with particular
reference to existing programs in Massachusetts, Illinois, Minnesota, and
Nebraska.

475 Rice, Joseph P. "Developmental approach to pupil acceleration."
     Clearing House 40(4): 216-20, December, 1965.
Author explores various aspects of acceleration and recommends a positive
course of action. Points out that accelerated pupils need more special
counseling opportunities. Discusses commonly used acceleration programs.

476 Richards, Stanley E. "A study of early admission students at the
     University of Utah." For a summary see: Diss Abstr Int 27A(8):
     2407, February, 1967. (0 References)

477 Stanley, Julian C. "Accelerating the educational progress of intel-
     lectually gifted youths." Educ Psychol 10(3): 133-46, Fall, 1973.
     (15 References)
The author contends that aptitude and achievement tests designed for much
older students are invaluable for finding very high ability at younger
ages. The usual in-grade, non-accelerative "enrichment" procedures often
recommended for intellectually gifted children are not advocated here.

478 ————. "Identifying and nurturing the intellectually gifted."
     Phi Delta Kappan 58(3): 234-37, November, 1976.
Describes the author's John's Hopkins program of radical acceleration for
highly gifted math students. Makes a case for acceleration over other
forms of enrichment.

479 Stephens, Thomas M., and Gibson, Arthur R. Acceleration and the
     gifted. Columbus, Ohio: Ohio Division of Special Education, 1963.
     73p.
The monograph consists of five introductory articles in addition to the
project reports. Covers articles on advanced placement in arithmetic,
English and chemistry.

480 Stephenson, Carolyn. "The gifted child: reflections on his place
     in school and in society." Orbit 5(3): 12-14, June, 1974.
This article from the journal of Ontario,Canada's Institute for Studies
in Education focuses on acceleration and enrichment programs and practices for the gifted.

481 Twitchell, Theodore G. "Programs initiated by institutions of
     higher learning for gifted high school students of California."
     For a summary see: Diss Abstr Int 25(3): 1672-73, September,
     1964. (0 References)

482 Ward, Virgil S. "Educating the most educable: the nature and sig-
     nificance of the task." Va J Educ 59(7): 16-17, March, 1966.
Discusses the necessity of differential education for the gifted. Author
feels that gifted's education can and should be compacted into a shorter
time span so as to release the creative and productive energies for
service to mankind.

483 Weinstein, Beatrice; Mitchell, Patrick; Schwartzstein, Morton; et.
     al. "The adjustment of children in a suburban community who were
     accelerated in elementary school." J Sch Psychol 5(1): 60-63,
     Fall, 1966. (1 Reference)
The results of the study indicate that of those children who had been
accelerated, more boys than girls experienced some difficulty in one or
more of the academic, social or emotional areas.

484 Williams, George. "Early admission for high school students."
     Plan Higher Educ 3(4): 9-10, August, 1974.
Academic planning at many colleges and universities has recently focused
on early admission programs for high school students. The pros and cons
of the policy are examined.

485 Wootton, Richard R. "High school students can handle college
     courses." Sch Couns 16(5): 394-97, May, 1969. (0 References)
The successful performance of forty-eight Provo, Utah high school students
in college classes in the area of their greatest academic strengths proves
the author's hypothesis.

                         3. Enrichment

486 Addy, Sandra T. "Effects of an evaluative thinking game on class-
     room interaction." For a summary see: Diss Abstr Int 35A(7):
     4278-79, January, 1975. (0 References)

487 Barbe, Walter B. "Chattanooga's program for talented youth."
     Except Child 27(7): 350-52, March, 1961 (0 References)
Reports on gifted children conference and program which resulted. Lists
the programs established in extracurricular time with volunteer community
help and resources.

488 Berkowitz, Harry. "An alternative position in preparing talented
     tots: some problems and implications." Gifted Child Q 11(4):
     241-47, Winter, 1967. (15 References)
Describes a program in which the child's own interests determine the
area and scope of his involvement. Efforts are directed at increasing
communication either in written form, or orally, musically and artistically.

489 Blakeslee, Sandra. "A college for kids." Educ Dig 41(1): 36-37,
     September, 1975.
Describes Marin County, California's innovative enrichment program for
gifted children age five to sixteen. A total of 1,400 children from

fourteen school districts and thirty-two private and parochial schools
participated during 1974-75. The most popular mini-courses offered were
computers, speed-reading, electronics, and marine biology, which were
offered to all age levels on Saturdays, after school hours and during
summer vacations.

490   Bovee, Oliver H. "Evolution of a program for the gifted." Clearing
       House 38(7): 412-14, March, 1964. (0 References)
Describes an Arizona program which provided enrichment for the gifted in
humanities, social sciences, applied sciences, and creative activities.

491   Broome, Elizabeth, ed. Educating for the future: 21st century
       teaching. Raleigh, North Carolina: State Department of Public
       Instruction, Division of Exceptional Children, 1973. 71p.
Compiled for use with gifted children, is a collection of activities and
lesson plans developed by teachers of the gifted at a summer institute.

492   Cameron, Sue. "Define a perfect pupil." Times Educ Suppl 3070:
       17, March 29, 1974. (0 References)
Report stresses the need for enrichment programs for gifted children,
so they can remain in ordinary classes, yet still be given headroom to
develop particular talents.

493   Campbell, Richard D. "Special workshop for the gifted." Todays
       Educ 58(9): 32-33, December, 1969. (0 References)
Describes Greenwich, Connecticut's enrichment program for intellectually
talented upper elementary school pupils who spend two half-day sessions
each week at the Workshop.

494   Cohen, Joseph W., ed. The superior student in American higher edu-
       cation. New York: McGraw-Hill, 1966. 299p.
Edited by the former director of the Inter-University Committee on the
Superior Student (ICSS), this is a collection of writings on honors programs in American institutions of higher education. There is a section
on honors programs in secondary schools and one on evaluation.

495   "Cooperation: the gifted-college for school kids." Nations Sch
       Coll 2(4): 23-26, April, 1975.
Reports on a Marin County, California special program which allows hun-
dreds of the areas brightest elementary school children to attend the
county's two community colleges on a no-grade, no-credit basis. With
instruction available in such diverse subjects as computer technology,
foreign languages, geology, electronics, and creative writing, more than
1,400 youngsters enrolled in ninety classes during academic year 1974-
75.

496   Dailey, Rebecca F. "Media in the round--learning in the special
       experience room." Teach Except Child 4(1): 4-9, Fall, 1971.
       (0 References)
Learning in this Pennsylvania comprehensive elementary school, which
includes physically and mentally handicapped as well as academically
talented students, centers around a unique room where sensory experiences
form the core of the curriculum, bringing various concepts to life and
adding new dimensions.

497 Dunn, Barbara J. "The El Monte project for high risk talent re-
     trieval." Gifted Child Q 16(3): 235-39, Fall, 1972. (0 References)
Describes the bussing of gifted sixth to eighth graders to the campus of
California State College, Los Angeles for four extended day experiences
with the college facilities. An open education concept model is proposed
to correct the program's deficiencies.

498 Dunn, Harry C. "Gifted children find research can be fun." Gifted
     Child Q 12(1): 10-13, Spring, 1968.
Describes a project in descriptive research which was carried out by
Bradley University's cooperative program in education of the academically
talented. A fourth grade survey of student transportation is included to
give teachers an indication of the scope and structure of the project.

499 Elkind, David. "Preschool education: enrichment or instruction?"
     Child Educ 45(6): 321-28, February, 1969. (20 References)
Concerned with the pre-school education of the middle-class child, the
author presents the contrasting arguments of the enrichment-instruction
conflict. He discusses readiness, pressure and the fostering of self-
expression and creativity.

500 Evyatar, A. "Enrichment therapy." Educ Res 15(2): 115-22,
     February, 1973. (5 References) (U.K.)
The author, a mathematician at Israel's Institute of Technology, describes
programs for very gifted children at the Technion from 1969-1971. The
basic principle was that the courses should be child-centered and try to
counteract "negative-gifted-child-syndrome,"by improving emotional balance
and developing capabilities. In addition to courses in computer programing, electronics, mathematics and other sciences, experiments were made
with some humanities courses. The eleven to thirteen year olds involved
made progress in both cognitive and affective domains.

501 Frankel, Edward. "Effects of a program of advanced summer study on
     the self-perceptions of academically talented high school students."
     Except Child 30(6): 245-49, February, 1964. (7 References)
The student body of 158 gifted boys and girls attending the Advanced
Studies Program at a New Hampshire school were rated on self-attitudes
at the beginning and end of the six-week session. They showed growth in
self-image, and satisfaction and developed the incentives to maintain
higher levels of aspirations.

502 Gold, Marvin J. "Introducing the gifted brief." Except Child
     37(8): 593-96, April, 1971. (0 References)
Presents file-size activity cards designed to reinforce and extend curricular goals. The cards outline activity objectives, major skills
employed, materials, procedures, an illustration, and variations.

503 Gruber, Joseph J. "Effects of enriched academic environment on
     scholastic achievement of culturally deprived pupils." Am Correct
     Ther J 29(2): 47-50, March/April, 1975.
A study of forty-one high school students who had completed two years in
a special residential school for intellectually superior but economically
deprived or culturally different students. It concludes that an enriched
environment significantly improves the scholastic achievement of disadvantaged students, with the greatest improvement occurring in the first
year.

504   Hanson, Verlan J.   "The enrichment program for high ability students in the Sweetwater Union High School district."   For a summary see: Diss Abstr Int   29A(2):   405-6, August, 1968.   (0 References)

505   Lazar, Alfred L.; Gensley, Juliana; Gowan, John C.   "Developing positive attitudes through curriculum planning for young gifted children."   Gifted Child Q   16(1):   27-31, Spring, 1972.
Describes enrichment program with visitation designed to change attitude of gifted toward handicapped and/or creative people.   Proved that enrichment tasks that challenge the gifted learner can result in enhancement of positive attitudes.

506   Lemen, Robert F.   "A summer school for the gifted."   Sch Soc   89(2194):   270-71, Summer, 1961.
Reports on a summer institute for 502 Missouri gifted.

507   Lessinger, Leon M.   "Enrichment for gifted pupils: its nature and nurture."   Except Child   30(3):   119-22, November, 1963.   (6 References)
Discusses enrichment in education of the gifted: considerations, definition, illustrations, and role of the teacher.

508   Levitin, Sonia.   "What's good for the gifted is good for everyone."   Parents Mag   46(9):   62-63+, September, 1971.   (0 References)
An in-depth presentation of one California school district's enrichment program for bright children which has upgraded the teaching--and the performance--of all the pupils in the schools.

509   Martinson, Ruth A.   Curriculum enrichment for the gifted in the primary grades.   Englewood Cliffs, New Jersey: Prentice-Hall, 1968.   115p.   (Bibliography)
Special planning for the gifted was first developed at the secondary school level, but this paperback book stresses identification and education of gifted children at the point of entry during early school years.   Principles for curriculum planning and detailed descriptions of specific practices in social studies, science, mathematics, language arts, music, and art are presented.   Included is a checklist for evaluation of any school's program for gifted children.

510   Meyers, Elizabeth S.; Ball, Helen H.; Crutchfield, Marjorie.   "Specific suggestions for the kindergarten teacher and the advanced child."   Gifted Child Q   18(1):   25-30, Spring, 1974.   (13 References)
A kindergartener who is not physically or emotionally ready for the first grade but who shows advanced development in some areas must be given day-to-day challenges in his special skill.   Suggestions for resources and activities are offered.

511   Miller, Sue E.   "Mural and music depicted U.S. history: Juneau's elementary gifted/talented children's enrichment program."   Instructor   85(2):   50-52, October, 1975.
Reports an award winning program on bicentennial themes.   History of the United States in art, song, and dance was the theme of the special program of the gifted.

512   Pinellie, Thomas E. "Utilizing community resources in programming
      for the gifted." Gifted Child Q 17(3): 199-202, Fall, 1973. (0
      References)
Briefly described is a six-week cooperative program involving community
resources to provide grade eleven and twelve gifted students with opportunities to exercise abilities and make realistic vocational choices.

513   Pringle, Robert G.; Webb, Judith G.; Warner, Dennis A.; et. al.
      "Innovative education for gifted children in rural elementary
      schools." Elem Sch J 73(2): 79-84, November, 1972. (2 References)
The authors describe a program of enrichment for academically talented
third, fourth, and fifth graders involving thirteen rural school districts in Washington state. While the participating pupils and their
parents were enthusiastic about the program, teachers of regular classes
expressed negative reactions.

514   Renzulli, Joseph S. "The enrichment triad model: a guide for
      developing defensible programs for the gifted and talented." Gifted
      Child Q 20(3): 303-26, Fall, 1976. (0 References)
Questions the appropriateness of many activities that are included in
gifted education and presents an enrichment model that can be used as a
guide in the development of qualitatively different programs in this
area of special education.

515   Rogers, Lloyd. "Our endangered species." Mensan 10(11): 25-27,
      November, 1974.
Suggests to Mensa members potential activities for gifted children,
including Saturday seminars, weekend trips to art galleries and museums,
and involvement in research projects at local colleges.

516   Sharp, Bert L. "The use of educational television in large classes
      of pupils with above and below average I.Q.'s." Florida J Educ Res
      4(1): 3-9, January, 1962. (2 References)
Studied the result of using television with large classes of students of
high (115+) I.Q. and low (-85) I.Q. The majority of the comparisons
showed no significant differences for either group of pupils.

517   Sheehy, Sister Gregory. "Motivation and enrichment for the gifted."
      Cathol Sch J 67(2): 31-32, February, 1967. (0 References)
Takes the position that the gifted make up 20 percent of our school population. Discusses ways teachers can identify able learners and enrichment opportunities that can be offered within the framework of the regular
classroom.

518   Sisk, Dorothy A. "Humanism as it applies to gifted children."
      Talents Gifts 18(2): 25-30, January, 1976.
Discusses the application of humanistic and affective educational principles in a Saturday morning enrichment program for gifted children from
four to seventeen years of age. Lesson plans are given for ten
"Encounter-Lessons" which emphasize each pupil's self-concept, potential,
and relationship with others.

519   Sonntag, Joyce. "Sensitivity training with gifted children." Gifted
      Child Q 13(1): 51-57, Spring, 1969. (6 References)
Recounts the author's experience with a one month summer workshop for
gifted children of nine to ten years at a California state college.

Objectives were to develop sensitivity by providing experiences in attending, receiving, responding, and valuing. The action oriented curriculum
allowed much discussion of the feelings engendered, and encouraged interpersonal feedback.

520   Walker, Joseph J. "Genies in the magic bubble." Teach Except Child
      8(3): 110-11, Spring, 1976.
Gifted children from Atlanta's inner-city take fantasy trips under the
sea, into space and to foreign lands in a teacher constructed "magic
bubble." The bubble provides the children with a vehicle which encourages
creative expression and communication in the form of art, writing, and
research projects.

521   Zaslow, Edmund M. "Talent in the ghetto." Am Educ 3(3): 24-27,
      March, 1967. (0 References)
Describes New York programs for intellectually gifted children. Mentions
many curriculum projects and some problems.

4. Individual Study

522   Chickering, Arthur W. "Dimensions of independence." J Exp Educ
      32(3): 313-16, Spring, 1964.
The development of independence is a major objective of the college where
the author teaches. Independent study seems to be a primary factor in
helping students achieve this independence.

523   Cooke, Gwendolyn J. "Alternative programing for the gifted through
      the university without walls." Talent Gifts 18(2): 18-21, January,
      1976.
The U.W.W. project offers gifted high school graduates the opportunity
to design their own collegiate learning programs from community and
college resources.

524   Gallagher, James J.; Greenman, Margaret; Karnes, Merle; et. al.
      "Individual classroom adjustments for gifted children in elementary
      schools." Except Child 26(8): 409-22+, April, 1960. (12 Refer-
      ences)
A case study approach was used to adjust the environment of fifty-four
highly gifted pupils (I.Q. 150+) in grades two to five. Objective
reports of parents and teachers suggested that they had observed considerable gains in their children in all areas of development during the
program.

525   Hymes, Rita M., and Bullock, Franklin O. "Alternative schools:
      answer to the gifted child's boredom." Gifted Child Q 19(4):
      340-45, Winter, 1975. (5 References)
The counselors at two Los Angeles alternative secondary schools describe
the individualized learning programs designed to provide a more congenial
learning environment for gifted students disillusioned by the regular
school programs.

526   Markwalder, Winston. "Design for a process oriented learning con-
      tract appropriate for high ability students." South J Educ Res
      10(3): 124-34, Summer, 1976.
Presents a revised contract form which has been modified to match the
process, rather than the product-oriented learning patterns of the gifted.

527   Martinson, Ruth A.; Hermanson, David R.; Banks, George. "An independent study seminar program for the gifted." Except Child 38(5):
421-26, January, 1972. (1 Reference)
Describes a program in which forty highly gifted students from three high
schools were allowed a high degree of autonomy, and self-determination in
learning. It is compared to other, more prestructured, programs for the
gifted.

528   Plowman, Paul D. "Programming for the gifted child." Except Child
35(7): 547-51, March, 1969. (7 References)
Stresses individualized instruction for the gifted, but also discusses
regular class instruction, private study, acceleration, counseling and
the need for ongoing evaluation.

529   Ramos, Suzanne. "Don't forget the gifted." Teacher 93(4): 46-48,
December, 1975.
Topics covered here include educational alternatives, partial programs,
problems of gifted underachievers, and classroom strategies, such as
individualized activities.

530   Renzulli, Joseph S., and Gable, Robert K. "A factorial study of the
attitudes of gifted students toward independent study." Gifted
Child Q 20(1): 91-99+, Spring, 1976. (0 References)
The attitudes of 305 gifted high school students were evaluated. The
Student Attitude Toward Independent Study Questionnaire was used to
examine five factors. Student response was positive on each of the five.

531   Suchman, J. R. "Inquiry training: building skills for autonomous
discovery." Merrill-Palmer Q 7: 147-69, July, 1961. (15 References)
Describes the "discovery" approach to concept attainment with the resulting intense motivation and deep insight. The dramatic results of its use
in a number of experimental mathematics, science and social studies curricula for able learners attracted national attention.

532   Treffinger, Donald J. "Teaching for self-directed learning: a
priority for the gifted and talented." Gifted Child Q 19(1):
46-59, Spring, 1975. (18 References)
The author corrects some of the common misunderstanding about self
directed learning, then describes several proposals for helping the
gifted move toward that goal.

5. General Provisions

533   Bereday, George Z., and Lauwerys, Joseph A., eds. "Concepts of
excellence in education." In: Yearbook of education. New York:
Harcourt, Brace and World, 1961. 503p.
Contributors from a variety of countries were asked to analyze and to
interpret what happens when attempts are made on a national scale to
discover and to educate gifted young people in all ranks of the population. Section I treats the concept of excellence in diverse cultures,
Section II contains area studies on provisions for talented children,
and Section III provides case studies.

534   ————, eds. "The gifted child." In: Yearbook of education. New
York: Harcourt, Brace and World, 1962. 541p.

This volume continues the discussion of the gifted begun in the 1961 Yearbook. It gives high priority to the various psychological aspects of the education of the talented, and examines in detail the science of providing for the gifted as a logical extension of the liberal arts notions on the subject. Contributors are forty-one educators representing nations in North and South America, Europe, Asia, and Africa.

535   "A better break in schools for gifted children." U. S. News World
      Rep 80(15): 56-57, April 12, 1976. (0 References)
An overview for the general public of what is being done for the gifted and talented. Cites federal efforts, state programs, and innovative local efforts. Identification, segregation, enrichment and acceleration are discussed.

536   Bridges, Sydney A. I.Q.--150. London: Priory Press, 1973. 160p.
      (Bibliography)
Bridges believes that the education of gifted children must be a coopera-tive effort involving education authorities, teachers, parents, and the children themselves. Since many potentially gifted youngsters are being missed at present in British schools, he stresses ways of identifying such children early enough in life for them to be given help toward a proper development.

537   Cole, Nina M. "An investigation of the implementation and articula-
      tion of the Wichita, Kansas program for the gifted." For a summary
      see: Diss Abstr Int 29A(8): 2602-3, February, 1969. (0 References)

538   Collins, Joseph L. "An appraisal of the Milwaukee public schools
      superior ability program." For a summary see: Diss Abstr Int
      33A(12): 6724-25, June, 1973. (0 References)

539   Crow, Lester D., and Crow, Alice, eds. Educating the academically
      able: a book of readings. New York: McKay, 1963. 433p. (Biblio-
      graphy)
This book of readings brings together basic principles and practices dealing with the education of gifted learners. Special consideration has been given to the identification and needs of the gifted, as well as to their personal and educational problems.

540   Cruickshank, William M., and Johnson, G. Orville, eds. Education
      of exceptional children and youth. 3rd ed. Englewood Cliffs, New
      Jersey: Prentice-Hall, 1975. 708p. (Bibliography)
Brings together the basic information regarding the education of the major groups of exceptional children. Chapter 4 deals specifically with gifted, dealing with screening, the enriched school program, illustrative activities, levels of programming, etc.

541   Dickey, Marguerite. Specialized instruction for gifted pupils in
      the public schools, fall 1968. Washington, D.C.: National Center
      for Educational Statistics, 1971. 17p. (Bibliography) (For sale
      by the Superintendent of Documents, U.S. Government Printing Office)
Data presented here shows the extent to which national interest in academically gifted pupils had been translated into educational commit-ment by 1968.

542 Dickinson, Rita M. Caring for the gifted. North Quincy, Massachu-
        setts: Christopher Publishing House, 1970. 112p. (Bibliography)
Sets forth the author's beliefs and ideas, based on nearly twenty years
of research and experience. Intended for parents, community leaders,
school boards, teachers and for the gifted themselves, to help them
achieve self-realization.

543 Dillon, Elizabeth A. "Guidelines for the development of a K-12
        program for gifted students." For a summary see: Diss Abstr Int
        30A(7): 2903-4, January, 1970. (0 References)

544 Douglass, Carol C. "Some considerations in facilitating the develop-
        ment of giftedness during elementary school years." For a summary
        see: Diss Abstr Int 23(11): 4164, May, 1963. (0 References)

545 Duncan, Donald K. "Programs for mentally gifted minors and other
        gifted students in the unified school districts of California."
        For a summary see: Diss Abstr Int 25(6): 3426-27, December, 1964.
        (0 References)

546 Dunlop, James M. "The education of children with high mental
        ability." In: Cruickshank, William M., and Johnson, Orville G.,
        eds. Education of exceptional children and youth. 3rd ed.
        Englewood Cliffs, New Jersey: Prentice-Hall, 1975. 149-99.
A comprehensive discussion of problems involved in identifying and making
adequate educational provisions for intellectually gifted students. Case
studies are included and 161 references cited.

547 Everett, Samuel, ed. Programs for the gifted: a case book in
        secondary education. New York: Harper, 1961. 299p.
This anthology contains papers by many noted authorities in the field,
including Paul Witty, William H. Kilpatrick, and Cristian L. Arndt. Its
three sections include "Orientation," "Programs from Abroad," and
"Programs in the U.S."

548 French, Joseph L., ed. Educating the gifted: a book of readings.
        Revised ed. New York: Holt, Rinehart and Winston, 1964. 514p.
Drawn primarily from professional journals, this is a collection of
articles which attempts to present a balanced view of educational practices, surface the problems inherent in educating the gifted, and report
research findings in the field.

549 Furr, Karl D., et. al. "Canadian programming for the gifted."
        Gifted Child Q 16(1): 32-40, Spring, 1972.
Discusses placement practices and program development for the gifted.
Emphasizes the use of culture-free tests with Canada's multi-cultural
school population.

550 Goodwin, Dalyta. "Relationship between student participation in
        the secondary gifted seminar program (San Diego Unified School
        District) and school behaviors and attitudes." For a summary see:
        Diss Abstr Int 33A(11): 6173, May, 1973. (0 References)

551 Hennes, James D. "Illinois television project for the gifted."
        Am Sch Board J 151: 30, September, 1965.
Describes an educational television program devised for gifted. Found

that, in general, success in the courses was not related to student ability scores.

552   Horan, Susan S. "Demographic,personnel, and philosophical factors
      related to the selection of provisions for gifted public elementary
      students in the Ingham Intermediate School District." For a summary
      see: Diss Abstr Int 32A(9): 4921-22, March, 1972. (0 References)

553   Johnson, Harriette W. "Analysis of educational provisions for
      gifted children in selected public elementary schools: the metro-
      politan area of the District of Columbia and specific reference to
      Washington, D.C." For a summary see: Diss Abstr Int 30A(6):
      2255-56, December, 1969. (0 References)

554   Lanza, Leonard G., and Vassar, William G. "Designing and implement-
      ing a program for the gifted and talented." Natl Elem Princ 51(5):
      50-55, February, 1972. (0 References)
Demonstrates the planning that is necessary for developing a program for
the gifted and talented by reconstructing a dialogue that took place
between the authors (State Consultant for the Gifted, and school principal) prior to implementing a gifted and talented program in the elementary
schools of Simsbury, Connecticut.

555   Love, Harold D. Educating exceptional children in regular class-
      rooms. Springfield, Illinois: Thomas, 1972. 235p. (Bibliography)
The author presents the view that exceptional children can be educated in
the regular classroom. An informative chapter on the gifted is included.

556   McBride, Vearl G. Damn the school system--full speed ahead!
      Jericho, New York: Exposition Press, 1973. 160p.
An angry critic of the system presents methods for training rapid reading,
spelling mastery, and rapid arithmetic, with specific instructions for
classroom teaching. Includes strong denunciations of current practices
on the elementary school level, particularly with regard to the suppres-
sion of unusual talent and ability.

557   Martinson, Ruth A. Educational programs for gifted pupils. Sacra-
      mento, California: California State Department of Education, 1961.
      274p.
Final report on the California Pilot Project which involved nearly 1,000
pupils, plus controls in several different grade levels and curriculum
organizations. Results were generally positive.

558   Monell, Ralph P. "Criteria for the education of gifted and talented
      children in a small city school system." For a summary see: Diss
      Abstr Int 28A(4): 1249, October, 1967. (0 References)

559   Otterness, June. "A gifted child program for rural schools." Gifted
      Child Q 15(1): 49-50, 56, Spring, 1971. (0 References)
Reports on a program that provides a specialized training program for
teachers of the gifted, a program for identification and selection of
gifted, develops techniques and procedures for gifted, and disseminates
the information.

560   Paschal, Elizabeth. Encouraging the excellent: special programs
      for gifted and talented students. New York: The Fund for the

Advancement of Education, 1960. 79p.
Describes many special programs for able students which were initiated
or undertaken within the decade prior to publication.

561   Passow, A. Harry, and Goldberg, Miriam L. "The talented youth
      project: a progress report, 1962." Except Child 28(5): 223-31,
      January, 1962. (35 References)
Summarizes various programs for the gifted and reports on their findings.

562   Plowman, Paul D., and Rice, Joseph P. California Project Talent.
      Sacramento: California State Department of Education, 1967. 148p.
A variety of education programs for the gifted in California are examined
in this volume.

563   ———. Final report: California Project Talent; demonstration of
      differential programming in enrichment, acceleration, counseling,
      and special classes for mentally gifted pupils. Sacramento: Cali-
      fornia State Department of Education, 1969. 133p. (Bibliography)
The first four sections summarize the four demonstrations in California's
federally-funded program from 1963-1966. Also included is a compilation
of position papers presented at the Project Talent Western Regional Dis-
semination Conference in 1966. In the summary is presented the educational philosophy of Project Talent.

564   Rabenstein, John E. Exceptional children: an overview. New York:
      MSS Information Corporation, 1962. 183p.
A collection of articles which have appeared in journals dealing with
exceptional children. Two studies on programs for the gifted and
familial cultural background of the gifted are included.

565   Renzulli, Joseph S. "The evolution of programs of differential
      education for the gifted." For a summary see: Diss Abstr Int
      27A(11): 3731-32, May, 1967. (0 References)

566   ———. "Identifying key features in programs for the gifted."
      Except Child 35(3): 217-21, November, 1968. (4 References)
Determined which features and characteristics of programs for the gifted
are considered to be the most necessary and sufficient for comprehensive
programming lists the seven key features and discusses their important
dimensions.

567   Rice, Joseph P. "California Project Talent: a unique educational
      development." Clearing House 42(5): 305-12, January, 1968.
California Project Talent was a three-and-one-half year project which
demonstrated four types of programs for gifted children and youth:
enrichment, acceleration, counseling, and special classes.

568   Rice, Joseph P., and Banks, George. "Opinions of gifted students
      regarding secondary school programs." Except Child 34(4): 269-73,
      December, 1967. (1 Reference)
In San Diego, 119 gifted secondary students were interviewed to obtain
their recommendations for academic program change. It was shown that
gifted students are capable of providing meaningful insights about the
nature of their educational programs.

569   Roeper, Annemarie. "Gifted preschooler and the Montessori method."
       Gifted Child Q 10(2): 83-89, Summer, 1966. (18 References)
Here the headmistress of a school for gifted children compares the traditional nursery school method with those of the Montessori School, then
relates these to the approach used with pre-schoolers in her own school.

570   Smythe, P. E., and Stennett, R. G. "Elementary education for gifted
       students: a review of research and current trends." Spec Educ Can
       47(2): 17-24, January, 1973. (14 References)
Describes methods of identifying able students in Canada, and provisions
for educating them by special classes, acceleration, and enrichment.
Program effectiveness and cost effectiveness are also treated.

571   Taba, Hilda. "Learning by discovery: psychological and educational
       rationale." Elem Sch J 63(6): 308-16, March, 1963.
This concept, made popular by the new curriculum in mathematics and
science is especially important in the teaching of the gifted. Teachers
must set conditions to make discovery possible.

572   Tannenbaum, Abraham J. "A backward and forward glance at the gift-
       ed." Natl Elem Princ 51(5): 14-23, February, 1972. (21 Refer-
       ences)
Reviews the sporadic attempts to establish special programs for the
gifted and talented during the 50's and 60's. Attributes failures to
provide consistent and adequate programs to American ideational conflicts
between "excellence" and "equality." Stresses need for multi-faceted
enrichment of the gifted capitalizing on their exceptional measure of
social concern.

573   ————. "Recent trends in education of the gifted." Educ Forum
       26(3): 333-43, March, 1962. (0 References)
Says that enrichment, telescoped courses, mechanized teaching, research
and talent searches have increased services to gifted.

574   Tannor, Shirley. "Survey on the gifted in cities over 250,000
       population." Except Child 32(9): 631-32, May, 1966. (4 Refer-
       ences)
Author describes results of a questionnaire which summarizes programs for
gifted in larger American cities. Eighty-five percent of the cities
responding had a formal program for the gifted. Discusses screening,
enrichment, policy making and other survey results.

575   Tempest, N. K. "Gifted and handicapped?" Spec Educ: Forward Trends
       1(1): 14-16, March, 1974. (2 References)
The author, a British professor of education, cites the American custom
of grouping highly intelligent children under the heading of "exceptional" and including them with the handicapped. He discusses how
"clever" children may actually be handicapped and goes on to compare
special provisions for the gifted such as segregation and enrichment in
the regular classroom.

576   Torrance, E. Paul. Gifted children in the classroom. New York:
       Macmillan, 1965. 102p. (Bibliography)
The author highlights some concepts about the nature of giftedness, and
treats briefly the goals of education of gifted children, problems of
identification and motivation, and development of giftedness during the

pre-school years. Three chapters are devoted to the development of creative readers and to the teaching of research concepts and skills.

577 ————. "How gifted high school students can continue growing intel-
     lectually." Gifted Child Q 12(1): 3-9, Spring, 1968. (7
     References)
Offers eight suggestions for intellectual stimulation to talented teenagers who find little challenge in the usual high school curriculum.
Suggestions are reinforced by examples of some of history's most eminent
people who employed these techniques as teenagers.

578 Trezise, Robert L. "The gifted child: back in the limelight."
     Phi Delta Kappan 58(3): 241-43, November, 1976.
Many signs indicate that programs for the gifted are returning to favor.
Here, Michigan's coordinator of such programs discusses twelve pilot
programs in his state which may be models for the nation.

579 Tucker, James A. "Structure of Intellect programming: some initial
     considerations." Talents Gifts 18(3): 19-21, March, 1976.
The Structure of Intellect profile is discussed in terms of planning
educational programs for gifted students. The relationship of mental
age to chronological age and the relationship of the divergent production
score to other dimension scores are considered.

580 Vasishta, V. S. "Educating the gifted child." Assoc Educ Psychol
     J Newsl 3(1): 42-45, Spring, 1972.
Discusses the use of acceleration, enrichment, and special groupings or
classes for gifted children. The role of the school psychologist in
evaluating students and counseling parents and teachers is discussed.

581 Verma, P. S. "Educating the talented." J Vocat Educ Guid 16(1-2):
     48-53, June/December, 1974.
Examines the problems associated with curriculum development and teaching
methods for the talented. Four special classroom techniques are examined.

582 Wall, W. D. "Highly intelligent children part II." Educ Res (U.K.)
     2(3): 207-17, June, 1960. (45 References)
Deals with early identification, creativity, enrichment and acceleration
of gifted children.

583 Ward, Virgil S. Educating the gifted: an axiomatic approach.
     Columbus, Ohio: Merrill, 1961. 240p. (Bibliography)
This book sketches a foundation in basic principles for the educational
experience of children and youth who form the topmost level of brightness
and who are intrinsically motivated toward literary, scientific, or other
academic accomplishments. The educational levels considered include the
intermediate grades through general college.

584 White, M. Judson. "The case for specifically designed education for
     the gifted." Gifted Child Q 14(3): 159-62, Fall, 1970. (0
     References)
Outlines a program for developing and utilizing special talents of exceptional individuals. Deals with identification, diverse programs and
society's responsibility regarding the gifted.

585   Willhoit, Amos J.   "A study of methods of instruction for the
      intellectually gifted student at the elementary level in Southern
      California schools."   For a summary see: Diss Abstr Int   31A(7):
      3188-89, January, 1971. (0 References)

B. Curricular Offerings

1. Language Arts

586   Adalbert, Sister Mary. "Language arts and the gifted." Cathol Sch
      J 66(3): 47-48, March, 1966. (0 References)
Discusses reading advanced works, varying levels of meaning, the challenge of writing and speaking. Makes practical suggestions for advanced
work in language arts.

587   Bamman, Henry A. "Language arts for the academically talented."
      In: Smith, Helen K., ed. Meeting individual needs in reading.
      Newark, Delaware: International Reading Association, 1971. 143-49.
Defines the talented child and then makes suggestions for programs for
the gifted in handwriting, spelling, writing, and reading.

588   Barbe, Walter B., and Norris, Dorothy E. "Reading instruction in
      special classes for gifted elementary children." Read Teach 16:
      425-28, May, 1963. (0 References)
Describes Cleveland reading program for gifted. Discusses skill instruction, intensive and collateral reading.

589   Burrows, Alvina T. "Encouraging talented children to write" Educa-
      tion 88(1): 31-34, September/October, 1967. (4 References)
Examines the needs and potentials of verbally gifted youths and considers
ways in which they may be stimulated to write.

590   Chomsky, Carol. "Creativity and innovation in child language." J
      Educ 158: 12-24, May, 1976. (0 References)
This paper, an address to the NCTE Elementary Language Arts Conference
in Boston in 1975, discusses two kinds of linguistic innovation in children: language acquisition and invented spelling systems. The latter
can be used by bright four and five-year olds to write words exacly the
way they sound.

591   Criscuolo, Nicholas P. "Open discovery spots for gifted readers."
      Gifted Child Q 18(2): 72-73, Summer, 1974. (0 References)
Suggests fifteen mini interest centers to be located in elementary classrooms. These can extend and enrich reading skills in creative manner,
and take the boredom out of reading for the gifted.

592   ————. "Teaching the superior reader." Education 84(3): 163-65,
      November, 1963. (5 References)
Author says superior readers must be given opportunities to develop reading skills in depth as well as develop areas of strength. Discusses ways
of creating these opportunities.

593   Cushenbery, Donald C., and Howell, Helen. Reading and the gifted
      child: a guide for teachers. Springfield, Illinois: Thomas, 1974.
      181p. (Bibliography)
Designed to dispel teachers' idea that gifted children need no special

program "since they can get it on their own." Presents teaching suggestions which have been classroom-tested and a variety of useful appendices.

594   De Boer, John J.   "Creative reading and the gifted student."   <u>Read
      Teach</u> 16:   435-41, May, 1963.   (3 References)
A former president of the National Council of Teachers of English notes
the high correlation between mental ability and reading comprehension,
but warns that many bright students are underachievers in reading.   He
suggests as major tasks involved in creative reading the following: (1)
creative inquiry, (2)   creative interpretation, (3)   creative integration,
(4)   creative application, and (5)   creative criticism.

595   Engle, John D., Jr.   "Giftedness and writing: creativity in the
      classroom."   <u>Gifted Child Q</u> 14(4):   220-29, Winter, 1970.   (0
      References)
The author, an associate editor of <u>Writer's Digest</u>, describes the unusual
success his high school creative writing students have had in publishing
their stories, poems, and articles in nationally circulated periodicals.

596   Gensley, Juliana T.   "Let's teach the gifted to read."   <u>Gifted Child
      Q</u> 19(1):   21-22, Spring, 1975.   (0 References)
Reading for the gifted should be a process of gathering information,
interpreting information, processing, analyzing, synthesizing, evaluating
and using information.

597   ————— .   "A new method of evaluation for gifted students: a diary
      of learning."   <u>Gifted Child Q</u> 13(2):   119-25, Summer, 1969.   (2
      References)
Dissatisfaction with conventional methods of evaluating student achievement has caused Dr. Gensley to describe a cooperative method of assess-
ment--a daily diary.   This type of evaluation involves the gifted child
in using criteria and standards for appraising his own progress.

598   Hanke, Jeannette J.   "Filmmaking--some experiences with the gifted."
      <u>Engl J</u> 60(1):   121-25, January, 1971.   (0 References)
Recounts author's attempts to create films with Advanced Placement senior
English students.   Benefits of the project lie in the fact that each
student thought originally, creatively and clearly; he organized, planned,
and revised; and he learned to cooperate with others in order to create
an artistic whole.

599   Isaacs, Ann F.   "What to do when you discover a child is gifted and
      interested in language."   <u>Gifted Child Q</u> 17(2):   144-49, Summer,
      1973.   (0 References)
This listing of 100 ways to stimulate creativity and enrichment in the
language arts would be of use to parents and classroom teachers.

600   Kender, Joseph P., ed.   <u>Emerging concerns in reading: highlights
      of the 21st annual reading conference of Lehigh University</u>.   Dan-
      ville, Illinois: Interstate Printers and Publishers, 1973.   146p.
This volume contains conference papers addressing topical and methodolog-
ical concerns in reading.   Essays such as "Poetry with Gifted Children"
and "Creative Writing in the Elementary School" will interest teachers
of talented students.

601   Knight, Lester M. Language arts for the exceptional: the gifted
      and the linguistically different. Itasca, Illinois: Peacock, 1974.
      157p. (Bibliography)
Part 2 of this book, "Maximizing the Language Power of the Gifted," is
concerned with identification of gifted children and the construction of
an appropriate language arts program for them.

602   Labuda, Michael. "Meeting the reading needs of gifted children in
      the elementary school." For a summary see: Diss Abstr Int   29A(6):
      1681-82, December, 1968. (0 References)

603   ———, ed. Creative reading for gifted learners: a design for
      excellence. Newark, Delaware: International Reading Association,
      1974. 141p.
It is the intent of this volume of papers to indicate both the nature of
children who possess traits of giftedness and creativity and the comprehensive educational procedures required to meet their needs.

604   Langston, Genevieve R. "A study of the effect of certain structured
      experiences in science, social science, and mathematics on beginning
      reading in gifted five year olds." For a summary see: Diss Abstr
      Int   25(2): 1049, August, 1964. (0 References)

605   Larrick, Nancy. "Poetry is for everyone." Gifted Child Q   20(1):
      42-46, Spring, 1976. (14 References)
Teachers of gifted elementary grade children may encourage interaction
with poetry through exposure to poems grouped by theme (such as animals),
and activities involving the writing or multi-media interpretation of
poetry.

606   National Council of Teachers of English. English for the academi-
      cally talented student in the secondary school. Revised ed.
      Washington, D.C.: National Education Association, 1969. 109p.
This is the 1969 revision of the Report of the NCTE's Committee on English
Programs for High School Students of Superior Ability. Nine essays are
contributed by members.

607   Quisenberry, Nancy L. "Developing language fluency in the gifted
      culturally different child." Gifted Child Q   18(3): 175-79,
      Autumn, 1974. (3 References)
In assessing ability of minority children, teachers often "measure their
intellect" in adult majority dialect, and so never realize the potential
giftedness in the culturally different or disadvantaged child.

608   Rogers, Wanda, and Ryan, Susan . "Extending reading skills into
      today's world." Teach Except Child 5(2): 58-65, Winter, 1973.
      (0 References)
Forty accelerated fourth, fifth, and sixth grade pupils in a Michigan
school were selected for a special reading class. A content area approach
based on today's changing world provided the relevant context. The
following units were presented: study skills, the newspaper, speech,
social studies, science, poetry, the short story, and drama. "Work type"
reading was alternated with "enjoyment" reading to maintain maximum
interest.

609   Roody, Sarah I.   "Teaching Conrad's Victory to superior high school
        seniors." Engl J 58(1): 40-46, January, 1969. (0 References)
Designed to train gifted students to read literary classics sensitively,
these lessons have been used successfully with twelfth grade candidates
for the Advanced Placement Examination in English.

610   Rowe, Ernest R.   "Creative writing and the gifted child." Except
        Child 34(4): 279-82, December, 1967.
An outgrowth of the author's experience in a self-contained classroom of
highly gifted sixth grade children in California. Covers motivational
techniques and evaluation of creative efforts. Contains examples of
student writing.

611 Sabaroff, Rose E.   "Challenges in reading for the gifted." Elem
        Engl 42(4): 393-400+, April, 1965.
Discusses a program for the gifted in reading which includes basal reading skills, reading in the content areas, and children's literature and
poetry.

612   Sebesta, Sam L.   "Language arts programs for the gifted." Gifted
        Child Q 20(1): 18-23+, Spring, 1976. (17 References)
Developers of language arts programs for the gifted need to examine
language structure, language function, and motivational activities to
develop syntactical modeling, vocabulary, spelling, and creative writing.

613   Sisk, Dorothy A.   "Communication skills for the gifted." Gifted
        Child Q 19(1): 66-68, Spring, 1975. (0 References)
A teacher training coordinator stresses the importance of developing
gifted children's communication abilities and briefly describes two group
dynamics activities for building listening, interpretation and discussion
skills.

614 ———.   "Discussion: a strategy for discovering values." Gifted
        Child Q 20(1): 105-8, Spring, 1976. (1 Reference)
Teachers can use discussion to develop critical thinking skills in gifted
children at all levels. Controversial topics can help students discover
feelings and differentiate between facts and values.

615   Stewig, John W.   "I absolutely refuse to be an onion." Gifted Child
        Q 20(1): 31-39, Spring, 1976. (13 References)
Suggested are ways to use creative dramatics with gifted children to encourage changes in impressive, expressive, communicative, social, and
creative behavior.

616   Torrance, E. Paul.   "Helping gifted children read creatively."
        Gifted Child Q 7(1): 3-8, Spring, 1963. (16 References)
Describes creative children who are becoming creative readers. Intended
for parents and teachers, this article presents two major ideas which
can be used to help gifted readers.

617 ———.   "Ten ways of helping young children gifted in creative
        writing and speech." Gifted Child Q 6(4): 121-27, Winter, 1962.
        (11 References)
The ten practical suggestions presented here for helping gifted youngsters
improve their language skills are meant for parents. They can be used to
supplement school efforts in this area.

618   Walker, Charles R. "Comparison of the compressed speech machine and
       the self-improvement method: two techniques for increasing the rate
       of reading of sixth grade gifted pupils." For a summary see: <u>Diss</u>
       <u>Abstr Int</u> 31A(6): 2625-26, December, 1970. (0 References)

619   Ward, Nancy. "MGM: program for the mentally gifted minor."
       <u>Instructor</u> 85(9): 73-75, May/June, 1976.
A California school librarian describes her district's program for stimulating interest in children's literature in gifted elementary pupils.
Cites some of the children's classics that have proved popular with different age groups, and suggests sample questions that can elicit provoca-
tive discussions by able readers.

620   Witty, Paul A. "Fostering creative reading." <u>Highlights Teach</u> 25:
       1-4, 1971. (21 References)
Presents techniques for identifying the creative student and describes
the differences between gifted and creative children. Stresses the role
of the teacher in fostering creativity.

621   ————. "The gifted pupil and his reading." <u>Highlights Teach</u> 7:
       1-4, 1967. (14 References)
Describes the characteristics of the gifted, then suggests methods of
teaching and specific literary selections that may meet the personal and
social needs of these able pupils. A list of coordinators of gifted programs and a professional bibliography are included.

622   ————. "The librarian as a talent scount." <u>Top News</u> 28(1): 34-
       37, November, 1971.
Witty cites the neglect of gifted children in many homes and schools
throughout the nation, and encourages the librarian to play a vital role
in the education of these children. He offers several examples of gifted
behavior to aid librarians in the important task of identification.

623   ————, ed. <u>Reading for the gifted and the creative student.</u> Newark,
       Delaware: International Reading Association, 1971. 63p.
This publication discusses the position of the gifted in education today
and presents several innovative programs. It also characterizes the
gifted child and defines the role of the parent and teacher.

624   Witty, Paul A.; Freeland, Alma M.; Grotberg, Edith H. <u>The teaching</u>
       <u>of reading: a developmental process.</u> Boston: Heath, 1966. 434p.
       (Bibliography)
Although this book is basically a developmental text, it does give some
special attention to challenging the superior and gifted student.

2. Mathematics

625   Bezuzska, Stanley J. "Math Rx: a new level of excitement and
       insight." <u>Learning</u> 3(7): 27-35, March, 1975. (0 References)
Replete with strategies and activities that tap the innate curiosity and
tremendous imagination of bright children.

626   Fehr, Howard F. "The Secondary School Mathematics Curriculum Im-
       provement Study: a unified mathematics program." <u>Math Teach</u> 67(1):
       25-33, January, 1974.
This article describes the content of an experimental curriculum for the
highly capable mathematics student in junior and senior high school.

627 Flagg, Elinor B. "Mathematics for gifted children. an experimental
     program." Educ Leadersh 19(6): 379-82, March, 1962. (0 Refer-
     ences)
Describes a program in mathematics for gifted fifth graders.

628 Fox, Lynn H. "Career education for gifted pre-adolescents." Gifted
     Child Q 20(3): 262-73, Fall, 1976. (4 References)
Describes a career awareness program consisting of four mini-courses, one
each in geometry, statistics, probability, and computer science. Twenty-
four fourth, fifth and sixth grade gifted students participated.

629 _____. "Facilitating educational development of mathematically
     precocious youth." J Spec Educ 9(1): 63-77, Spring, 1975.
     (5 References)
Seven case studies of mathematically precocious males are presented,
along with ideas for educational counseling and individualization of
school programs for the gifted.

630 George, William C. "Accelerating mathematics instruction."
     Gifted Child Q 20(3): 246-61, Fall, 1976. (29 References)
Another account of the operating procedure of the very successful Study
of Mathematically Precocious Youth carried out by personnel at Johns
Hopkins University.

631 Lansdown, Brenda. "Exploring rate graphs with gifted ten-year-
     olds." Arith Teach 11(3): 146-49, March, 1964.
The author explored graphs with gifted fifth graders in a New York City
private school. Results showed that children of ten years can handle
concepts of straight-line and parabolic graphs, can think in the
principles of analytic geometry, use the graphs for finding new relationships, and relate practical, theoretical, and graphical ideas to
form a pattern of thinking.

632 Laycock, Mary. "Creative mathematics at Nueva." Arith Teach
     17(4): 325-28, April, 1970.
Describes a creative mathematics program which fits the individual
needs of children. Gives examples of use of counting beads in kindergarten, Cuisinaire rods in first grade, weighing in second grade, multiplication, geometry in third grade, etc. Creative mathematics spring-
board.

633 McCormack, Marilyn J. "Computational program for gifted students."
     Math Teach 69(5): 365, May, 1976.
Describes an individualized mathematics program designed for academically
gifted intermediate students from five Pennsylvania school districts.
Participants who are recommended by their teachers and score above 130 on
individual I.Q. tests meet in groups of eight for two-and-one-half hours
a week. This non-graded program supplants regular classroom instruction
and covers grade-level competencies, enrichment, and individual research.

634 Millikin, Gloria, and Siegel, Darby. "A kit for teaching calculat-
     ing and computing devices." Teach Except Child 3(1): 17-22,
     fall, 1970. (42 References)
Authors describe a kit designed as an aid for conducting a special workshop for gifted junior high students. It introduces the basic concepts
involved in understanding computers and outlines more advanced activities
which may be used to teach computer construction and operation.

635   Passow, A. Harry; Goldberg, Miriam L.; Link, Frances R.   "Enriched
       mathematics for gifted junior high school students." <u>Educ Leadersh</u>
       18(7):   442-48, April, 1961. (0 References)
Study on relative effectiveness of varied approaches to mathematics for
gifted. Acceleration in content and instructional tempo produced increased achievement.

636   Pielstick, N. L.   "Gifted children and learning experiences."   <u>J
       Educ Res</u> 57(3):   125-30, November, 1963. (29 References)
Discusses inquiry training, new approaches to teaching mathematics and
developing of divergent thinking and creativity and summarizes the implications for work with the gifted.

637   Poole, M. A.   "The M.A.T. mathematics problem competitions." <u>Aust
       Math Teach</u> 28(1):   11-12, March, 1972.
Describes a mathematical enrichment program used in Australia to identify
talented secondary school mathematicians.

638   Runnels, Patricia, and Runnels, L. K.   "A kindergarten mathematics
       program." <u>Sch Sci Math</u> 74(5):   361-65, May/June, 1974. (5
       References)
Reports on a training program for able kindergarten pupils, age four to
five-and-one-half, during which they were exposed to primary arithmetic
three times daily. At the end of the first semester of first grade all
were well beyond grade level in both computation and reasoning.

639   Snow, C. P.   "Our obligation to gifted children." <u>Instructor</u>
       79(5):   96-97, January, 1970.
Deals with mathematics for the gifted. Tells what Russia has done with
mathematically gifted. Uses as illustration to propose that elitism for
the gifted should be practiced.

640   Solano, Cecilia H., and George, William C.   "College courses and
       educational facilitation of the gifted." <u>Gifted Child Q</u> 20(3):
       274-85, Fall, 1976. (11 References)
Describes the highly gifted seventh and eighth graders who take college
courses in science and mathematics at Johns Hopkins University under the
aegis of the Study of Mathematically Precocious Youth (SMPY).

641   Stanley, Julian C.   "Intellectual precocity." <u>J Spec Educ</u> 9(1):
       29-44, Spring, 1975. (51 References)
The director of the Study of Mathematically and Scientifically Precocious
Youth at Johns Hopkins University reviews earlier studies of intellectual
giftedness, cites recent examples of precocity, and describes many of the
"radical accelerants" discovered by his study. These twelve to thirteen
year old junior high students were outstandingly successful in mathematics
and science courses at selective colleges.

642   Stanley, Julian C.; Keating, Daniel P.; Fox, Lynn H., eds. <u>Mathe-
       matical talent: discovery, description, and development</u>. Baltimore:
       Johns Hopkins University Press, 1974. 215p. (Bibliography)
The research and discussion in the nine separate papers in this volume
stem directly from the Study of Mathematically and Scientifically Precocious Youth, a five-year project at Johns Hopkins University. The editors
are all directors of the project.

643 Suppes, Patrick. "Accelerated program elementary school mathematics:
the second year." Psychol Sch 3(4): 294-307, 1966.
Describes thirty-four bright second graders in the second year of an
accelerated math program who work at their own rate. The author felt that
continual practice on drills and maintenance of previously acquired skills
should be undertaken, as he was not satisfied with the mastery of the
basics as reflected in the results.

644 Suppes, Patrick, and Ihrke, Constance. "Accelerated program in
elementary school mathematics: the third year." Psychol Sch 4(4):
293-309, 1967. (7 References)
The thirty-four bright pupils in this program still show great variation
in acquisition and error rates in basic arithmetic skills. As third
graders, they are working on fourth to sixth grade problems, and have
some difficulty in perfecting needed skills.

3. Science

645 Brandewein, Paul F. Teaching gifted children science in grades
seven through twelve. Sacramento: California State Department of
Education, 1975. 58p.
Offers teachers and administrators recommendations for curriculum development and science instruction for the gifted. Among the curricular
strategies discussed are programmed materials, a conceptually based
curriculum, and instruction in investigative arts.

646 Bryan, J. Ned. "Identifying and planning for the gifted in science."
Instructor 73(5): 61-62+, January, 1964.
Discusses the three factors necessary for an effective program for gifted
science students: the child's unique characteristics, educational environment, and nature and purposes of science.

647 Cooper, Carolyn R. "The English and ecology mix." Clearing House
47(7): 423-26, March, 1973. (0 References)
The experiential learning of bright students is described as they participate in a ten day specimen collecting trip in the South Carolina swamps.

648 Fox, Robert P. "A study and analysis of twenty-three programs for
gifted science students in high schools of the United States." For
a summary see: Diss Abstr Int 21(10). 3015, April, 1961
(0 References)

649 Pavey, O. "Junior explorers in art and science." Athene 13(2):
8-13, 1968.
A junior workshop for gifted children in West London is described. Here
the children are free to come and explore their talents in art and
science, whether it is designing space capsules or finger painting.

650 Riley, Reed F., and Overberger, C. G. "A summer research participation program for high school students." J Chem Educ 38(8):
424-27, August, 1961. (0 References)
Describes a summer chemistry program for bright students. Includes
objectives, selection and specific information about the program. ·
Would be of use to chemistry teachers.

651   Roth, Eleanor. "Columbia University helps exceptional high school
       students." Gifted Child Q 13(3): 181-85, Fall, 1969.
A report of the Science Honors Program conducted at Columbia University
on Saturdays through the support of the National Science Foundation.
Covers admission criteria and student evaluation.

652   Ryder, Virginia P. "A docent program in science for gifted elemen-
       tary pupils." Except Child 38(8): 629-31, April, 1972.
       (1 Reference)
 Describes a docent program in which gifted fifth graders study museum
biological and physical science exhibits and serve as museum guides for
their peer visitors.

653   Saslaw, Milton S. "Gifted young scientists laboratory research
       program." Gifted Child Q 5(1): 3-4+, Spring, 1961.
Describes the Young Scientists Laboratory Research Program which provides
extracurricular enrichment for high school students with I.Q.'s of 135
or better. Benefits include increased student motivation, appreciation
of scientific method, and development of good work habits.

654   Schwartz, Pearl W. "Compendium of methods for the teaching of
       science to gifted children." Sci Educ 52(2): 130-38, March, 1968.
Not only a resource compendium, but also suggests and amplifies ideas
for teachers for the gifted child in science.

655   Sikes, William N. "A study of the nature and effectiveness of the
       teaching of environmental problems to gifted science students in
       Texas public schools." For a summary see: Diss Abstr Int 34A(2):
       635, August, 1973. (0 References)

656   Starr, Robert J. "Structured oral inquiry improves thinking."
       Am Biol Teach 34(7): 408-9, October, 1972. (4 References)
The author compared talented ninth grade biology students using the
Biological Sciences Curriculum Study Invitations to Inquiry Materials
to a control group using regular textbooks. At the end of the eight
weeks instruction, there was a significant gain in critical thinking of
pupils who had used the inquiry materials.

657   ———. "A study of Invitations to Inquiry and their effect on
       student knowledge of science processes." Sch Sci Math 72(8): 714-
       17, November, 1972. (4 References)
Post-test results are given on the Processes of Science test with able
secondary school students who experienced the Biological Sciences
Curriculum Study Program, Invitations to Inquiry.

658   Wiesner, Jerome B. "Education for creativity in the sciences."
       Daedalus 94(3): 527-37, Summer, 1965.
A "prescription" formulated for the educational needs of future research
scientists.

4. Music

659   Gibberd, Kathleen. "Virtuoso from start to finish: Yehudi Menuhin
       School for musically gifted children." Educ Dig 31(6): 48-49
       February, 1966. (0 References)
Discusses Yehudi Menuhin School for the musically gifted and its program.

In its program, the boarding school students study their instruments,
practice, listen to visiting virtuosos, listen to student performances
every evening, and a teacher concert once a week.

660 Graham, Richard M. Music for the exceptional child. Reston,
      Virginia: Music Educators National Conference, 1975. 251p.
A compilation of thirteen papers is given to provide help for the music
educator who encounters exceptional children but lacks training in special
education. Included among the ten entries regarding specific areas of
exceptionality is a paper on the gifted by M. M. Vaughan.

661 Hartshorn, William E. "Musical education of the gifted." Music
      Educ J 54(6): 76-80, February, 1968.
Outlines types of learning in the field of music that should be available
to gifted in elementary schools. Among the suggestions for enrichment in
kindergarten through sixth grade are:create original music and poetry for
the autoharp, create dramatic interpretations of songs, sing descants,
learn to recognize composers' styles.

662 Isaacs, Ann F. "More than one-hundred ways to polish your talent in
      music." Gifted Child Q 18(2): 128-33, Summer, 1967. (11 Refer-
      ences)
Lists 146 suggestions for improving music ability. Very practical.

663 Povey, Robert M. "Educating the gifted." Assoc Educ Psychol J
      Newsl 3(9): 1-4, Summer, 1975.
Examines the views of thirty leading British performers on the question
of providing special schooling for gifted young musicians and dancers.
Most were opposed to segregated education, stressing instead a broad
course of academic study not removed from normal life.

664 Tirro, Frank. "Development of an elementary instrumental music
      program." Music Educ J 51(1): 56+, September, 1964.
Discusses an instrumental program instituted at a school for gifted.
Briefly discusses some of the musical content, methods of scheduling,
instruments used, and rationale of the program. By the program's second
year, the orchestra had grown to thirty pieces, and a band was started;
ample proof of successful program.

665 Wollel, J. W. "Problems of the talented child in music." Gifted
      Child Q 7(1): 9-12, Spring, 1963. (20 References)
This article criticizes music education as currently practiced. The
constructive suggestions can raise the level of music learning and teaching immeasurably.

5. Art

666 Alkema, Chester J. Art for the exceptional. Boulder, Colorado:
      Pruett, 1971. 100p. (Bibliography)
Suggests specific art activities for each of the areas of exceptionality,
including the gifted child. The gifted use their fluent imaginations to
produce work that is sensitive, original and of a high esthetic standard.
They are easily motivated and quick to discover new and unusual uses of
materials.

667   Brown, D. Sydney. Teaching gifted students art in grades seven
        through nine. Sacramento: California State Department of Education,
        Bureau of Publications, 1973. 37p.
This guide gives concrete suggestions for teaching art to adolescents.
Aesthetic perception and lack of inhibition are stressed.

668   Eisner, Elliot W. "Arts curricula for the gifted." Teach Coll Rec
        67(7): 492-501, April, 1966. (8 References)
The writer argues that the art curriculum ought to be viewed within the
context of the secondary school curriculum as a whole. The critical and
historical aspects of the arts should also be included with the productive
aspects in the curriculum for the gifted.

669   Hurwitz, Al. "The U.S. and U.S.S.R.: two attitudes toward the
        gifted in art." Gifted Child Q 20(4): 458-65, Winter, 1976. (9
        References)
Contrasts the American idea of art as a frill or avocational activity
receiving little financial assistance to the Soviet support of the arts
as a key area of national policy. Gifted artists in Russia are selected
for ability and then given complete support through special art academies
and young Pioneer Places. They are expected to use their talents and
training in the interests of the state.

670   Lake, Thomas P. "The arts and humanities come alive for gifted and
        talented." Except Child 41(4): 261-64, January, 1975. (0
        References)
Sponsored by the South Dakota Division of Elementary and Secondary Education, U. S. Office of Education, a temporary community of artists,
teachers and state and national leaders convened in October of 1974 to
explore the arts and humanities and their implications for gifted and
talented youth. Several programs for gifted and talented youth presented
at the conference are discussed here.

671   Lally, Ann. "Encouraging development of the talented in the fine
        arts." Education 88(1): 43-46, September/October, 1967. (6
        References)
Suggests a variety of ways of providing for children talented in fine
arts, but points out that a number of problems may be encountered.

672   Luca, Mark C., and Allen, Bonnie. Teaching gifted children art in
        grades four through six. Sacramento: California State Department
        of Education, Bureau of Publications, 1973. 43p.
This guide for teachers of gifted upper elementary children gives concepts and suggestions for development of an art program. Contribution
of art to the cultural heritage is stressed.

673   McFee, June K. "Art education for special groups: the talented."
        In: The encyclopedia of education. Vol. I. New York: The
        Macmillan Company and the Free Press, 1971. 316-20. (24
        References)
Author discusses behavior, ability evaluation and curricula for the
gifted art student. Believes that because of diversity of talents and
methods, there is no one best curriculum. Their program should be
stimulating and encourage creativity.

674 "Perspectives on talent: how to search for and nurture talent in
     the arts." Talents Gifts 18(2): 5-14, January, 1976.
Presents the texts of brief speeches by eminent performers in the arts.
Speakers recount their own artistic development and give such advice to
young people as getting a thorough liberal arts education.

675 Saunders, Robert J. "The role of the arts in creativity for the
     gifted." Gifted Child Q 12(2): 120-24, Summer, 1968. (14
     References)
Saunders, Art Consultant for the Connecticut State Department of Education, describes the attitudes of the public and general educators who
view art as "a frill" or insignificant part of the curriculum. He
advocates a better balance in education of the gifted, so that they are
not just mentally gifted, academically gifted, or artistically gifted,
but are totally gifted.

676 Sawdey, Russell M. "A comparison of the opinions of a group of out-
     standing professional artists and a group of art teachers concerning
     guidance and instruction of the artistically gifted child." For a
     summary see: Diss Abstr Int 25(3): 1669-70, September, 1964.
     (0 References)

677 Schultze, Mildred. "Art experiences and divergent thinking." Sch
     Arts 65(7): 37-39, March, 1966.
Any creative art experience will develop intuitive and intellectual
processes, but since the former process is generally less used than the
latter, art educators can formulate controlled situations in which in-
stinctive processes are put into play. The thinking process is extended
and divergent, or creative, thinking results.

678 Vautour, J. A. Camille. "Discovering and motivating the artistically
     gifted child." Teach Except Child 8(2): 92-96, Winter, 1976.
Children with specific learning disabilities who are identified as artistically gifted participate in a reading program which taps their artistic
talent. They write and illustrate original stories and use an audio
dictionary to practice new skills.

                    6. Social Studies

679 Anderson, Robert. "Illinois multi-talent program." Scholastic
     Teach 24-26, December, 1973.
The Illinois State Department of Education has identified four areas of
student talent not identified by conventional testing: creative thinking,
critical thinking, talent in human relations, and independent thinking.
Teachers are being trained at regional centers and at summer curriculum
writing workshops to develop these divergent thinking talents. A sample
lesson plan for social studies is included.

680 Eibling, Harold H. "History in depth." Ohio Sch 44(8): 21,
     November, 1966. (0 References)
This short article makes useful suggestions for history studies for able
students.

681 Graves, Herman. "A program in social studies and English for
     talented pupils in the Marion Junior High School." Ill J Educ
     56(6): 38-40, October, 1965. (0 References)

Describes the educational innovations employed in Marion Junior High School, a demonstration center for gifted seventh, eighth and ninth grade students. Both social studies and English are taught inductively to students selected for the "gifted" classes on the basis of test scores, teacher recommendations and prior grades. An in-service program is offered to teachers who need to develop new strategies for meeting this challenge.

682   Mehorter, James T. "Self and Society: an independent study course for gifted high school students." For a summary see: Diss Abstr Int 25(7): 3979, January, 1965. (0 References)

683   Neff, Herbert B. "Ways to help gifted students like social studies." Gifted Child Q 11(2): 108-11, Summer, 1967. (6 References)
Although gifted students are generally characterized by social sensitivity." a strong social conscience and an interest in people and social relationships, they often are turned off by classes in social studies taught by poor teachers, usually coaches.

684   Sandberg, John H. "Introduction to the Social Sciences: an independent study course for gifted high school students." For a summary see: Diss Abstr Int 24(6): 2385-86, December, 1963. (0 References)

7. Other/All

685   Barbe, Walter B., and Frierson, Edward C. "Psychological concepts for gifted preadolescents: pilot study." Psychol Rep 13(1): 112, August, 1963.
The results of this pilot study involving fifteen high-achieving sixth grade students who met three hours daily for five weeks during a summer suggest that mental giftedness extends to precocity in understanding psychology and that this precocity can be further developed by providing psychological terminology and activities.

686   Emerson, Arthur. "Help the gifted move ahead, with tapes." Grade Teach 85(1): 74, September, 1967. (0 References)
Describes an educational program built around the use of standard audio-visual equipment, primarily tape recorders. With these the teacher can allow the gifted to proceed at their own pace, while giving attention to the rest of the class.

687   Guilford, J. P. "Creative thinking and problem solving." Educ Dig 29(8): 29-31, April, 1964. (0 References)
Creative thinking appears to depend on the ability to do divergent-productive thinking. Fluency, flexibility, elaboration, and redefinitions are factors playing significant roles in creative thinking and in the larger content of problem solving.

688   Herr, Edwin L. "Career education for the gifted and talented: some observations." Peabody J Educ 53(2): 98-103, January, 1976. (8 References)
Discusses issues in planning career education programs for gifted and talented children. Lists nine characteristics of career education, and offers a definition of gifted children. A need for training the gifted in career-decision making skills is recognized.

689 Howitt, Lillian C. "Let us not waste our gifted." High Points
      43(9): 35-39, December, 1961.
Deals with identification, grading, and articulation of curricula for
gifted in the subject areas of social studies, language arts, and science.

690 Hoyt, Kenneth B., and Hebeler, Jean R., eds. Career education for
      gifted and talented students. Salt Lake City: Olympus, 1974. 293p.
      (Bibliography)
Summarizes two conferences on career education for gifted and talented
students sponsored by USOE. Chapters treat the future of work, identification and characteristics of the gifted, value issues, policy considerations, and administrative issues as well as exemplary programs in career
education.

691 Iarusso, Marilyn B. "Creative children: children as filmmakers."
      Top News 28(1): 60-67, November, 1971.
The author, an audio-visual specialist with The New York Public Library's
Office of Childrens Services, sees films as an ideal medium of self-
expression for talented children, particularly for disadvantaged children,
who are often non-verbal, lacking in confidence, and who may face a
language problem as well. She visited four filmmaking centers in Man-
hattan which offer classes to children, and describes here the creative
efforts of their Puerto Rican students.

692 Lake, Thomas P. "Their classroom is the world." Teach Except Child
      6(1): 6-15, Fall, 1973. (0 References)
Through the efforts of the ten Regional U.S. Offices of Education, 10,000
gifted and talented applicants were screened and 158 students went on
expeditions of from one to eight weeks. Called The Exploration Scholarship Program, this is an on-the-job training and apprenticeship opportunity for able students. Results show growth in intellectual and personal-
social skills, and a renewed appreciation and understanding of life in
the U.S. because of experiences in foreign cultures.

693 Maley, Donald. "Talent for education." J Ind Arts Educ 27(2):
      16-20, November, 1967. (0 References)
Deals with definitions of the gifted, enrichment possibilities for the
industrial arts curriculum, and recommendations for the industrial arts
teacher of the gifted.

694 Mull, Kenneth V. "The religious education of the gifted." For a
      summary see: Diss Abstr Int 23(9): 3247, March, 1963. (0 Refer-
      ences)

695 Newburger, Doris. "The effect of speech therapy on behavior and
      academic achievement of high I.Q. children." For a summary see:
      Diss Abstr Int 28A(12): 4956, June, 1968. (0 References)

696 Phillips, Mark. "Confluent education, the hidden curriculum, and
      the gifted child." Phi Delta Kappan 58(3): 238-40, November,
      1976. (4 References)
Confluent education encompasses purposes and techniques likely to be
widely adopted in years to come. Phillips explains why the movement is
so important, particularly in the education of the gifted, broadly defined.

697   Pittman, David F. "Gifted child: religious education of the
        gifted." <u>Relig Educ</u> 63(5): 365-70, September/October, 1968. (14
        References)
The author, a Baptist minister in North Carolina, makes a plea for
enlightened concern for the gifted child in church and synogogue.

698   Plowman, Paul D. "Encouraging the development of the talented in
        academic areas." <u>Education</u> 88(1): 35-42, September/October,
        1967. (8 References)
Defines the parameters of educating the gifted and suggests ways of
extending appreciations and stimulating growth.

699   <u>Principals, objectives, and curricula for programs in the education</u>
        <u>of mentally gifted minors; kindergarten through grade twelve.</u>
        Sacramento: California State Department of Education, 1971. 125p.
        (Bibliography)
This is a concise description of California's successful program for
gifted students. It is enlightening in its presentation of the application of the learning theories of Guilford, Piaget, Bloom, and Phenix to
actual curricula in seven subject areas, including art and music.

700   Prokes, Dorothy. "Exploring the relationship between participation
        in creative dramatics and development of the imaginative capacities
        of gifted junior high students." For a summary see: <u>Diss Abstr Int</u>
        32A(5): 2555-56, November, 1971. (0 References)

701   Shirey, Sharon M. "The academically talented student in business
        education." <u>Bus Educ World</u> 54(3): 26-27, January/February, 1974.
The upper fifteen to twenty percent of secondary school students may be
provided for through enrichment within existing classes, ability
grouping, and acceleration. A number of recommendations are made.

702   Smith, Robert M. "Industrial arts activities for children with
        individual differences." <u>J Ind Arts Educ</u> 23(5): 21-24, May,
        1964. (0 References)
Discusses how socio-drama and individual-small group approach can be
used with gifted. Gives specific examples.

703   Spragens, Jane. "Recreation for the gifted child." <u>J Health Phys</u>
        <u>Educ Recreat</u> 36(4): 53-55, April, 1965.
Points out that gifted groups achieve unusually fine success in athletic
and social activities. Points out that extremely high I.Q. child often
cannot acquire physical accomplishments in keeping with mental capacities.
Teacher should work for attitude of acceptance of skills and limitations.
Includes concrete guidelines for teachers working with gifted.

704   Stadstad, Curtis A. "Humanistic education for the gifted." For a
        summary see: <u>Diss Abstr Int</u> 34A(10): 6467, April, 1974. (0
        References)

705   Toomin, Marjorie K., and Toomin, Hershel. "Bio-feedback: fact and
        fantasy! Does it hold implication for gifted education?" <u>Gifted</u>
        <u>Child Q</u> 17(1): 48-55, Spring, 1973. (20 References)
Because there is some slight evidence that increasing the percent and
amplitude of alpha brain waves has some positive effect on mental
efficiency, authors discuss research on benefits of increasing alpha and
theta brain waves to enhance giftedness.

706   Torrance, E. Paul. "Give the gifted children of the world a chance
      to solve future problems." Talents Gifts   18(3): 22-24, March,
      1976.
Suggestions for gifted children include team competition in future problem solving, a battery of future problem solving tasks, and studies to
determine what questions gifted children ask about the future.

707   ———. "Ways gifted children can study the future." Gifted Child
      Q 18(2): 65-71, Summer, 1974. (16 References)
Describes a few of the methods that are emerging for helping children
study the future. They appeal especially to the gifted because they are
challenging and stretch their minds, imaginations, and aspirations.

708   Torrance, E. Paul, and Myers, R. E. "Teaching gifted elementary
      pupils research concepts and skills." Gifted Child Q 6(1): 1-6,
      Spring, 1962.
The able children described here learned to formulate hypotheses, test
them and report results. A test showed that the high achievers class
had a good grasp of the fundamentals of research.

709   Walden, James D. "An action program for gifted students." Gifted
      Child Q 20(1): 24-30+, Spring, 1976. (2 References)
Provides suggestions to encourage gifted students in creative and intellectual endeavors. These include growing plants, listing community
resources, using photography to enhance idea expression, and performing
pantomime skits.

710   Walker, Joseph J. "Developing values in gifted children." Teach
      Except Child 7(3): 98-100, Spring, 1975.
Stresses the importance of ethical and moral training to influence the
affective behavior of the gifted. Teaching methods and class activities
for this purpose are suggested.

711   Worcester, D. A. "Curriculum for the gifted." Am Sch Board J
      146(6): 13-14, June, 1963. (0 References)
An insightful address on variations among the gifted and implications
for curriculum in various subject areas for the gifted.

C. Administrator Role

712   Ackerman, Paul R., and Weintraub, Frederick J. "Summary analysis
      of state laws for gifted children." Except Child 35(7): 569-76,
      March, 1969. (0 References)
A state-by-state analysis of the state laws for gifted children. As
of writing, seventeen states have laws applying to the gifted. Of
those, ten provide legal guidelines or definitions. Sixteen states
describe some criteria for service programs.

713   Armstrong, Kenneth. "A survey of Kansas elementary school princi-
      pals' opinions of the education of gifted children." For a summary
      see: Diss Abstr Int 28A(11): 4367, May, 1968. (0 References)

714   Ashpole, Kenneth M. "The development of a model for legislative
      special state financial aids to programs for academically gifted
      students." For a summary see: Diss Abstr Int 33A(6): 2603-4,
      December, 1972. (0 References)

715   Brodinsky, Ben. "The Connecticut story," <u>Todays Educ</u> 65(1):   40-42,
      January/February, 1976. (0 References)
Connecticut with strong state support for programs for the gifted and
talented has been cited for leadership in this area. A number of exemplary district programs from the 70 formal programs in operation are
outlined here.

716   Bryan, J. Ned. "Education of the gifted." <u>Sch Life</u> 44(6):   13-15,
      April, 1962.
Presents a policy statement on the education of the gifted developed by
the Council of Chief State School Officers. Describes the characteristics
of gifted students and lists the responsibilities of state departments
of education for programming for them.

717   ────. "Education of the gifted: report on a conference." <u>Sch</u>
      <u>Life</u> 44(9):   13-14, July, 1962.
The Office of Education specialist for the education of gifted and
talented youth discusses a conference which he directed. The 12 states
with full-time directors of education for the gifted sent them to the
conference where they report on innovative and exemplary programs
being implemented in their states.

718   Bryan, J. Ned, and Chalfant, James C. "Elementary and Secondary
      Education Act of 1965: potential for serving the gifted."
      <u>Except Child</u> 32(3):   147-55, November, 1965. (3 References)
Discusses Act which provides assistance for education of children of
low income families; school library resources and instructional
materials; educational centers and services; educational research and
training; and strengthening state departments of education. Suggestions
for implementation are offered.

719   Buerki, Virginia V. "Antidote for mediocrity: encourage ability
      and intelligence." <u>Ohio Sch</u> 40(9):   12-13, December, 1962. (0
      References)
Lists author's suggestions for gifted - small class size, testing,
homogeneous grouping, instruction over years by same teacher and 6
others.

720   Chansky, Norman M. "Report card choices of gifted junior high
      school pupils." <u>Gifted Child Q</u> 7(2):   64-65, Summer, 1963.
The Report Card Preference Inventory was administered to gifted junior
high school pupils. Results show that boys prefer cards which restrict
judgments of achievement to academic subjects, while girls prefer cards
which yield adjectival statements of achievement in academic as well as
non-academic areas.

721   Curtis, Carroll A. "Pupil identification, objectives, organization,
      and financing of state supported programs for the gifted in
      Pennsylvania schools." For a summary see: <u>Diss Abstr Int</u> 31A(2):
      577-78, August, 1970. (0 References)

722   Demarais, Roland W. "Planning occupational experiences for
      culturally disadvantaged gifted." <u>Gifted Child Q</u> 11(2):   79-85,
      Summer, 1967. (0 References)
Gifted junior high students in Chinatown benefit from smaller classes
and a home-school-community teacher as part of federally funded effort
to overcome disadvantaged home and social environment.

723   Drews, Elizabeth M. "Educational innovations for superior students."
      Mich J Second Educ 4(1): 44-54, Fall, 1962. (0 References)
In a vital letter to the secondary principal, Drews discusses the new
education for the gifted - revolution in curriculum, infiltration of new
methods, abundance of teaching resources, and changes in students.

724   ————. "Leading out and letting be." Todays Educ 65(1): 26-28,
      January/February, 1976. (0 References)
In this philosophical introduction to the gifted Dr. Drews stresses their
needs for both self-fulfillment and social awareness. An ideal education
is proposed, combining the "leading out" of the Western tradition with
the "letting be" of the Eastern.

725   Fincher, Jack. "Depriving the best and the brightest." Hum Behav
      5(4): 16-21, April, 1976.
Education for the gifted suffers from limited federal spending, inadequate
identifications measures, lack of public awareness and support, and
absence of validated curriculum approaches. Unchallenging school
experiences and social isolation can combine to deprive both the gifted
student and the nation of valuable talents.

726   Fine, Benjamin. Stretching their minds. New York: Dutton, 1964.
      255p.
The exciting new approach to the education of the gifted child pioneered
by the Sands Point Country Day School is described here by its director.

727   Finley, Robert M. "What are LEA's needs in gifted/talented education
      from the suburban viewpoint" Talent Gifts 18(3): 13, March, 1976.
      (0 References)
Suburban educational programs for gifted and talented students are
discussed in terms of strategies of preparation, barriers to be faced,
and types of delivery systems.

728   Flanagan, John C. "Project Talent: some early findings from a
      nationwide survey." NEAJ 53(1): 8-10, January, 1964.
Preliminary findings from a survey of 440,000 students and some follow-up
indicate that amount of student learning varies from school to school;
that guidance is of crucial importance, and that identification of
inadequately used talent is necessary.

729   Flanagan, John C., and Dailey, John T. "Project Talent - the
      identification,development and utilization of human talents,"
      Pers Guid J 38(6): 504-5, February, 1960. (0 References)
Describes Project Talent and results that should come out of it.

730   Fliegler, Louis A., ed. Curriculum planning for the gifted.
      Englewood Cliffs, New Jersey: Prentice-Hall, 1961. 414p.
      (Bibliography)
This test was designed for teachers, administrators and curriculum
specialists for developing concepts and materials for gifted students.
With chapters contributed by experts in each field, it is intended to
serve as a resource manual as well as a guide for a course in curriculum
planning for the gifted.

731   Fogarty, John E. "Stimulating special education through federal
      legislation." Except Child 31(1): 1-4, September, 1964. (0
      References)

Discusses congressional legislation for handicapped; however, it points out
that gifted are not provided for. Author welcomes proposals for legislation for the gifted.

732 Fox, Ann E. "Kindergarten: forgotten year for the gifted?"
     Gifted Child 15(1): 42-48, Spring, 1971.
Author believes that kindergarten is a place where gifted students can
easily be turned off to education and gives examples.

733 Frierson, Edward C. "Education of gifted youth in secondary school
     and college." Education 88(1): 25-29, September/October, 1967.
     (23 References)
Describes the significant administrative and instructional changes that
have occurred in secondary and college education for the gifted since
1950.

734 Geer, William C. "The education of the gifted." Except Child
     27(8): 436-38, April, 1961. (0 References)
Discusses a project designed to acquaint mature educational personnel
with the best knowledge presently available about the education of bright
and gifted children. Discusses program selection, procedures, personnel,
etc.

735 Ginandes, Shepard, M.D. The school we have. New York: Delacorte,
     1973. 273p.
Describes how troubled, fed-up adolescents interact with creative adults.

736 Gourley, Theodore J., and Breyley, Patricia. "Surprise, New Jersey
     does have some programs for the gifted." NJEA Rev 48(8): 27-28,
     April, 1975.
Discusses the needs of the state's gifted students and appropriate
programs designed to satisfy those needs.

737 Halpert, R. L., and Vredevoe, Lawrence E. "Administration and
     evaluation of programs for gifted students." Natl Assoc Second
     Sch Princ Bull No. 305: 69-83, December, 1965.
Deals with evaluating a program for the gifted. Includes a 10-page
evaluation form for the administrator to use. Also includes evaluation
key.

738 Hanna, Lyle. "An investigation of administrative procedures in
     gifted child programs." For a summary see: Diss Abstr Int
     25(7): 3931-32, January, 1965. (0 References)

739 Hermanson, David P. "One hundred recommendations for a senior high
     school gifted program," Gifted Child Q 15(4): 249-55, Winter,
     1971. (0 References)
Recommends subject matter in a variety of areas, e.g., individual
motivations and community resources: subjects are offered as discussion
topics for workshops, parent groups and individual schools when programs
for the gifted are being planned.

740 Hill, Frances. "Rich, privileged - and quite experimental."
     Times Educ Suppl 2922: 18, May 21, 1971. (0 References)
Describes Britain's Millfield School, a private institution of about
1000 students, reported to be the most expensive school in the world.

For its many gifted pupils (I.Q.'s 150+) Millfield provides the stimulus
of competition with peers and the chance to proceed at their natural fast
pace. They may study extra-curricular subjects such as computers and
astronomy as well as do university work during secondary years.

741 Hill, Thomas B. "Whatever happened to the gifted?" Educ Forum
     36(3): 323-26, March, 1972. (0 References)
This study challenges the national leadership to provide the resources
needed better to serve our gifted youth, so that the utilization of
human resources will be improved.

742 Irwin, Theodore. "Better schooling for bright youngsters"
     Parents Mag 45(1): 40-41+, January, 1970.
Gives many examples of innovative projects school systems all over the
country have initiated to provide enrichment for the intellectually or
artistically talented. Evaluates the benefits of many programs.

743 Isaacs, Ann F. "Guides for the administrator who would help gifted
     children." High Sch J 48(8): 484-90, May, 1965.
This overview of programs for the gifted deals with starting a program
for the gifted, factors necessary for gifted programs. Of special value
is an administrative acrostic for evaluating old and initiating new
programs for the gifted.

744 Jordan, June B. "Foundation for exceptional children addresses the
     needs of the culturally different gifted child." Except Child
     40(4): 279-83, January, 1974.
Reports on a conference which attempted to clarify major needs and
issues of culturally different gifted child identify barriers to
effective educational and social action and develop strategies to overcome them, and identify action to be taken.

745 Khatena, Joe. "Educating the gifted child: challenge and response
     in the U.S.A." Gifted Child Q 20(1): 76-90, Spring, 1976. (52
     References)
Reviewed are trends in the education of gifted children including
identification, teaching methods, problems of the highly gifted, support
for special educational opportunities, and future directions.

746 Kough, Jack. Practical programmes for the gifted. Chicago,
     Science Research Associates, 1960. 192p.
Deals with administrative programs for the gifted; identifying outstanding ability, special talents or disabilities of the gifted;
beginning a program for the gifted; motivation; significant programs;
the consultant's role; and special activities for the gifted.

747 Lyon, Harold C., Jr. "Education of the gifted and talented."
     Except Child 43(3): 166-68, November, 1976. (0 References)
Describes progress made in providing for the gifted since the national
effort began in 1970. Covers state leadership, appropriations and goals
of the multi-faceted program.

748 ————. "Gifted and talented: a new federal priority." Todays
     Educ 65(1): 33-35, January/February, 1976. (0 References)
Cites the federal governments concern with the nation's most neglected
and valuable natural resource, 2.5 million gifted and talented youth.

Efforts to strengthen state leadership, establish career education,
infuse the arts and humanities into all learning, and increase
cooperation between the community and the private sector are discussed.

749   Lyon, Harold C., Jr.   "The other minority."   Learning   2(5):
      65-66, January, 1974.
The director of Education for the Gifted and Talented in the USOE
discusses the smallest minority group of children neglected by the
school system - those of exceptional ability. He outlines plans of
his office to expand existing facilities and create innovative new
programs to insure the greatest contribution to society by the talented.

750   ————.   "Talent down the drain."   Am Educ   8(8):   12-16,
      October, 1972. (0 References)
The director of USOE's Office of Education for the Gifted and Talented
describes the more than two million such boys and girls in the nation's
elementary and secondary schools. He discusses past neglect of this
vast potential, and erroneous assumptions about them by educators and
public alike. Ends with description of plans and programs by USOE to
salvage this talent.

751   Magary, James F., and Freehill, Maurice F.   "Critical questions and
      answers relating to school and society in the education of the
      gifted."   Gifted Child Q   16(3):   185-94, Fall, 1972.
      (0 References)
Poses six questions related to societal expectations and obligations in
regard to the gifted. Following thoughtful discussion, eight questions
are raised and answered on school-related issues in the education of
talented minors.

752   Marland, Sidney P., Jr.   "Our gifted and talented children - a
      priceless national resource."   Intellect   101(2343):   16-19,
      October, 1972.
The U.S. Commissioner of Education cites past neglect of our most
valuable resource - our brightest, most talented, most skilled citizens.
In an effort to correct this he details the responsibilities,
activities, and plans of the federal government for the education of
the academically above-average.

753   Meeker, Mary N., and Mestyanek, Larry.   "Can gifted children be
      taught to be more intelligent?"   Gifted Child Q 20(2):   168-69,
      Summer, 1976. (0 References)
The author lists twelve critical issues which were of primary concern
to the educators who formulated the California State Framework for
Mentally Gifted Minors in 1971.

754   Ming, Roger W., and Gould, Noah.   "Meeting the needs of the
      gifted."   Educ Dig   38(6):   34-35, February, 1973.
Educators can do much with a small amount of money by freeing gifted
students to work under teachers who recognize and respect them.   The
authors point out that it is often community action that is the key to
providing the kind of needed education.

755   Newland, T. Ernest.   "On defining the mentally superior in terms
      of social need."   Except Child   29(5):   237-40, January, 1973.
      (0 References)

Varying claims that educational planning for mentally superior children should include from less than 1% up to 20% of the student population reflect an absence of clear conceptualization of the educational and social problems involved. Suggests an analysis of social needs which school programs for superior students could aim to fulfill.

756 Ogilvie, Eric. Gifted children in primary schools: the report of the Schools Council enquiry into the teaching of gifted children of primary age, 1970-71. London: Macmillan, 1973. 279p. (Bibliography)
When the British Schools Council set up a working party to study the teaching of gifted children in primary schools in 1969 they found that Local Education Authorities were poorly informed about current practices. This report describes their subsequent enquiry into local programs during the period 1970-71, and reports the findings resulting from it.

757 Olick, Alice. "Plight of the gifted." NJEA Rev 46(4): 26-27, 47, December, 1972.
Shows that only 21 states have legislation designed to aid gifted children, herein designated as those with I.Q. scores of 120 and above.

758 Olson, Thomas A. Raising consciousness of key publics about the needs of gifted and talented. Los Angeles: National/State Leadership Training Institute on the gifted and talented, 1975. 18p.
Presents a report of the 1974 planning conference on raising public consciousness about the needs of the gifted and talented. Stresses the fact that gifted and talented students can be found among various racial, ethnic and socioeconomic groups.

759 Passow, A. Harry, and Tannenbaum, Abraham J. "Some perspectives for the mid-70's. Education of the gifted and talented." Natl Assoc Second Sch Princ Bull 60(398): 3-12, March, 1976.
Covers past and present efforts in education of the gifted. Noted are problems such as inadequate funding and the paucity of legislation. Recent efforts to identify and develop talent in various ethnic and racial minorities are noted.

760 Patrick, Brother Charles, "Inter-parish cooperation: Monsignor William R. Kelly School, New York City." Natl Cathol Educ Assoc Bull 63(1): 425-26, August, 1966.
Discusses the community cooperation necessary for the success of an inner-city school for the gifted. Shows how a parochial school needs the cooperation of all.

761 Plowman, Paul D. "The California curriculum project for the gifted." Gifted Child Q 13(2): 113-15, Summer, 1969.
Describes the California State Department of Education's efforts to develop a framework in gifted child education, 31 curriculums, 35 exemplary curriculum guides, and a curriculum evaluation instrument, instrument package, and guidelines. This is to provide resources needed by 10,000 teachers and 254 school districts.

762 Problems, practices, procedures: experiences of 62 project schools. Chicago, Illinois: Segerdahl-Halford, 1964. 99 p.

This publication is the result of a survey by the North Central Association of Colleges and Secondary Schools of the 100 pilot high schools
which were selected in summer 1958 to participate in the 5 year
Superior and Talented Students Project.

763   Sanders, David C. Elementary education and the academically
       talented pupil. Washington, D.C.: National Education Association,
       1961. 96p.
This publication was prepared by educator-participants attending the
NEA conference on the Academically Talented Pupil. It is intended to
stimulate schools at the local level to reappraise their programs to
determine whether the needs of all children are being well met; and
provide some guidelines for sound appraisal and action.

764   Sato, Irving S. "The culturally different gifted child: the
       dawning of his day." Except Child 40(8): 572-76, May, 1974.
       (23 References)
The need for qualitatively differentiated program provisions for the
culturally different is discussed. Progress in fulfilling their needs
is noted, and information on the educational programs being instituted
throughout the U.S. is offered.

765   Smith, Mark C., Jr. "Administrative problems connected with
       special programs for gifted pupils in California junior high
       schools." For a summary see: Diss Abstr Int 21(10): 2971-72,
       April, 1961. (0 References)

766   Stewart, Jack C. "A survey of attitudes of superintendents toward
       educational programs for gifted children." For a summary see:
       Diss Abstr Int 33A(6): 2794, December, 1972. (0 References)

767   Syphers, Dorothy F. Gifted and talented children: practical
       programming for teachers and principals. Arlington, Virginia:
       Council for Exceptional Children, 1972. 84p. (Bibliography)
This small handbook should be of practical help to school principals.
It discusses methods and administrative procedures to show how theory
has been translated into practice. Included are scales for rating
behavior of both superior students and their teachers.

768   Torrance, E. Paul, ed. Talent and education: present status and
       future directions. Minneapolis: University of Minnesota Press.
       1960. 210p.
A compilation of papers presented at the 1958 Institute on Exceptional
Children. Part I deals with state's responsibility to gifted; Part II
deals with problems relevant to the identification of the talented.
Part III deals with eminent geniuses; Part IV offers three divergent
points of view concerning school provisions for meeting the needs of
gifted children.

769   U.S. Congress. House. Committee on Education and Labor, General
       Subcommittee on Education. Gifted and Talented Children Educational
       Assistance Act. Hearing on H.R. 4807 and H.R. 12814. 91st Congress,
       1st session, July 15, 1969.
Presents testimony at the House hearing on federal aid for the gifted and
talented. Experts in the field testifying before the committee included

James Gallagher, William Vassar, Joseph French, Marvin Gold and William Rogge who all advocated increased funding for gifted and talented programs.

770   U.S. Congress. Senate Committee on Labor and Public Welfare.
      A Bill to Amend the Elementary and Secondary Education Act of 1965,
      to Provide a Program for Gifted and Talented Children. Hearing on
      S. 1539. 93rd Congress, 1st session, 1973.
This is the bill sponsored by Senator Jacob Javits to support a
program for the gifted and talented at the federal level. While not yet
law, it is potentially landmark legislation.

771   U.S. Department of Health, Education and Welfare Office of
      Education. Talent development project, 1964. Washington, D.C.:
      Government Printing Office, 1964. 16p.
This small pamphlet is designed to acquaint the general public with the
Talent Development Project. It describes the background, goals,
activities and plans of the project. It concludes with identification
of project personnel and listing of publications available from U.S.
Office of Education on the gifted and talented.

772   U.S. Office of Education. Education of the gifted and talented:
      report to the Congress of the United States by the U.S. Commissioner
      of Education, and background papers submitted to the U.S. Office
      of Education. Washington, D.C.: U.S. Government Printing Office,
      1972. 324p. (Bibliography)
This comprehensive report is the result of a mandate from the U.S.
Congress to report on the status of education of gifted and talented
children. Volume 1 is an excellent, current source of U.S.-wide
programs, and planned federal objectives. Volume 2 is the background
papers for the study and constitutes valuable material contributed by
experts in the field, as well as the case studies of the four states
with the most successful educational programs for the gifted.

773   Ward, Frederick C. "Gifted children's educational assistance act."
      J Gen Educ 25(4): 247-52, January, 1974. (0 References)
An address by the Education Advisor of the Ford Foundation to the
Committee on Labor and Public Welfare of the U.S. Senate concerning
the purposes and aims of this bill. Covers attitudes toward the gifted,
undiscovered potential in women, lower economic and ethnic minority
groups, and stresses the need for full community involvement in
meeting the special needs of the gifted.

774   "What are you doing for your gifted?" Instructor 82(6): 80-83,
      February, 1973.
This article is intended to help elementary administrators build a case
and start a program for the gifted. It discusses identification,
presents program guidelines, and suggests several sources of help.

775   Wilcox, Edward T. "Seven years of advanced placement." Coll Board
      Rev 48(2): 29-34, Fall, 1962.
Describes program of advanced standing at Harvard. Explains methods of
selection of talented candidates, and programs offered. Would interest
administrators planning to offer advanced placement.

776   Williams, Jane C. Education for the gifted and talented: a role
       for the private sector. Washington, D.C.:   Office of Education,
       1974. 19p.
Reports the results of a survey of approximately 78 leaders in the field
of education for the gifted and talented who identified priority needs
and areas of potential for investment by the private sector.

777   Woolcock, Cyril W. The Hunter College High School program for
       gifted students. New York: Vantage, 1962. 166p.
The story of the nation's most famous school for intellectually gifted
girls - Hunter College High School - by its principal, the first male on
the faculty. Presently in its 90th year, the school enrolls girls with
I.Q.'s above 130 and offers them a broad liberal arts curriculum leading
to admission to the most selective colleges and universities.

778   ———. New Approaches to the education of the gifted. Morristown,
       New Jersey: Silver Burdett, 1961. 112p.
Presents some innovative administrative adaptations to meet the educational needs of the gifted.

                        D.   Teacher Role

779   Anzalone, Patricia. "Organizing your day around individuals."
       Instructor 77(10): 64, 70, 72. June/July, 1968. (0 References)
Stresses uniqueness and recommends a teaching program tailored to
individual needs and interests. Offers help to the teacher of a summer-
school program for the gifted by describing the interest centers which
will suit varying tastes and abilities.

780   Ashley, Rosalind M. Activities for motivating and teaching bright
       children. West Nyack, New York: Parker, 1973. 204p.
Many suggestions for classroom use are given for working with students
who are bright in the arts, science, mathematics, and language arts, as
well as those with aptitude in social studies and mechanics.

781   Barbe, Walter B., and Frierson, Edward C. "Teaching the gifted - a
       new frame of reference." Education 82(8): 465-67, April, 1962.
       (0 References)
Recognizes that teaching gifted children effectively requires a different concept of teaching. Contrasts product-oriented teaching with
process-oriented, and recommends the latter for gifted students.

782   Beck, Madeline H. "The attitudes, insight, and planning of students
       and experienced teachers in working with gifted intermediate grade
       pupils." For a summary see: Diss Abstr Int 29A(3): 829,
       September, 1968. (0 References)

783   Bishop, William E. "Characteristics of teachers judged successful
       by intellectually gifted, high-achieving high school students."
       For a summary see: Diss Abstr Int 28A(2): 487-88, August, 1967.
       (0 References)

784   ———. "Successful teachers of the gifted." Except Child 34(5):
       317-25, January, 1968. (8 References)
This study is concerned with personal and social traits and behaviors,
professional attitudes and educational viewpoints, and classroom

behavior patterns of effective teachers of gifted high school students.
Eleven characteristics are presented which differentiate successful
teachers of the gifted from their colleagues.

785 Blatt, Burton. "Preparation of special education personnel:
     gifted." Rev Educ Res 36(1): 151-61, February, 1966. (62
     References)
Summarized goals, offerings of college courses on gifted, and discovered,
based on a questionnaire to teachers, that there is a pressing need for
improved preservice teacher education on the gifted.

786 Boller, Jon D. "Sensitivity training and the school teacher: an
     experiment in favorable publicity." Pupil Pers Serv J 1(1): 24-30,
     1971.
Conducted a sensitivity training workshop for teachers of gifted.
Exercises were designed to promote self, group, and other awareness.
Tests after training suggest that relationships developed were more
positive than experimentors had anticipated.

787 Bridges, Sydney A. Gifted children and the Millfield Experiment.
     New York: Pitman, 1975. 185p.
Subtitled "New Work Since the Brentwood Experiment," this is a continua-
tion of the author's earlier study. It describes the work being done by
some of the British colleges in the area of education of the gifted.

788 Bridges, Sydney A., ed. Gifted children and the Brentwood Experi-
     ment. London: Pitman, 1969. 160p. (Bibliography)
The purpose of the present book is threefold. First it is to review
the work that is being done at England's Brentwood College of Education.
The second purpose is to record the lessons learned by the staff in the
course of the work, since these are important for all children. The
third purpose is to help those teachers who recognize the presence of
gifted children in their classes, but are unable to give these children
the help that they require.

789 Bruch, Catherine B. "Persistence of changes of attitudes toward
     gifted children." Gifted Child Q 7(3): 172-77, Autumn, 1967.
     (5 References)
Study of attitudinal changes of teachers dealing with gifted children.
More effective teaching of gifted children through an emphasis on
creativity is a trend that cuts across a multitude of courses.

790 Chambers, Dewey W. "Signposts for creative teaching." Instructor
     78(2): 57+, October, 1968.
Lists practices which can encourage creative thinking in students.

791 Coletta, Anthony J. "Reflective didactic styles for teachers of
     the young, gifted and poor children." Gifted Child Q 19(3):
     230-40, Fall, 1975. (18 References)
Demonstrates how the Flanders Interaction, the Bloom Taxonomy in the
cognitive domain, and the Gordon Teacher Effectiveness cues were combined into a workable framework for dealing with young, gifted, and
poor children.

792 Concannon, Sister Josephina. "The gifted: a major concern."
     Peabody J Educ 46(5): 274-77, March, 1969. (5 References)

Urges professional help for teachers who must identify the gifted among
their students, then make curriculum provisions, and provide assessment
and follow-up activities for those selected.

793 Cornish, Robert L. "You can challenge the gifted child." Grade
     Teach 85(3): 141-44, November, 1967.
Lists classroom-tested methods to challenge the gifted child at the
elementary level.

794 Cutts, Norma, and Moseley, Nicholas. Teaching the bright and
     gifted. Englewood Cliffs, New Jersey: Prentice-Hall, 1957. 268p.
     (Bibliography)
Gives practical help to classroom teachers. Deals with identification,
purpose and plans, methods and content, utilizing community resources,
special groups, acceleration, fundamentals, motivating, underachieving
mental hygiene, character development, educational and vocational
guidance and working with parents.

795 Drews, Elizabeth M. Learning together: how to foster creativity,
     self-fulfillment, and social awareness in today's students and
     teachers. Englewood Cliffs, New Jersey: Prentice-Hall, 1972.
     324p. (Bibliography)
The author concludes that youths protest mainly because a dehumanizing
society has left them unfulfilled. Teachers, she feels, must take the
lead in guiding students to the fullest development of their potentialities by implementing a humanistic-existential educational philosophy in
the manner of Rogers, Maslow, Allport and Fromm.

796 Feldhusen, John F. "Practicum activities for students and gifted
     children in a university course." Gifted Child Q 17(2): 124-29,
     Summer, 1973.
Dr. Feldhusen, Chairman of the Educational Psychology and Research
Department at Purdue University, here describes his three-tiered course
for undergraduate and graduate students entitled "Gifted, Creative and
Talented Children." He lists goals of the course, reading topics,
source books and films, and instructional activities. Of especial interest is the description of the practicum where college students work with
the gifted students on a one-to-one basis in cooperation with parents,
teachers, and under Dr. Feldhusen's direction.

797 Fredrickson, Ronald H., and Rothney, John W. "Statewide implementa-
     tion of classroom practices for superior children." Except Child
     35(2): 135-40, October, 1968. (3 References)
Describes a study which attempted to discover if teachers made changes
in practices with superior students following a university in-service
training program which encouraged implementation of 25 practices.

798 Freehill, Maurice F. "Intelligence, empathy and methodologic bias
     about teaching the gifted." Gifted Child Q 18(4): 247-48, Winter,
     1974.
Results of 3 tests administered to 93 educators in a workshop on gifted
education, which included The Concept Mastery Test, an Empathy Scale
based on Sherman and Scotland, and an interactionist vs behaviorist bias
scale.Yielded correlations between -0.2 and 0.12 between the measures.

799 French, Joseph L. "The preparation of teachers of the gifted."
     J Teach Educ 12(1): 69-72, March, 1961. (0 References)
Surveyed university courses on the gifted, summarized course outline and
provided names of contributing instructors.

800 Gallagher, James J. The gifted child in the elementary school.
     Washington, D.C. National Education Association, 1959. 32p.
     (Bibliography)
One of the monographs in the NEA's What Research Says to the Teacher
series. Its author, with the aid of several experts on education of the
gifted, has drawn from research materials on intellectually gifted
children in elementary schools, those items which promise to be of most
help to classroom teachers.

801 ————. Teaching the gifted child. 2nd ed. Boston: Allyn and
     Bacon, 1975. 431p. (Bibliography)
Gallagher's book emphasizes advances during the previous ten years.
While it treats matters of concern to administrators, primary consideration is given to the discussion of curriculum and pedagogy from the
teacher's standpoint. Case studies are used throughout the book to
illustrate theoretical points discussed.

802 Gallagher, James J., ed. Teaching gifted students: a book of
     readings. Boston: Allyn and Bacon, 1965. 326p. (Bibliography)
The set of articles collected here were chosen to supplement the author's
text Teaching the Gifted Child. The general sections of this book
parallel those in the text. Emphasis is placed on classroom environment,
new curriculum movements, and special teaching methods as opposed to
administrative provisions.

803 Gallagher, James J.; Aschner, Mary J.; Jenne, William. Productive
     thinking of gifted children in classroom interaction. Washington,
     D.C.: The Council for Exceptional Children, 1967. 103p.
The authors utilized tape recorders for making a permanent record of
classroom interaction. Thus they were able to identify and classify
productive thought processes expressed by intellectually gifted 12-14
year old students and their teachers. Previous observations were
confirmed regarding the crucial role played by the teacher as initiator
and determiner of the kinds of thought processes expressed in the
classroom.

804 Gray, Charles E., and Young, Richard C. "Utilizing the divergent
     production matrix of the Structure-of-Intellect model in the
     development of teaching strategies." Gifted Child Q 19(4):
     290-300, 271, Winter, 1975. (20 References)
Describes development of a program to train teachers to stimulate
hypothesis generation (creativity) in elementary and secondary students.

805 Hauck, Barbara B., and Freehill, Maurice F. The gifted-case
     studies. Dubuque, Iowa: W. C. Brown, 1972. 141p. (Bibliography)
Planned for use in preservice and inservice teacher training classes,
this small volume attempts to integrate data, theory, and cases. The
cases are written by experienced teachers and counselors and they provide
considerable material for thought, discussion, and planning.

806   Hecht, Kathryn A.   "Teacher ratings of potential dropouts and
       academically gifted children: are they related?"   J Teach Educ
       26(2):   172-75, Summer, 1975.   (9 References)
A large national sample of elementary school children were rated by
teachers as potential dropouts or academically gifted.   As expected
the PD's were assigned all the negative traits and the AG's all the
positive traits.   In addition the PD's were overrepresented on low
achievement variables and also on personal problems.

806a   Hildreth, Gertrude H.   Introduction to the gifted.   New York:
       McGraw-Hill, 1966.   572p.   (Bibliography)
This text has been organized for use in education and child psychology
courses, and for training courses preparing specialists in the field.
It gives a survey of developments through the years and alternatives in
educational adjustments for bright and talented children, but deals
primarily with educational theory and practice.   The Appendix comprises
a "Checklist for Gifted Children (ages 10 and over)."

807   Isaacs, Ann F.   "A survey of suggested preparation for teachers of
       the gifted."   Gifted Child Q   10(2):   72-77, Summer, 1966.   (18
       References)
In response to inquiries from teachers, state certification departments,
and school administrators about the training needed by teachers of the
gifted, the author conducted a questionnaire survey; items are ranked
according to respondents' replies.

808   Jacobs, Jon C.   "Teacher attitude toward gifted children."
       Gifted Child Q   16(1):   23-26, Spring, 1972.
Developed a measure for teacher attitude toward the gifted to determine
whether that attitude was positive or negative.   When administered to
private school teachers, positive attitudes were displayed toward gifted.
However when given to kindergarten and first grade teachers, they displayed more negative attitude toward gifted.   It is suggested that at
an early age the gifted child is taught that his inquisitive behavior is
less acceptable than that of other children.

809   James, Katherine G.   "The preparation of teachers for the gifted in
       the elementary schools with special reference to Southern
       Connecticut State College."   For a summary see: Diss Abstr Int
       21(10):   3005-6, April, 1961.   (0 References)

810   Josephina, Sister. "Teachers' reactions to gifted pupils."   Gifted
       Child Q   5(2):   42-44, Summer, 1961.   (0 References)
Sixty six teachers surveyed for attitudes revealed the following (1)
teachers for the gifted need superior intelligence and training (2) there
are more gifted boys than girls (3) acceleration is unwise but enrichment
is desirable.

811   Lyon, Harold C., Jr.   Learning to feel - feeling to learn.
       Columbus, Ohio: Merrill, 1971.   321p.   (Bibliography)
The author, Director of the Office of Education for the Gifted and
Talented, feels that teacher training is a crucial concern here.   The
gifted need "humanistic" teachers with a capacity to share their feelings
as well as their knowledge and experience.   This book goes beyond romantic
complaints and academic intellectualizations and presents actual humanistic innovations which worked in teacher education settings.

812 Malone, Charlotte E. "Cost little (or less than that): creative
     teaching ideas." Gifted Child Q 19(1): 68-70, Spring, 1975.
     (0 References)
Presented are creative teaching ideas for developing gifted students'
skills in locating, analyzing and evaluating information.

813 ———. "Implementing a differential school program for the gifted."
     Gifted Child Q 19(4): 316-27, Winter, 1975. (16 References)
Presents numerous suggestions for establishing an in-service education
program for teachers of gifted children. Techniques and criteria for
effective evaluation are also discussed.

814 Moore, George N., and Woodruff, G. Willard. Providing for children's
     differences. Wellesley, Massachusetts: Curriculum Associates, 1970.
Teachers seeking better use of learning time, space and materials, and
who wish to improve the child's school environment and meet demands of
curriculum will find this a particularly helpful book. Where special
programs for gifted are not provided, these suggestions will be most
useful.

815 Morrison, Charlotte. "A creative teacher shares notes to trainees
     in a gifted child training program." Gifted Child Q 14(2):
     97-105, Summer, 1970. (0 References)
This article is made up of daily handouts given to trainees at the start
of each demonstration class during the 1969 Creativity Workshop sessions
at San Fernando Valley State College, California.

816 Myers, Garry C. "Creative thinking in the classroom." Highlights
     Teach 3: 1-4, 1966. (11 References)
The editor of Highlights for Children describes the characteristics of
creative thinking persons and gives helpful suggestions to teachers who
want to foster creativity in their pupils.

817 Nelson, Joan B., and Cleland, Donald L. "The role of the teacher
     of the gifted." Education 88(1): 47-51, September/October, 1967.
Emphasizes the vital importance of the teacher's role in early recognition of superior ability and development of latent talents of the gifted.

818 Parker, Margaret, "Teachers talk with parents about bright kids."
     Kootenay Cent Gifted J 1(3): 11-17, October, 1973.
Maintains that teachers of gifted children can rate their interpersonal
skills on three scales of genuineness, nonpossessive warmth, and
accurate empathy.

819 Peterson, John F. "A study of the effects of giving teachers
     personal information about high-ability low-performing, secondary
     school students." For a summary see: Diss Abstr Int 27A(4):
     963-64, October, 1966. (0 References)

820 Ripin, Margaret. "Teaching: round table." J Emot Educ 9(1):
     33-39, Winter, 1969. (0 References)
Presents a discussion with four Gramercy Hill Institute teachers of the
gifted on differences between traditional teaching and a new form of
creative teaching which believes that a child's emotional needs are as
important as his intellectual and physical needs.

821   Salvia, John; Clark, Gary M.; Ysseldyke, James E.   "Teacher retention
       of stereotypes of exceptionality."   Except Child   39(8):   651-52,
       May, 1973.   (3 References)
Undergraduate teachers in training were asked to rate children labeled
"mentally retarded", "normal", or "gifted".   Children labeled "gifted"
were seen more positively than children labeled "normal", while those
labeled "retarded" were rated less favorably than those rated "normal".

822   Sanderlin, Owenita.   Teaching gifted children.   South Brunswick, New
       Jersey: Barnes, 1973.   190p.   (Bibliography)
Although the title would indicate that this book is mainly for teachers
it will probably find its greatest readership among parents and lay
leaders of the gifted.   Some of the topics treated are the issue of
whether education of the gifted is undemocratic, how children should be
grouped, and what parents of the gifted can do.

823   Shaffer, V. Faye, and Troutt, George E., Jr.   "Courses offered on
       the education of the gifted."   Gifted Child Q   14(1):   8-23,
       Spring, 1970.   (0 References)
College courses dealing with the gifted are listed by title; information
is provided in the name and location of the institution, the instructor,
time, whether it is graduate or undergraduate, and the credit it carries.

824   Sisk, Dorothy.   "Teaching the gifted and talented teacher: a
       training model."   Gifted Child Q   19(1):   81-88, Spring, 1975.
       (8 References)
A training model in teacher training for teachers of the gifted evolved
by the University of South Florida (Tampa) Teaching is seen as the
process of continuing learning at its highest level, that of a teacher
sharing learning with others - the students.

825   Skipper, Charles E.   "Intellectually gifted people and their
       potential as teachers."   Kappa Delta Pi Rec   10(3):   83-87,
       February, 1974.   (16 References)
Recounts a Miami University study in which female secondary teacher
candidates in the Honors Program were compared to an unselected group of
teacher candidates on a number of personal attributes.   Based on
attitudes toward teaching, values, vocational preferences and personal
preferences, it appears that gifted teacher candidates will be more
effective in working with children than the non-gifted, and will provide
worthwhile role models for pupils to emulate.

826   Stark, June B.   "Look on the bright side."   Early Years   6(9):
       40-42, May, 1976.
Many practical suggestions for the teacher desiring to further creativity
in bright students.   Recommends using brainstorming as a group activity,
and providing lessons which mesh affective and cognitive development in
the child.

827   Taylor, Calvin W.   "Be talent developers as well as knowledge
       dispensers."   Todays Educ   57(9):   67-69, December, 1968.   (0
       References)
Presents several student case studies showing examples of multiple
talents.   Suggests a grouping of talents based upon world-of-work needs
including academic, creative, evaluative or decision-making, planning,
forecasting, and communication talents.

828   Taylor, Calvin W. "Multiple talent teaching." Todays Educ 63(2):
      71-74, March, 1974.
Wants teachers to become miners of talent. Makes suggestions for
developing students' talents at forecasting and planning. Describes a
program in one school system and how tests proved that creative potential
is much improved with multiple-talent teaching.

829   Torrance, E. Paul. "Gifted child teacher." Instructor 77: 63-68+,
      June, 1968.
Torrance is editor of this section which has brief articles by different
authors of value to beginning teachers. Includes characteristics of
gifted, enrichment reading, references, advantages of summer programs
for the gifted, activities for the gifted, thinking games, and organizing
a teachers day.

830   ————. "What gifted disadvantaged children can teach their
      teachers." Gifted Child Q 17(4): 243-49, Winter, 1973. (2
      References)
At the conclusion of a summer creativity workshop for programmed 6-13
year old disadvantaged children the teachers were asked to list things
pupils had taught them, either directly or indirectly. Each teacher
cited 9-10 teachings of both kinds.

831   Vassar, William G., and Renzulli, Joseph S. "Course offerings on
      the psychology and education of the gifted." Gifted Child Q
      13(1): 37-44, Spring, 1969.
Presents the results of a periodic survey of college and university
courses dealing with education of the gifted. Of the 676 institutions
responding, 71 course offerings dealing with the gifted are reported.
Course titles, instructors, time of offering, level of courses and credit
hours are included.

832   Walker, Joseph. "Gifted teacher, know thyself." Gifted Child Q
      17(4): 288-92, Winter, 1973. (4 References)
Dr. Walker, a specialist in gifted education at the University of
Georgia, tells of a programmed instrument he developed to introduce to
teachers of the gifted the concept of self-assessment.

833   Wilson, Frank T. "Motivation of the gifted and teacher education."
      J Teach Educ 12(2): 179-84, June, 1961. (11 References)
The study of teachers' practices leads one to conclude that in order to
secure teachers who can nurture children possessing unusual capabilities,
special programs must be designed to improve preservice teacher
education.

834   Wilson, Sandra H. "Teacher self-perception and the self-concepts
      of disadvantaged, preschool, gifted children: an experimental
      investigation." For a summary see: Diss Abstr Int 34A(8):
      4939-40, February, 1974. (0 References)

835   Wilson, Sandra H.; Greer, Jack F.; Johnson, Russell M. "Synectics,
      a creative problem-solving technique for the gifted." Gifted
      Child Q 17(4): 260-67, Winter, 1973. (20 References)
Paper of practical use to teachers states that synectics (a group
problem solving activity wherein persons are stimulated to think

creatively under a loosely structured system) is a powerful tool for use
with gifted children. Gives creative examples for classroom use.

836   Yardley, Alice. Reaching out. young children learning series.
       New York: Citation Press, 1973. 112p.
One of a series of four books in which issues affecting the organization
and work of the British Infant School are discussed. Considers gifted
children, slow learners and the functions of the teacher.

E.   Guidance and Counseling

837   Barbe, Walter B., and Chambers, Norman S. "Career requirements of
       gifted elementary children and their parents." Vocat Guid Q
       11(2): 137-40, Winter, 1963. (1 Reference)
There was found no significant difference in career choice requirement
of gifted elementary children and their parents. The research
uncovers a greater need for the specialized guidance worker at the
elementary school than has ever been suspected.

838   Beery, Richard G. "Fear of failure in the student experience."
       Pers Guid J 54(4): 190-203, December, 1975. (11 References)
Considered in a four part article is the fear of failure which is
thought to dominate the lives of many high achieving and gifted college
students. Examples are given of the reactions of students to this
fear. Implications for counseling are clear.

839   Bose, K. "Guidance services for the talented." J Vocat Educ Guid
       16(1-2): 53-57, June/December, 1974.
Urges more attention to guidance services and resources for the gifted.
Divides the gifted into two groups: (a) The intellectually superior,
and (b) the societal leaders. Discusses 3 basic needs of gifted pupils.

840   Caldwell, Edward. "The effects of special counseling upon talented
       students with inferior grades." Florida J Educ Res 4(1): 11-16,
       January, 1962. (7 References)
Counseling of the social-casework type which includes parents was given
to underachieving talented students. Counseled students showed no
significant gains in grades over control group.

841   Culbertson, Edward L. "Changes in perceived attitudes of mentally
       gifted minors following individual and group counseling." For a
       summary see: Diss Abstr Int 33B(1): 419, July, 1972.
       (0 References)

842   Demos, George D., and Grant, Bruce. "If you are scholastically
       gifted." Gifted Child Q 10(1): 25-28, Spring, 1966. (0
       References)
The authors speak directly to the gifted about the variety of vocational
choice open to them. They suggest occupations suitable for the
academically gifted, and list those requiring bachelors, masters, and
doctoral degrees.

843   Drews, Elizabeth M. "Counseling for self-actualization in gifted
       girls and young women." J Couns Psychol 12(2): 167-75, Summer,
       1965. (19 References)

Various approaches to counseling and curriculum which emphasize being
and becoming show that gifted girls are helped to break through
restraining social sanctions and to move toward greater self actualization.

844 Drews, Elizabeth M. The creative intellectual style in gifted
       adolescents: being and becoming, cosmic approach to counseling
       and curriculum. East Lansing: Michigan State University, 1965.
       285p. (Bibliography)
Developed program which tried to make the gifted student more interested
in learning, more creative, and more sensitive to their fellow man.
Used adult models in films and textbooks to stimulate the students.
Study was successful.

845 Drews, Elizabeth M., ed. Guidance for the academically talented
       student. Washington, D.C.: National Education Association
       Project on the Academically Talented Student, 1961. 144p.
This publication, a result of the 1959 Washington Conference on Guidance
for the Academically Talented Student, contains both ideas for guidance
work with able youth and specific ways in which these ideas can be
actualized. Appendices describe in-school, summer, and out-of-school
programs designed for superior students.

846 Ewing, Thomas N., and Gilbert, William M. "Controlled study of the
       effects of counseling on the scholastic achievements of students
       of superior ability." J Couns Psychol 14(3): 235-39, May, 1967.
       (16 References)
Students who cooperated in this project whether counseled or not
showed more grade improvement than students who were uncooperative.
It was concluded that the evidence supports the hypothesis that
counseling can assist underachieving students to improve scholastically.

847 Ferguson, Donald G. "Professional roles in the vocational
       guidance of gifted children." Vocat Guid Q 11(4): 241-46, Summer,
       1963. (10 References)
Points out there is little literature on vocational guidance for
gifted. Nevertheless, the gifted need special guidance in handling
expectations and frustrations.

848 Forrest, Aubrey. "Counseling talented students in college choice,"
       Pers Guid J 40(1): 42-47, September, 1961. (5 References)
Discusses eight criteria for picking colleges listed by the talented
and makes recommendations.

849 Franklin, Anderson J. "To be young, gifted and black with
       inappropriate professional training: a critique of counseling
       programs." Couns Psychol 2(4): 107-12, 1971. (0 References)
States that the professional counselor must not lose his identity as
a black man. He should be an agent of social change. Outlines training
of prospective counselors.

850 Freehill, Maurice F. "School psychology and gifted children."
       Coll Educ Rec 40(2): 20-25, June 19, 1974. (20 References)
The work of school psychology has been predominantly directed to the
assessment of deficiencies and assignment to remedial programs.

Freehill feels that psychologists should concern themselves with the gifted, for among them psychologists will find maximized individual differences, variable and powerful learning styles and extreme impingements of personality on performance.

851   Gowan, John C.   "Issues on the guidance of gifted and creative children."   Gifted Child Q   11(3):   140-43, Autumn, 1967. (7 References)
Many of the special problems of academically talented children are different from those of the child of average ability. However, the same problems faced by both gifted and average children may simply occur at an earlier time for the gifted child.

852   Gowan, John C. et. al.   "New aspects in guiding the gifted in demonstration classes."   Gifted Child Q   13(2):   103-12, Summer, 1969. (7 References)
Recounts many instances of initial student maladjustment and subsequent resolution through effective counseling during summer creativity workshops which train teachers to work successfully with gifted elementary age children.

853   Gowan, John C., and Bruch, Catherine.   The academically talented student and guidance. Boston: Houghton Mifflin, 1971. 107p. (Bibliography)
This monograph attempts to relate a two-fold message: (1) gifted and talented students include not only those with high generalized abilities but also those with a variety of specific abilities, and (2) gifted and talented students experience many problems and need adequate guidance.

854   Gowan, John C.; Demos, George D.; Kokaska, J.   The guidance of exceptional children. New York: McKay, 1972.   300p.
A revision of the only book of readings on guidance of exceptional children.   Contains chapters on the gifted, creative and under-achievers.

855   Gumaer, Jim, and Voorneveld, Richard.   "Affective education with gifted children."   Elem Sch Guid Couns   10(2):   86-94, December, 1975.
Fourth grade gifted students participated in group counseling in which they received relaxation training and transactional analysis while fifth grade gifted pupils received only TA.   Results showed that the combination employed with fourth graders was more successful in reducing anxiety and improving inter-personal relations among students.

856   Hall, Eleanor.   "What will I be? A summer program for gifted students."   Innovator   7(8):   1-3, April, 1976. (0 References)
A two-week summer program for gifted junior high school students is held at the University of Michigan to allow pupils to explore career possibilities.   Participants are given aptitude and interest inventories and taken on field trips to interesting places.

857   Harris, Pearl, and Trolta, Frank.   "An experiment with under-achievers."   Education   82(6):   347-49, February, 1962.

Underachieving bright students were selected for group discussion.
After nine sessions, four students had improved their grades and two
showed minor improvement. Two showed no improvement. Study shows that
group discussion was of value in helping underachieving bright
students. Interestingly, the students had not thought of themselves as
having problems, thus some time was spent in making them see they had
problems.

858   Henjam, Raymond J., and Rothney, John W. "Parental action on
      counselor's suggestions." Vocat Guid Q 18(1): 54-58, September,
      1969. (5 References)
Results suggested that a large majority of parents of superior students
want to help with educational planning, especially vocational planning.
College-educated parents were more willing to help their children in
career planning.

859   Hill, Charles H. "On learning to abide fools gladly." Sch
      Community 58(8): 26-27,41, April, 1972. (18 References)
The author suggests that there are characteristics of the gifted that
require differential counseling by virtue of their presence, intensity
or timing. Assuming the burden of guidance for gifted children rests
with the professional educator. The writer presents various specific
suggestions.

860   Hutson, Thomas, and Osen, Deborah. "A multi-media approach
      to gifted in a high school group psychology - counseling seminar."
      Gifted Child Q 14(3): 186-90, Fall, 1970. (6 References)
Seminar using closed circuit TV enabled pupil participants to view
themselves and give honest feedback. Sessions were designed to
develop intellectual freedom through critical thinking.

861   James, Newton E. "A motivational and surveillance program for
      talented college students." Pers Guid J 40(8): 723-27,
      April, 1962. (2 References)
Describes a motivational program to stimulate scholarship. The grade
point averages of the counseled talented students were not different
from all those counseled but there was less attrition by talented
students.

862   Jenkins, James J., and Fullerson, Donald C., eds. Studies in
      Individual Differences: the Search for Intelligence. New York:
      Appleton-Century Crofts, 1961. 774p.
Presents some of the challenging problems involved in the conservation
of human talent. Stresses the role of education and counseling in
reducing occupational maladjustment in our society.

863   Joesting, Joan, and Joesting, Robert. "Future problems of gifted
      girls." Gifted Child Q 14(2): 82-90, Summer, 1970. (51
      References)
Paper summarizes studies on gifted girls,indicates that gifted girls do
tend to be beset by problems, sexist and otherwise, and makes suggestions
for counselors of gifted girls.

864   Koeppe, Richard P., and Rothney, John W. "Evaluation of first
      steps in the counseling of superior students." Pers Guid J
      42(1): 35-40, September, 1963. (4 References)

Seventy-five gifted high school freshmen from 25 Wisconsin high schools
were selected by their teachers to participate in a Guidance Laboratory.
Although one day of counseling was insufficient to produce extensive
changes in behavior, some significant changes were observed by
teachers, parents, and students themselves.

865   Martinson, Ruth A. "Guidance of the gifted." Education   82(6):
         342-46, February, 1962. (5 References)
Discusses the guidance counselor's concerns with the gifted -
identification, grading, planning, parents, vocational guidance, and
evaluation.

866   Miller, Leonard M., ed. Guidance for the underachiever with
         superior ability. Washington, D.C.: U.S. Department of Health,
         Education, and Welfare, Office of Education, 1961. 85p.
A useful guide for the counselor who is working to motivate the able
underachiever to use his talents.

867   Ratna, Ved. "Guidance for the talented selected under the
         National Science Search scheme." J Vocat Educ Guid   16(1-2):
         44-47, June/December, 1974.
Discusses the special counseling needs of gifted students in the
context of the National Science Talent Search. Three pilot NSTS
programs are described which have been implemented with success, to
help maximize the potential of gifted students.

868   Rothney, John W. "A state-wide approach to the discovery and
         guidance of superior students." Sch Soc   89(2194): 271-74,
         Summer, 1961.
Describes a University of Wisconsin laboratory project in identifying,
testing, and counseling gifted high school students.

869   Rothney, John W.,and Sanborn, Marshall P. "Wisconsin's Research-
         Through-Service Program for superior high school students."
         Pers Guid J   44(7): 694-99, March, 1966. (9 References)
Describes Research and Guidance Laboratory at University of Wisconsin
which helps with identification, guidance, and educational and
vocational development of superior students. Long-range follow-up is
stressed.

870   Sanborn, Marshall P., and Wasson, Robert M. "Guidance of
         students with special characteristics." Rev Educ Res   36(2):
         308-326, April, 1966. (87 References)
A summary of research reports and selected writings that appear to
have implications for school counselors.

871   Scarvelis, Stephen M. "Guidance procedures supported by Elementary
         School Counselors and Counselor Educators of Ohio for the
         identification and guidance of the gifted." For a summary see:
         Diss Abstr Int   30A(6): 2342-43, December, 1969. (0 References)

872   Searles, Aysel Jr. "The effectiveness of limited counseling in
         improving the academic achievement of superior college freshmen."
         Pers Guid J   40(7): 630-33, March, 1962. (3 References)
Describes a three-interview counseling procedure for 62 freshmen. Did
not seem to have any effect an academic grades of students.

873 Semke, Charles W.   "A comparison of the outcomes of case study
     structured group counseling with high ability, underachieving
     freshmen." For a summary see: Diss Abstr Int 29A(1): 128,
     July, 1968. (0 References)

874 Sippel, Raymond G. "Relationship of perceptions held by San Diego
     gifted seniors and their intergrade advisors of the advisor's
     role in the college decision." For a summary see: Diss Abstr Int
     32A(2): 812, August, 1971. (0 References)

875 Shouksmith, George A., and Taylor, J. W. "The effect of counseling
     on the achievement of high-ability pupils." Br J Educ Psychol
     34(1): 51-57, February, 1964. (11 References)
Authors conclude from a three-group experiment that counseling does
have a positive effect on under-achieving pupils of high ability.

876 Winborn, Bob, and Schmidt, Louis G. "Effectiveness of short-term
     group counseling upon the academic achievement of potentially
     superior but underachieving college freshmen." J Educ Res
     55(4): 169-73, December/January, 1961. (3 References)
Investigation found that short-term group counseling did not increase
academic grades of gifted college freshmen. Long-term counseling was
recommended.

877 Wyne, Marvin D., and Skjei, Priscilla. "The counselor and
     exceptional pupils: a critical review." Pers Guid J 48(10):
     828-35, June, 1970. (19 References)
Suggests that school counselors do not deal systematically or consistantly
with exceptional children's needs. Counselors' work with gifted
students is appraised.

F. Parental Management

878 Beck, Joan. How to raise a brighter child. New York, Trident,
     1967. 273p.
The purpose of this book is to report to parents, presenting research
from scientific journals, learned symposiums and experimental laboratories in a form that will be useful to those who live and work with
small children.

879 Bricklin, Barry, and Bricklin, Patricia M. Bright child-poor
     grades. New York: Delacorte, 1967. 150p.
This book aims to change attitudes. Changes in significant parental
attitudes will increase the child's efficiency. Part I of the book
discusses what attitudes need to be changed, and furnishes the understanding that must come before such change is possible. Part II is
concerned with positive recommendations.

880 Brumbaugh, Florence N., and Roshco, Bernard. Your gifted child:
     a guide for parents. New York: Collier, 1962. 160p.
This readable little paperback consists of three parts: Understanding
Giftedness, How to be a Gifted Parent, and Working with the Gifted
Child.

881 Cheyney, Arnold B. "Parents view their intellectually gifted
     children." Peabody J Educ 40(2): 98-101, September, 1962. (0
     References)

Interviewed 500 sets of parents of gifted. 82% recognized their children
were gifted. Usually schools had made the parents aware of their students'
abilities. Parents most often used books as a method to foster their
childrens' giftedness.

882 Cutts, Norma E., and Moseley, Nicholas. Bright children: a guide
     for parents. New York: Putnam, 1953. 238p. (Bibliography)
This guide book for parents of bright children offers many useful
suggestions on discipline, mental hygiene, choice of school and college
and vocational guidance. It includes references to many relevant books
and articles and helpful personal accounts by bright children and their
parents.

883 Deakin, Michael. The children on the hill: the story of an
     extraordinary family. Indianapolis: Bobbs-Merrill, 1973. 125p.
Recounts one family's bold experiment with a new way of learning and
growing. Offers creative suggestions for parents of the gifted.

884 De Haan, Robert F. Guidelines for parents of capable youth.
     Chicago: Science Research Associates, 1961. 48p.
In order to assist parents to gain information about their gifted youngsters, the Superior and Talented Secondary Schools' Project asked the
author to think through the main questions confronting parents of able
youth, and to give some practical suggestions as they work toward understanding and helping their talented teen-agers.

885 Dunn, Harry C. "A study of parental attitudes concerning a program
     for academically gifted children." For a summary see: Diss Abstr
     Int 30A(11): 4678-79, May, 1970. (0 References)

886 Engelmann, Siegfried, and Engelman, Therese. Give your child a
     superior mind: a program for the pre-school child. New York:
     Simon and Schuster, 1966. 317p.
This programmed guide is designed for parents. It gives explicit
instruction and information on how to develop the intellect of the preschool child. Also useful for elementary teachers.

887 Ennis, Authur L. "Raising brighter children." Ill Med J 137(1):
     38-39, January, 1970.
Dr. Ennis, a general practitioner interested in infants' mental as well
as physical development, presents some practical suggestions to new
mothers. His ideas on early mental stimulation may be useful to pedia-
tricians, nurses, and pre-school teachers as well.

888 Frazer, Donald W. "A study of parental attitudes toward the special
     education class for the mentally gifted sixth grade students in
     Atchison,Kansas." For a summary see: Diss Abstr Int 25(7): 3929,
     January, 1965. (0 References)

889 Gensley, Juliana. "The gifted isolate, or where are the peers?"
     Gifted Child Q 16(3): 246-47, Fall, 1972. (2 References)
In the average small elementary school the gifted child is liable to be
without peers of comparable ability and similar interests. Some
suggestions are given to parents on how to help the gifted adjust to
others and develop many peer groups.

890 Gensley, Juliana. "Parent perspective: the bored child." Gifted
     Child Q 15(1): 60-61, Spring, 1971. (0 References)
Practical advice for the parents of bored gifted youngsters.

891 ———. "The pre-school gifted child." Gifted Child Q 17(3):
     219-20, Fall, 1973. (0 References)
Suggestions for parents of gifted preschool children include talking to
the child as an individual, listening perceptively, finding ways to
round out knowledge for development of true concepts, and providing a
good learning environment.

892 Grost, Audrey. Genius in residence. Englewood Cliffs, New Jersey:
     Prentice-Hall, 1970. 224p.
This is a mother's story of how a "normal" American family raised a most
unusual child - a child with an I.Q. "too high to be meaningfully
measured". Despite her personal involvement, Mrs. Grost maintains a
great deal of perspective and insight, both on the experiences of her
son and the attitude of those in the outside world who "experience" him.

893 Jacobs, Jon C. "Evaluation of mother teaching style in high ability
     families." Gifted Child Q 15(1): 32-35, Spring, 1971. (4
     References)
Describes 20 mothers of gifted children who were varied in their teaching
styles. Eight were restrictive, nine were expansive, and three varied
greatly. Thus, the implications from literature that mothers of gifted
are uniformly expansive is not born out.

894 Keller, George, C. "Bright kids." Am Educ 3(3): 28-32, March,
     1967.
Written for parents, this comprehensive overview of the gifted touches
identification of the gifted, I.Q. levels, a brief summary of Terman's
studies, importance of home stimulation, and just about anything the
layman would want to know about the gifted. Very knowledgeable and
readable.

895 Klemm, Eugene. "Family help for gifted children." Education
     88(1): 22-24, September, 1967. (4 References)
The author suggests ways in which parents, through careful advice and
stimulation, may help gifted children meet the problems of adolescence and
maturity.

896 Love, Harold D. Parental attitudes toward exceptional children.
     Springfield, Illinois: Thomas, 1970. 167p.
This book is designed to help educators, ministers, physicians,
psychologists and other interested personnel to analyze parental
attitudes and to counsel parents who have exceptional children. Chapter
VI, dealing with the gifted child, covers definition, incidence, adjustment, education and guidance and gives many suggestions for parental
handling of superior children.

897 Mackinnon, Frederick A. "The relationship of perceived patterns of
     parent-child decision making to divergent thinking ability in
     gifted children." For a summary see: Diss Abstr Int 27A(11):
     3726-27, May, 1967. (0 References)

898   Malone, Charlotte E.   "Education for parents of the gifted."
       Gifted Child Q   19(3):   223-25, Fall, 1975.   (0 References)
Parents are requesting help in the guidance of their atypical, gifted
children.   They do not have the standard societal models to direct their
interaction with their children and they are aware that the potential
for productivity is greater in their children than in most.   In
addition, adult education for parents of gifted is needed to interpret
school placement and programs.

899   Maynard, Fredelle.   Guiding your child to a more creative life.
       New York: Doubleday, 1973.   369p.
A highly useful guide to activities and supportive materials and books
for helping cultivate and develop children's creativity.   Chapters deal
with play, music, arts and crafts, dance and rhythm, family games and
activities, books and the growing child.

900   Mentally gifted children and youth: a guide for parents.   Harris-
       burg: Pennsylvania State Department of Education, 1973.   25p.
A brochure intended to help parents understand and aid their gifted children in home, school, and community.

901   Myers, Kent C.   "The relationship of special programming for gifted
       children to parent attitudes toward schools."   For a summary see:
       Diss Abstr Int   24(3):   1034, September, 1963.   (0 References)

902   Oppen, M. "Gifted child in a small town: a parent's point of view."
       Gifted Child Q   14(2):   92-95, Summer, 1970.
A parent describes her attempts to bring up her gifted child in a small
town with no enriching facilities in school or elsewhere.

903   Rankin, Allen.   "Prodigy from Plumtree."   Read Dig   109(652):
       54-58, August, 1976.
Presents a case history of a highly gifted child (I.Q. 200+) born to an
average family in North Carolina.   His special interest in science is
discussed and also his reactions to the dread leukemia which is
destroying him.

904   Sanderlin, Owenita.   "Gifted child emeritus: John Owen Sanderlin."
       Gifted Child Q   17(4):   279-84, Winter, 1973.   (0 References)
The mother of a gifted leukemic boy who died before his 16th birthday
tells of learning about special educational needs of the gifted as she
guided her son's education at home.

905   Stern, Aaron.   The making of a genius.   Miami, Florida: Hurricane
       House, 1971.   172p.
A discussion, sometimes egotistical, of how the author created a physical
and emotional environment that enabled his daughter to become a genius.
Of interest to administrators working with parents of the gifted, are
the author's negative views on public education.

906   Strang, Ruth.   Helping your gifted child.   New York: E. P. Dutton,
       1967.   270 p.   (Bibliography)
This parents' guide, now in its fourth printing, includes information on
varieties of giftedness and ways of supplying supportive opportunities
for gifted children at all ages, as well as a good section on problems
of gifted children in schools.

907 Truax, Charles B. "Effective interaction with gifted children."
     Kootenay Cent Gifted J 1(3): 4-10, October, 1973.
Questions parents ask teachers about giftedness are posed and
answered. Stresses ways parents can help their gifted child.

VI

Special Problems of the Gifted

A. Underachievement

908 Abraham, Willard. "Motivating the gifted underachiever." Education
     82(8): 468-71, April, 1962. (0 References)
Presents a framework composed of seven recommendations and ideas to help
solve the problems of lack of motivation or under-achievement.

909 Bachtold, Louise M. "Personality differences among high ability
     underachievers." J Educ Res 63(1): 16-18, September, 1969. (7
     References)
Study found credulity, self-confidence, and self-control were components
in successful female achievement. Emotional stability, seriousness,
and sensitivity were components in successful male achievement.
Underachievers differed in personality factors according to type of
underachievement. Unachieving female groups differed in credulity,
self-control, self-confidence, and excitability. Underachieving male
groups differed in emotional stability, cheerfulness, and sensitivity.

910 Burrows, L. J. "Provisions for the ascertainment and assessment of
     the intelligent child." Proc R Soc Med 66(12): 1201-3, December,
     1973. (0 References)
This paper, presented at the Royal Society of Medicine's Conference on
the under-achieving intelligent child, cites data to support widespread
underachievement by the gifted. Lack of teacher awareness and limitations of available tests are held responsible for much current neglect.

911 Bush, Wilma J. "A comparative study of the WISC test patterns of
     the bright and gifted under-achievers with the test patterns of
     under-achievers with normal intelligence." For a summary see:
     Diss Abstr Int 32A(9): 5066, March, 1972. (0 References)

912 Bush, Wilma J., and Mattson, Bruce D. "WISC test patterns and
     underachievers." J Learn Disabil 6(4): 251-56, April, 1973.
     (11 References)
Compared WISC test patterns of gifted underachievers with those of
gifted achievers. Also compared normal-level underachievers with
achievers at that level. Significant differences were found between
underachievers and achievers at both levels.

913 Capponi, Attilio. "The relation between academic underachievement
     and depression: an exploratory study." For a summary see: Diss
     Abstr Int 34B(7): 3488-89, January, 1974. (0 References)

914   Carter, Harold D.   "Overachievers and underachievers in the junior
        high school."   Calif J Educ Res   12(2):   51-56, March, 1961.   (5
        References)
Paper presents the results of correlation analysis involving intelligence,
achievement, and personality tests.   Over-achievers are happier, have
more self-confidence and better morale.   They have more intellectual
curiosity and better study habits, being more systematic.

915   Cauthen, Janet.   "Gifted underachiever ."   Tex Outlook   48(4):
        30-31, April, 1964.
Discusses suggestions for the teacher of the gifted underachiever.
Suggests teacher study permanent records, keep a case study, use outside
help if necessary, and include him in an enrichment program.

916   Combs, Charles F.   "Perception of self and scholastic underachieve-
        ment in the academically capable."   Pers Guid J   43(1):   47-51,
        September, 1965.   (8 References)
Junior high school boy underachievers with I.Q.'s over 115 perceived
themselves as less adequate, and less acceptable to others.   They
perceived their peers and adults as less acceptable.   They showed an
inefficient approach to problems and less adequacy of emotional
expressions.

917   Davids, Anthony.   "Psychological characteristics of high school
        male and female potential scientists in comparison with academic
        underachievers."   Psychol Sch   3(1):   79-87, January, 1966.   (5
        References)
Brown University accepted high school students in two special programs:
one for academically successful students who had demonstrated outstanding potential in science, and the other for bright underachievers.
The high-achievers possess many similar characteristics to the successful
college student.   The underachievers, on the other hand, are considerably
lower than average high school students on psychological measures indica-
tive of socialization, emotional maturity, intellectual efficiency and
achievement potential.

918   Davids, Anthony, and Sidman Jack.   "A pilot study: impulsivity,
        time orientation, and delayed gratification in future scientists
        and in underachieving high school students."   Except Child   29(4):
        170-74, December,1962.
Describes both a science program for the gifted and a program for
underachieving gifted.   Boys in the high achieving group were less
compulsive, more future oriented, and less concerned with immediate
gratification.

919   Douglas, J. W.   "The under-achieving intelligent child: other
        social factors."   Proc R Soc Med   66(12):   1204-7, December, 1973.
        (4 References)
Dr. Douglas discusses how far the standard of achievement of pupils is
influenced by the kinds of school they go to and the quality of teaching
they receive.   He notes the difficulty of tailoring education to meet
special needs of various groups, and advocates eliminating regional
inequalities in educational provisions.

920   Dulles, Robert J.   "The myth of underachievement."   J Educ Sociol
        35(3):   121-22, November, 1961.   (4 References)

Dulles suggests that changing the terminology from "underachieving" to "over-predicted" would lessen the judgmental aspect of the school situation and thus relieve pressure on the student. The "real" capacity of a student should be his actual level of performance, not what people predict for him.

921   Elkind, Joel. "The gifted child with learning disabilities."
    Gifted Child Q   17(2): 96-97, 115, Summer, 1973. (6 References)
Paper includes the definition, identification and ameliorative procedures and programs for gifted children with learning disabilities.

922   Fine, Benjamin. Underachievers: How they can be helped.
    New York: Dutton, 1967. 253p. (Bibliography)
The author, headmaster of the Sands Point Country Day School for the Gifted and former education editor of the New York Times, stresses the importance of a child's self-concept in determining achievement, and the vital role of the parents in forming this self-concept. Suggestions are given for help from parents, teachers, and community.

923   Finney, Ben C., and Van Dalsen, Elizabeth. "Group counseling for
    gifted underachieving high school students." J Couns Psychol
    16(1): 87-94, January, 1969. (8 References)
Sixty-nine academically gifted but underachieving sophomores were given group counseling. There was no improvement in grade point average, but they were rated by their teachers as being more cooperative and absent less.

924   French, Joseph L. "Characteristics of high ability dropouts."
    Natl Assoc Second Sch Princ Bull   53(334): 67-79, February, 1969.
    (0 References)
Each year more than 80,000 youth who are within the top 25% of the nation's population intellectually and who have the scholastic potential for higher education and a high level job leave school before graduation. This study surveys bright dropouts in Pennsylvania, and compares them to school persisters in vocational interest, personality, and attitude.

925   Furneaux, William D. The chosen few. London: Oxford University
    Press, 1961. 245p.
This volume presents the results of the Nuffield Investigation, a 10-year examination of certain aspects of the problems of university selection in Great Britain. It was prompted by a concern with the fact that only 1 applicant out of 54 could be accepted by many highly selective departments, and that among the highly qualified chosen for admission the failure rate was frequently 50%.

926   Goldberg, Miriam L. "Studies in underachievement among the
    academically talented." In: Frazier, A., ed. Freeing the
    Capacity to Learn. Washington, D.C.: Association for Supervision
    and Curriculum Development, 1960. 56-73.
Describes two studies of underachievement, one on self-concepts and ideal concepts, one on geometry. Two factors are crucial for underachievers: a supportive teacher, and assistance in mastering learning skills missed earlier.

927   Green, Donald A. "A study of talented high school dropouts."
      Vocat Guid Q 10(3): 171-72, Spring, 1962. (3 References)
A comparison of 21 talented dropouts with 21 talented persisters
found that there was a significant difference between the mean high
school grade point average. However there was no difference between
the means on standardized achievement tests. Persisters were more
involved in extra-curricular activities, their fathers occupations
were slightly higher, and their absence ratio was lower.

928   Harrison, Edna L. "Elementary school counselor and the gifted
      underachiever." Pers Guid J 41(8): 716-19, April, 1963.
      (4 References)
Discusses methods of placing a student in a special room for the gifted,
including teacher recommendations and testing. Also discusses
responsibility for underachievers and working with parents.

929   Hinkelman, Emmet A. "Academic actualization of gifted elementary
      school children." Gifted Child Q 10(2): 66-71, Summer, 1966.
      (7 References)
The author used sample 11-year-old boys with I.Q.s over 140 who were
admitted to a prestigeous New York private school. While generally
better in reading and arithmetic than typical children, 86 to 100
percent of the subjects were underachievers in relation to their
mental potentials.

930   Holmes, Frances B. "A study of the psychological, emotional,
      and intellectual factors associated with academic underachievement."
      Indep Sch Bull 62-63(1): 54-59, November, 1962.
The underachiever appears from this study to have many individual
emotional and personality problems which are interfering with effective
intellectual functioning and which need to be investigated, understood,
and helped. In many cases poor parental relationships or sibling
rivalry were strong factors.

931   Howald, Betty L. "An investigation into anxiety factors in
      achieving and underachieving gifted children at the fifth-grade
      level." For a summary see: Diss Abstr Int 25(3): 1746-47,
      September, 1964. (0 References)

932   Illingworth, Ronald S. "The backward intelligent child."
      Clin Pediatr 4(10): 615-18, October, 1965. (6 References)
Dr. Illingworth, author of The Childhood of the Famous, cites many
examples of illustrious men who were labeled dull or backward at
school. He attributes their underachievement to four factors: the
teacher, the methods of assessment, the home and parents, and the
child's personality.

933   ———. "Under-achieving children destined for fame." Proc R Soc
      Med 66(12): 1207-8, December, 1973. (2 References)
This paper from a British medical conference presents many instances of
school "backwardness" or failure by persons of intellectual eminence.
Cites cases of underachievement in math and languages among scientists,
authors, and statesmen later recognized as "geniuses."

934   Isaacs, Ann F. "Role expectancy and its effect on performance and
      achievement among gifted students." High Sch J 48(2): 107-16,
      November, 1964. (19 References)

Discusses some reasons for failure among the gifted, i.e., resisting
identification, rejecting teachers identified with the gifted, disliking
the greater demands on the gifted, and mixed up expectations for the
gifted. Says that for success, the gifted need models with whom to
identify, accepting parents and teachers, and an encouraging public
climate.

935   Karnes, Merle B. et. al. "Factors associated with underachievement
      and overachievement of intellectually gifted children." Except
      Child 28(4): 167-75, December, 1961. (42 References)
Study suggests that the high educational achievement of intellectually
gifted pupils in the elementary grades is related significantly to
creativity and a high degree of perceived peer acceptance.

936   Karnes, Merle B.; McCoy, George; Zehrbach, Richard R.; et. al.
      "The efficacy of two organizational plans for underachieving
      gifted children." Except Child 29(9): 438-46, May, 1963.
      (9 References)
Study which investigated the efficacy of placing a small proportion
of gifted underachievers in homogeneous classes with high achievers.
Study found that underachievers did make gains, were slightly more
creative, and parents' attitudes toward the underachievers were better
than in the contrasting group of underachievers in heterogeneous
classes.

937   Kornrich, Milton, ed. Underachievement. Springfield, Illinois:
      Thomas, 1965. 670p. (Bibliography)
Fifty-one contributions to this volume represent a sample selected
from five hundred published and unpublished papers. Most of them are
reports of research in the formal sense, and clinical case studies,
and are of recent origin. Much of the research is directed toward the
intellectually gifted underachiever, because the disparity between
his I.Q. and his performance is so striking.

938   Kowitz, Gerald T., and Armstrong, Charles M. "Underachievement:
      concept or artifact?" Sch Soc 89(2197): 347-49, October 21,
      1961. (5 References)
In a longitudinal study of pupils at 3rd, 6th, and 9th grade, some
evidence was found that school policy has an effect on the pattern
of achievement of its students. However, over-achievement was more
prevalent than under-achievement.

939   Laird, Albert W., and Cangemi, Joseph P. "The lost ones - the
      gifted." Gifted Child Q 17(3): 175-81, Fall, 1973.
      (5 References)
Examined are societal and educational practices responsible for loss
of gifted children and adolescents at a time when world problems
require abilities that the gifted possess.

940   Langan, Sylvia W. "A comparative study of a number of variables
      assumed capable of accounting for differences between intellectually
      gifted achievers and under-achievers in the New York City high
      schools." For a summary see: Diss Abstr Int 23(3): 926-27,
      September, 1962. (0 References)

941 Mehta, Perin H. "The self-concept of bright underachieving male
     high school students." Indian Educ Rev 3(2): 81-100, 1968.
The self-concept of bright achievers and under-achievers were compared.
Under-achievers were characterized by negative aspects of self-concept,
achievers by positive aspects.

942 Newman. C. Janet; Dember, Cynthia F.; Krug, Othilda. "He can but
     he won't.": A Psychodynamic Study of So-Called "Gifted Under-
     achievers." Psychoanal Study Child 28: 83-129, 1973.
     (47 References)
Reviews the background of psychiatric thinking on underachieving
highly intelligent children. In addition, findings are discussed that
have a bearing on the understanding of some of the pathogenic influences
on the development of intelligence and the ability to achieve.

943 Norman, Ralph D.; Clark, Betty P.; Bessemer, David W. "Age, sex,
     I.Q., and achievement patterns in achieving and non-achieving
     gifted children." Except Child 29(3): 116-23, November, 1962.
     (10 References)
Two groups, achievers and non-achievers, were studied. Major findings
indicated that achievers were younger than non-achievers, and that
achievers had significantly higher language I.Q.s, non-achievers had
significantly higher non-language and total I.Q.s.

944 O'Shea, Arthur J. "Low-achievement syndrome among bright junior
     high school boys." J Educ Res 63(6): 257-62, February, 1970.
     (13 References)
Three instruments evaluating interest and personality were administered
to 284 bright junior high school and low-achieving boys to determine
whether the two groups differed significantly on certain of the scales.
Low achievers described themselves as having weaker achievement
motivation, less satisfactory family relationships, as being less
aggressive, less persistent, less conforming, and as having stronger
heterosexual interests.

945 Packard, Vance O. Do Your Dreams Match Your Talents? Chicago:
     Science Research Associates, 1960. 43p.
A frank and forthright discussion of some of the causes of under-
achievement and waste of talent among capable young Americans.
Includes sections on motivation and planning for the future.

946 Parks, Emory C. "Factors relating to underachievement."
     Sch Community 49(3): 22-23, November, 1962. (0 References)
Principals studied 94 pupils, examined their records and found the
following about the underachievers. The majority lived with both
parents, had several siblings, their mothers had a more intensive
formal background than their fathers, attendance in early grades was
significant, only 28% had stayed in one elementary school. Teachers
felt the underachievers were motivated, relatively healthy, less
anxious about tests than they actually were. The students felt happy,
but about 43% thought they could do better.

947 Perkins, Hugh V. "Classroom behavior and underachievement."
     Am Educ Res J 2(1): 1-12, January, 1965. (12 References)
Study identifies student behavior, learning activity, teacher behavior,
and teacher-role variables related to lack of achievement in high-
ability fifth grade pupils.

948   Pierce, James V.   "Personality and achievement among able high
      school boys."   J Individ Psychol   17(1):   102-7, May, 1961.
      (7 References)
Fifty-two high achievers were compared with fifty-two low achievers.
Authors found that high achievers show more favorable personality
characteristics such as responsibility and tolerance, higher motivation,
greater involvement in achievement tasks, and more school-related
interests.   Also, mothers of high achievers tended to be less authoritarian.

949   Pringle, M. L. Kellmer   Able Misfits.   London: Longman, 1970.
      171p.   (Bibliography)
One of the titles in the "Studies in Child Development" series done by
Britain's National Bureau for Cooperation in Child Care, this volume
examines the educational and behavioral difficulties of 103 very
intelligent children (I.Q.s 120-200).

950   ————.   "Social adversity and its effects on the intelligent
      child's achievement."   Proc R Soc Med   66(12):   1203-4, December,
      1973.   (24 References)
Dr. Pringle of England's National Children's Bureau reviews the
research of the 50's and 60's on the effects of social deprivation on
school achievement.   The role of motivation and parental concern and
interest is stressed, and the association between under-achievement
and broken homes is noted.

951   Purkey, William W.   An Independent Study Project for Gifted
      Underachievers: Project Self Discovery.   Gainesville, Florida:
      University of Florida, College of Education, August, 1967.   42p.
This research project is the result of a contract with the Office of
Education.   The study attacks the problem posed by gifted underachievers.
The research was carried out in two phases: (1) Preparation of
"Project Self Discovery" materials, involving student participation,
and (2) Evaluation of the efficacy of project.   There is helpful
material for teachers.

952   Radin, Sherwin S., and Masling, Joseph.   "Tom: a gifted under-
      achieving child."   J Child Psychol Psychiatry   4(3):   183-97,
      December, 1963.   (4 References)
This paper describes the school behavior, test results and psycho-
therapy of Tom, an extremely gifted 10-year-old, who was referred for
treatment because of impending school failure.   Implications for
treatment of such a child are examined, as are the special problems
involved for school personnel who deal with such children.

953   Raph, Jane B.; Goldberg, Miriam L.; Passow, A. Harry.   Bright
      Underachievers: Studies of Scholastic Underachievement Among
      Intellectually Superior High School Students.   New York:
      Teacher's College Press, 1966.   289p.
The authors present a thorough review of the research literature and
a complete summary of their own work comparing achievers and non-
achievers.   They comment on the great waste of talent which occurs
among the underprivileged because of adverse learning conditions both
at home and at school.

954 Roth, Robert M. Underachieving Students and Guidance. Boston:
     Houghton Mifflin, 1970. 90p. (Bibliography)
Presents a discussion of underachievement as well as the results of
several years of systematic research which moves from identification
of types of underachievers to the actual treatment intervention
employed. Closes with a discussion of the implications for
elementary, secondary, and college counseling programs.

955 Seiden, Dorothy S. "Some variables predictive of low achievement
     by high ability students." For a summary see: Diss Abstr Int
     29A(9): 3009, March, 1969. (0 References)

956 Shaw, Merville C., and Alves, Gerald J. "The self concept of
     bright academic underachievers." Pers Guid J 42(4): 401-3,
     December, 1963. (3 References)
The authors attempt to verify the findings of a previous study of
high school underachievers through the use of a more objective measure
of self-concept. Results tend to confirm earlier findings and point
strongly to a direct association between negative self-attitudes
and academic underachievement, when ability levels are equal.

957 Shaw, Merville C.; Edson, Kenneth; Bell, Hugh M. "The self-
     concept of bright underachieving high school students as
     revealed by an adjective check list." Pers Guid J 39(3):
     193-96, November, 1960. (7 References)
Study found differences in self-concept between achievers and underachievers. Male underachievers have more negative feelings about
themselves; the female underachievers are ambivalent.

958 Shaw, Merville C., and McCuen, John T. "The onset of academic
     underachievement in bright children." J Educ Psychol 51(3):
     103-8, June, 1960. (6 References)
Authors hypothesize "that underachievement among bright students is
not a problem which has genesis within the educational framework, but
rather one which the underachiever brings with him, at least in
embryo form, when he enters high school." This intensive study of
small number of gifted underachievers found an underachievement
pattern present by grade 5.

959 Sher, Ellen O. "The 'under-achiever': a comparison of high-
     achieving and low-achieving high I.Q. boys." For a summary see:
     Diss Abstr Int 34B(7): 3509-10, January, 1974. (0 References)

960 Thorndike, Robert L. The Concepts of Over- and Under-achievement.
     New York: Bureau of Publications, Teachers College, Columbia
     University, 1962. 78p. (Bibliography)
Monograph written for educators who might set up a research study in
over-achievement and underachievement. Examines concepts, points out
problems and errors.

961 Torrance, E. Paul. "Who is the under-achiever?" NEAJ 51(8):
     14-17, November, 1962.
Takes a hypothetical classroom and looks at the cases of five underachievers. Easy to read.

962   Torrance, E. Paul, and Strom, Robert D., eds. Mental health and
      achievement. New York: Wiley, 1965. 417p. (Bibliography)
Although this book deals largely with the slow learner, chapters 25, 27,
and 33 are of value. Chapter 25 deals with different kinds of learning.
Chapter 27 discusses continuity in the creative development of young
children. Chapter 33 addresses itself to motivating children with
school problems. Very readable and contains many practical suggestions
and cases.

963   Wonderly, Donald M., and Fleming, Elyse S. "Under-achievement and
      the intelligent creative child." Except Child 31(8): 405-9,
      April, 1965. (10 References)
292 bright children were evaluated for relative emotional adjustment and
personality characteristics. Neither the emotional adjustment nor the
personality characteristics of these creative children were significantly
affected by their achievement level.

964   Zilli, Marie G. "Reasons why the gifted adolescent underachieves
      and some of the implications of guidance and counseling to this
      problem." Gifted Child Q 15(4): 279-92, Winter, 1971. (20
      References)
This review has found correlations between underachievement and lack of
motivation, desire for peer acceptance, excessive authoritarianism at
school, poor teaching, and complex of personality characteristics. Also
related were parental overprotection, authoritarianism, or excessive
permissiveness and a large family. One study demonstrated that manipu-
lating the educational environment was more effective in raising
achievement than was direct counseling thus counselor should work at
changing educational milieu.

B.   Social Adjustment

965   Anastasiow, Nicholas J. "Sex differences in self-concept scores of
      high and low ability elementary students." Gifted Child Q 11(2):
      112-15, Summer, 1967. (11 References)
Not succeeding in academic areas is associated with a negative self-
evaluation. Unsuccessful girls not only have lower self-concepts than
their unsuccessful male counterparts and the more successful girls but
these low scoring girls also see the future as hopeless.

966   Cazzola, Gus. "The oiled hinge of giftedness." NJEA Rev 47(1):
      45,66, September 1973.
Author considers the problems of the gifted student and suggests the
methods teachers should use to integrate such children into the school
system.

967   Grotberg, Edith H. "Adjustment problems of the gifted." Education
      82(8): 474-76, April, 1962. (12 References)
Early research endeavors found that the gifted were generally well
adjusted. The author reviews several studies on adjustment then presents a summary of her study of institutionalized gifted in an Illinois
State Hospital, as compared to non-gifted fellow patients.

968   Lansing, Cornelius. "Problems of adjustment of gifted children."
      North Carolina Med J 21(10): 441-45, October, 1960. (6 References)
Describes public attitudes toward gifted children before the classic

Terman study, and at the present time. Characteristics of these children are given, and incidence and type of maladjustment among them are covered. The highly gifted are compared to the moderately gifted, and are found to be more frequently maladjusted.

969   Mirman, Norman. "Are accelerated students socially maladjusted?" Elem Sch J 62(5): 273-76, February, 1962. (1 Reference)
Study indicates that personal adjustment is "not appreciably affected by acceleration" and that acceleration could be used more widely, though decisions on acceleration should be made only after careful consideration of all factors.

970   O'Shea, Harriet E. "Friendship and the intellectually gifted child." Except Child 26(6): 327-35, February, 1960. (7 References)
This paper reaffirms the assumption that "the power fields of friends strengthen each other". Assuming that genuine interaction with other persons does many favorable things – then it is urgent that arrangements be made for intellectually gifted children which will offer them appropriate contacts to enable them to build friendships.

971   Powell, Douglas H. "Special problems of precocious youth." Int Psychiatry Clin 7(3): 49-65, 1970. (5 References)
From his experiences counseling intellectually gifted Harvard under-graduates, astronauts, and New England prep school students the author describes the problems this top 2-3% of our youth face. Problem areas discussed are those of family relationships, school, peer relations, and career choice.

972   Silverstein, Samuel. "How cliquish are intellectually superior children in regular classes?" Elem Sch J 62(7): 387-90, April, 1962. (7 References)
Study shows that intellectually superior students are no more cliquish than their classmates and will cross ability levels to find friends.

973   ———. "How snobbish are the gifted in regular classes?" Except Child 28(6): 323-24, February, 1962. (6 References)
350 5th graders were given the Ohio Social Acceptancy Scale test. The gifted were found to be no more snobbish than the other children in regular classes.

974   Thomas, Susan B. "Neglecting the gifted causes them to hide their talents: let's stop shortchanging our gifted children." Gifted Child Q 17(3): 193-98, Fall, 1973. (17 References)
Examined are causes of negative self-concept in many gifted children, programs for disadvantaged gifted children, and the trend toward more research on the gifted.

975   Wood, Donald W. "An analysis of peer acceptance and perceived problems of gifted junior high school students." For a summary see: Diss Abstr Int 26(8): 4515, February, 1966. (0 References)

VII

Longitudinal Studies

A. Educational Achievement

976 Alexakos, C. E.; Stankowski, W. M.; Sanborn, Marshall P. "Superior high school students'thoughts about the future and their later college achievements." Vocat Guid Q 15(4): 273-80, June, 1967. (7 References)
Personal essays written by 73 gifted high school students were analyzed. The study concluded that in general the subjects showed more optimism about their own personal futures than about the world situation. Only three subjects were pessimistic about their futures. Typical of the students who achieved well in college were statements containing humanistic ideals and/or concern for society. Study suggests that superior student's college performances are as highly related to ideals, concerns, and attitudes as to past scholastic performances and test scores.

977 Alexander, Karl L., and Eckland, Bruce K. "Sex differences in the educational attainment process." Am Sociol Rev 39(5): 668-82, October, 1974.
Used longitudinal data on a national sample of 2,077 students between 1955 and 1970 to assess the effects of sex on academic achievement. Results showed that status background influences were highly important for females, while academic ability was more important for males, at both the high school and college levels.

978 Auger, John G. "A study of the effect of participation in the advanced placement program of the College Entrance Examination Board on academic performance at the University of Colorado." For a summary see: Diss Abstr Int 30A(3): 1067, September, 1969. (0 References)

979 Bishop, John E., Jr. "A study of four hundred and three intellectu-ally gifted 1957-58 Missouri high school graduates." For a summary see: Diss Abstr Int 20(9): 3587, March, 1960. (0 References)

980 Braunstein, Florence L. "The effect of an elementary school experience in a fast learner program on academically talented children in Valley Stream, New York." For a summary see: Diss Abstr Int 28A(10): 3989-90, April, 1968. (0 References)

981 Cozy, Helen M. "Post high school academic achievement in the con-tent of specified value indicants in high school cumulative records of scholastically superior women." For a summary see: Diss Abstr Int 33(8): 4084-85, February, 1973. (0 References)

982   Eberle, Betty J.   "Mathematics program for gifted high school
       students: a participant follow-up, summers 1964 through 1969 at The
       Ohio State University." For a summary see: Diss Abstr Int   31A(9):
       4378-79, March, 1971. (0 References)

983   Faunce, Patricia S. "Academic careers of gifted women."   Pers Guid J
       46(3):   252-57, November, 1967. (3 References)
Seven hundred and twenty three gifted freshmen women who graduated were
compared on certain academic variables with 526 who did not graduate.
The results are discussed in relation to findings of a larger study
concerning personality characteristics and vocational interests of gifted
women and a follow-up study of the nongraduates.

984   Hitchfield, E. M.   In search of promise: a long-term national study
       of able children and their families. London: Longman, 1973. 219p.
       (Bibliography)
This is the report of a British study of 238 gifted children who were
identified by multiple criteria including views of teachers, parents,
and the children themselves.

985   Kincaid, Donald. "A study of highly gifted elementary pupils."
       Gifted Child Q 13(4):   264-67, Winter, 1969.
Report of a 1963-64 longitudinal study of intellectually gifted pupils with
an I.Q. 150 and above by the Los Angeles city schools. A total of 561
highly gifted pupils were identified in grades K-6. A large proportion
of the group did not appear to be achieving to expectancy. Of special
concern was the large percentage of average or below average marks
received by pupils in science, arithmetic, and social studies.

986   Koehn, Edna B. "The relationship of the basic skill development of
       sixth grade gifted children to ninth grade achievement in the content
       fields." For a summary see: Diss Abstr Int   21(1):   133-34, July,
       1960. (0 References)

987   Macdonald, Barry; Gammie, Alistair; Nisbet, John. "The careers of
       a gifted group." Educ Res (U.K.) 6(3):   216-19, June, 1964.
A follow-up of pupils who obtained very high scores on verbal reasoning
tests at the time of transfer from primary to secondary school.
University enrollment of the subjects revealed great differences by sex
and social class.

988   Meeker, Mary N. "Differential syndromes of giftedness and
       curriculum planning: a four-year follow-up." J Spec Educ   2(2):
       185-96, Winter, 1968. (16 References)
Describes identification, procedure and results of a follow-up of a
special elementary program for the gifted. After 4 years, 75% of the
67 students were still above 90th percentile. Oddly enough, the I.Q.
scores from earlier tests did not correlate highly with the tests
given 4 years later. In fact, none of the teachers even knew their
pupils had been previously judged as gifted. The students' grades on
achievement tests were still high, but were lower than in elementary
school. The author concludes that it is questionable whether the elementary program had impact at the high school level. Children who test at
a gifted level early do not necessarily remain so in high school, and
potential later achievers are lost as a consequence of inadequate attention
in secondary school.

989   Montour, Kathleen. "Three precocious boys: what happened to them."
     Gifted Child Q 20(2): 173-79, Summer, 1976. (7 References)
An interesting account of three boys who began their college careers
between the ages of 12 and 14. All were extremely versatile and able to
excell in whatever field they attempted. The author traces their lives
to the present time to document the success they achieved.

990   Nichols, Robert C., and Astin, Alexander W. "Progress of the merit
     scholar: an eight-year follow-up." Pers Guid J 44(7): 673-81,
     March, 1966.
Merit scholars from 1956-1959 were followed up in 1964 to obtain information about their academic and vocational achievement, current activities, hobbies and interests, future plans, and other data.

991   Nisbet, John, and Gammie, Alistair. "Over 135 I.Q." Educ Res
     (U.K.) 4(1): 53-55, November, 1961. (0 References)
Scottish study used local records to trace gifted pupils in Aberdeen.
Half went on to college training. Those with fathers in professions
were more likely to graduate.

992   Oden, Melita H. "The fulfillment of promise: 40-year follow-up of
     the Terman gifted group." Genet Psychol Monogr 77(1): 3-93,
     August, 1968.
Presents data obtained in the 1960 follow up of the Terman group.
Compares 100 most successful and least successful men to identify factors
which influence achievement. The differentiating factors are enumerated.

993   Pressey, Sidney L. "Fordling accelerates ten years after." J
     Couns Psychol 14(1): 73-80, 1967. (11 References)
In 1966 three universities examined the alumni records of those students
who in 1951-54 were given Ford scholarships to enter college early - 42%
after completing only 10 years of schooling and 29% under the age of 16.
The majority went on to obtain advanced professional training and completed their work about two years earlier than their classmates. Many
of them, already into outstanding careers, report no harm from skipping
the high school work, and a gain from early beginning of career.

994   Richards, Berna F. "A predictive longitudinal study of intellective
     and non-intellective factors affecting school achievement of
     gifted children." For a summary see: Diss Abstr Int 22(10):
     3526-27, April, 1962. (0 References)

995   Sanborn, Marshall P. "Vocational choice, college choice, and
     scholastic success of superior students." Vocat Guid Q 13:
     161-68, 1965. (1 Reference)
Studied both successful and unsuccessful college students to see what
factors were involved in performance. Realism of educational goals
seemed to be responsible for success or failure.

996   Schreffler, Roy H. "Six year study of three groups of students
     screened for sixth grade major work classes: special and regular
     class students of high Binet I.Q., and pseudogifted students."
     For a summary see: Diss Abstr Int 29A(10): 3473, April, 1969.

997   Smilansky, Moshe, and Nevo, David. "A longitudinal study of the
     gifted disadvantaged." Educ Forum 39(3): 273-94, March, 1975.
     (6 References)

Authors analyzed the process of modernization as an answer to the basic question of how to plan and develop educational policies for the gifted culturally disadvantaged.

998 Svensson, Nils-Eric. "Ability grouping and scholastic achievement." Educ Res (U.K.) 5(1): 53-56, November, 1962. (0 References)
Report on a five-year follow-up study in Stockholm. Study concluded attainment of pupils in advanced classes did not correlate with previous schooling. There was a slight tendency towards superiority of pupils in early streamed classes, but it was erased by grades 8 and 9. Localization of classes had no bearing on achievement of pupils, and on low-ability levels, the time of streaming appeared to have no effect on attainments.

999 Tempest, N. R. "Gifted children in the primary school." Adv Sci 27(133): 255-64, March, 1971. (9 References)
In this conference paper presented to the British Association for the Advancement of Science Tempest notes the general neglect of the gifted in English schools. He describes his own 5-year study of gifted children from ages 7-11, and discusses (a) the identification of gifted children and the problems posed by them in the primary classroom, (b) providing methods and materials to challenge them, (c) some possible directions for future work in this field.

1000 Torrance, E. Paul. "Prediction of adult creative achievement among high school seniors." Gifted Child Q 13(4): 223-29, Winter, 1969. (7 References)
Describes a follow-up study of a group of Minnesota high school seniors who had been administered the original version of the Torrance Tests of Creative Thinking seven years previously. Results showed that those who had scored highest had not only amassed an extraordinary record of creative achievement in literature, science, music, and art, but had far out-shone low scorers in number of graduate academic degrees.

1001 Torrance, E. Paul; Bruch, Catherine B.; Morse, Jean A. "Improving predictions of the adult creative achievement of gifted girls by using autobiographical information." Gifted Child Q 17(2): 91-95, Summer, 1973. (8 References)
Gives the findings of a long-range predictive validity study of the Torrance Tests of Creative Thinking. Responses of female subjects suggest that the Alpha Biographical Creativity Scale was significantly related to creative achievement.

1002 Watley, Donivan J., and Kaplan, Rosalyn. "Merit Scholars and the fulfillment of promise." Natl Merit Scholarsh Corp Res Rep 6(3): 1-17, 1970. (3 References)
Presents information about progress made by over 3,000 Merit Scholarship winners. About 75% were satisfied by progress they were making toward long-range goals, while 25% were dissatisfied or expressed mixed feelings.

B. Vocational Choice

1003 Holland, John L. "Explorations of a theory of vocational choice and achievement: II. a four-year prediction study." Psychol Rep 12(2): 547-594, April, 1963. (24 References)
A four-year longitudinal study of high aptitude students finishing high school and again as college seniors. Found that student stability and

achievement are more closely related to personal attributes than to institutional attributes.

1004 Isaacs, Ann F. "Giftedness and careers." Gifted Child Q 17(1): 57-59, Spring, 1973. (0 References)
Discusses early career goal setting by some gifted children, while others show ambivalence and vacillation throughout their school years and job history.

1005 Lutz, Sandra W. "The educational and vocational planning of talented college-bound women." For a summary see: Diss Abstr Int 35A(6): 3427, December, 1974. (0 References)

1006 Messing, Jeffrey K. "A study of relationships among stated occupational choice, occupational value rankings, and patterns of manifest needs, for gifted high school students." For a summary see: Diss Abstr Int 27A(12): 4101-2, June, 1967. (0 References)

1007 Torrance, E. Paul. "Career patterns and peak creative achievements of creative high school students twelve years later." Gifted Child Q 16(2): 75-88, Summer, 1972. (7 References)
In a follow-up study of almost 400 former students identified as highly gifted in high school it was found that previously administered creativity tests served as significant predictors of creative achievement, especially in the case of men.

1008 ———. "Is bias against job changing bias against giftedness?" Gifted Child Q 15(4): 244-48, Winter, 1971. (3 References)
Study to explore a possible employment and promotion bias against gifted young who make frequent job changes early in their careers. Changes were related to Torrance Creative Thinking Test - predictions of creativity. It is suggested that early job mobility should not be a criterion for lack of job promotion, since such individuals are among the most talented.

1009 Watley, Donivan J. "Career progress: a longitudinal study of gifted students." J Couns Psychol 16(2): 100-108, March, 1969. (6 References)
Study of 1014 male and 368 female Merit Scholars and level of college education attained. Levels differed markedly. Factors pertaining to family background and scholar personality characteristics appeared to be related to level of education attained.

1010 ———. "Career progress of Merit Scholars." Natl Merit Scholarsh Corp Res Rep 4(1): 1-23, 1968. (8 References)
Purpose of this study was to assess the variability in career progress made by highly gifted students seven to eight years after entering college; and also to identify factors that possibly contributed to the differential progress observed.

1011 ———. "Stability of career choices of talented youth." Natl Merit Scholarsh Corp Res Rep 4(2): 1-13, 1968.
Reports the pre-college career plans of Merit Scholars and traces the extent to which they remained stable. Considerable change among men was found. Among men, engineering suffered the greatest loss of talent. Education subsequently lost many women.

1012   Watley, Donivan J., and Kaplan, Rosalyn.   "Career or marriage?
       aspirations and achievements of able young women." J Vocat Behav
       1(1): 29-43, January, 1971. (5 References)
Women who won National Merit Scholarships during the years 1959-1960 were
followed up in 1965 to determine their marriage and/or career plans. The
educational and career field aspirations of these groups differed
considerably, however, and those seeking an immediate career scored
higher on scholastic ability tests than those who either planned no
career or who planned to delay entering them.

1013   Werts, Charles E. "Career choice patterns: ability and social
       class." Natl Merit Scholarsh Corp Res Rep 2(3): 1-17, 1966.
       (9 References)
Data from 76,015 male and 51,110 female college freshmen from 248
colleges and universities were analyzed to determine the relationship of
social class and ability to career choice. In general, it was found
that students at each ability level tend to have different career
choices, depending on their class backgrounds.

1014   ———. "Paternal influence on career choice." Natl Merit
       Scholarsh Corp Res Rep 3(2): 1-19, 1967. (11 References)
Father's occupation was compared with son's career choice for a sample
of 76,015 male college freshman at 4-year colleges. Results indicated
that certain types of father's occupations were associated with similar
types of career choices by sons.

C. General

1015   Broman, Sarah H.; Nichols, Paul L.; Kennedy, Wallace A. Preschool
       I.Q.: prenatal and early developmental correlates. Hillsdale,
       New Jersey: Laurence Erhbaum Associates, 1975. 326p. (Bibliography)
A seminal contribution to this theoretically and socially relevant issue,
this study is important because of the size of the sample and the number
of cognitive characteristics evaluated. After a longitudinal study of
nearly 27,000 children of mothers receiving pre- and post-natal care in
the project clinic the authors concluded that socio-economic class and
parents occupation made the largest contribution to four-year-olds'
I.Q.'s. In fact, the correlation was so large it dwarfed the effect of
all the other variables.

1016   Brown, Janet L. "Precursors of intelligence and creativity: a
       longitudinal study of one child's development." Merrill-Palmer Q.
       16(1): 117-37, January, 1970. (28 References)
Presents a longitudinal study of a highly creative girl from birth to
eight years. Concentrates on infant behavior and creative drawings.
Outstanding characteristics were depth and focus of attention, unusual
visual awareness, inner-directedness, and good fine motor coordination.

1017   Bruch, Catherine B., and Morse, Jean A. "Initial study of
       creative (productive) women under the Bruch-Morse model."
       Gifted Child Q 16(4): 282-89, Winter, 1972. (11 References)
Creative women who had participated in Torrence's long study were
studied after 12 years and finding suggest that creative characteristics
are stable over time. The authors discovered a significant relationship
between subject complexity and creativity predictor variables.

1018 Hall, Richard L. "Gifted underachievers and highachievers five
      years following high school graduation." For a summary see:
      Diss Abstr Int 26(6): 3152, December, 1965. (0 References)

1019 Hartz, John D. "A cross-historical comparison of ten year follow-up
      studies of talented young people." For a summary see: Diss Abstr
      Int 35A(1): 188, July, 1974. (0 References)

1020 Lee, Raymond E., and Newland, T. Ernest. "Small community and its
      gifted school children." Educ Forum 30(3): 363-8, March, 1966.
Information selected on post-eighth grade youngsters over a nine-year
period depicts intellectual erosion in the community. After graduation,
nearly 63% of the brighter children had left the community. Only one
especially bright one remained. Discusses implications of brain drain
on small communities.

1021 Lewis, Charles W. "Prediction of four-year post-high school
      accomplishments of superior students." For a summary see: Diss
      Abstr Int 29A(12): 4286-87, June, 1969. (0 References)

1022 Owen, Cramer. "An investigation of creative potential at the
      junior high level." Stud Art Educ 3(2): 16-33, 1961/1962.
Study investigated the growth of creativity in 30 art students.
Describes results of longitudinal study designed to stimulate original
thinking.

VIII

Related Research

A. Creativity Studies

1023 Anastasi, Anne, and Schaefer, Charles E. "Note on the concepts of
       creativity and intelligence." J Creat Behav 5(2): 113-16, 1971.
       (10 References)
In general, creativity-test scores correlate almost as highly with
intelligence-test scores as the individual test scores within either
domain correlate with each other. Correlations of the creativity scores
with grades are of the same magnitude as those with I.Q.

1024 Bachtold, Louise M. "The creative personality and the ideal pupil
       revisited." J Creat Behav 8(1): 47-54, 1974. (3 References)
Teachers, parents, elementary and junior high school students, all gave
their perceptions of the ideal person. Sixty-two characteristics were
rated by subjects as either desirable, undesirable or most important.
Most selected behaviors or characteristics were not facilitative of
creative productivity.

1025 Bachtold, Louise M., and Warner, Emmy E. "An evaluation of
       teaching creative skills to gifted students in grades 5 and 6."
       J Educ Res 63(6): 253-56, February, 1970. (15 References)
To assess practice effects of verbal tasks which elicit divergent and
evaluative thinking, high I.Q. students were given written assignments in
creative thinking every week for a period of 8 months. Boys scored
higher on tests requiring divergent thinking and girls scored higher on
those requiring evaluative thinking.

1026 Bedmar, Richard L., and Parker, Clyde A. "The creative development
       and growth of exceptional college students." J Educ Res 59(3):
       133-36, November, 1965. (9 References)
Guilford tests administered to 90 students in an honors program at
Brigham Young University revealed no significant relationship or growth
during three years.

1027 Beggs, Berenice B. "How do we educate this child for the future?
       Don't curb the creative appetite." Sch Community 52(8): 14+,
       April, 1966.
Makes suggestions for stimulating creativity and providing an atmosphere
where it may be nourished and inspired. Reminds that beginning years are
crucial; creativity grows faster during the first 10 years of life than
the second 10 years.

1028   Boersma, Frederick J., and O'Bryan, Kenneth. "An investigation of
the relationship between creativity and intelligence under two
conditions of testing." J Pers 36(3): 341-48, September, 1968.
(19 References)
Nonverbal intelligence tests were administered to 46 fourth grade boys.
After being randomly assigned to two equal groups, completion and
unusual uses tests were administered to one group a day later. The
following day the second group was tested but without restrictions of
time or setting. The second group scored significantly higher on creativity tests and displayed a substantial reduction in correlation between
intelligence and creativity variables.

1029   Bonsall, Marcella R. "Developing creativity in gifted children."
Gifted Child Q 12(4): 223-26, Winter, 1968. (8 References)
Since each stage of the creative process demands a certain thinking
operation as well as a definite attitude on the part of the student, it
behooves the teacher to apply a particular teaching principle at the
most opportune time. A schematic design is offered to help each teacher
devise a personal approach to teaching for creativity.

1030   Bradley, R. C., ed. The education of exceptional children. Wolfe
City, Texas: The University Press, 1970.
The gifted and creative are described in the chapter entitled "Children
with original and novel ideas." They are characterized as stronger and
healthier with fewer defects than their average peers, and are said to
possess favorable personal and social qualities. In addition, they are
able to produce work that has freshness, vitality, and uniqueness.

1031   Broderick, Mary. "Creativity in children: some case studies."
Natl Elem Princ 46(2): 18-24, November, 1966. (0 References)
Presents four case studies exploring individual differences among students
and offers implications for the education of boys and girls. Defines
enrichment, presents depth and scope in planning learning opportunities,
and provides opportunities for creative and critical thinking and
expression.

1032   Bruch, Catherine B. "Assessment of creativity in culturally
different children." Gifted Child Q 19(2): 164-74, Summer, 1975.
(32 References)
Discusses issues in the measurement of gifted black children, and makes
concrete suggestions for testers.

1033   Burt, Cyril L. "The psychology of creative ability." Br J Educ
Psychol 32(3): 292-98, November, 1962. (0 References)
In this criticism of Getzels and Jackson's study Burt states that the
weight of evidence is strongly against the simplified interpretation
that there are just two basic cognitive or intellective modes, the
"creative" and the "intelligent" and similarly, two distinct types of
"gifted students". Suggests expansion and extension of creativity-
intelligence investigation as needed area of British research.

1034   Callahan, Carolyn, and Renzulli, Joseph. "Development and
evaluation of a creativity training program." Except Child 41(1):
44-45, September, 1974. (1 Reference)
Describes and evaluates Renzulli's New Directions in Creativity, a three
volume creativity training program. Each volume contains 24 types of

creativity training activities and a teacher's guide that includes
suggestions for individualized instruction and follow-up programming.
In a field study with 35 experimental classes using the materials for
eight weeks both teacher and student response was positive.

1035 Callaway, Webster R. "A holistic conception of creativity and its
      relationship to intelligence." Gifted Child Q 13(4): 237-41,
      Winter, 1969. (13 References)
Callaway presents the results of a study concerning the relationship
between personality characteristics closely associated with creativity
and intelligence as measured by verbal I.Q. His hypotheses of a high
positive correlation between six personality dimensions and verbal
intelligence were born out for his sample of 180 bright eleventh grade
students.

1036 Carroll, James L., and Laming, Lester R. "Giftedness and creati-
      vity: recent attempts at definition: a literature review."
      Gifted Child Q 18(2): 85-96, Summer, 1974. (78 References)
While a single definition of "gifted" is not used universally, this
article points out the consensus of many distinguished experts. Two
tables bring together comparative data, one on Criteria Used to Measure
Giftedness and one on Characteristics Ascribed to Gifted Children. The
bibliography attests to the research for the article.

1037 Cicirelli, Victor G. "Form of the relationship between creativity,
      I.Q., and academic achievement." J Educ Psychol 56(6): 303-8,
      December, 1965. (9 References)
Questions whether creativity is independent of the general intelligence
factor. Concludes that creativity did not interact with I.Q. to boost
achievement of the sample in this study.

1038 Clark, Charles M.; Veldman, Donald J.; Thorpe, Joseph S. "Conver-
      gent and divergent thinking abilities of talented adolescents."
      J Educ Psychol 56(3): 157-63, June, 1965. (15 References)
The investigators reported a creativity-intelligence dichotomy consistent
with that described in Getzels and Jackson's 1962 study.

1039 Crockenberg, Susan B. "Creativity tests: a boon or boondoggle for
      education." Rev Educ Res 42(1): 27-45, Winter, 1972. (44
      References)
The disenchantment of many educators with I.Q. tests led to the
proliferation of creativity tests, which were viewed as consistent with
the continuing search for greater educational equality. Much research
on creativity tests is available, but the profusion of tests, the
complexity of the results, and the dispersion of the research articles
have hindered translation of scientific findings into educational
policies.

1040 Damm, Vernon J. "Creativity and intelligence: research
      implications for equal emphasis in high school." Except Child
      36(8): 565-69, April, 1970. (24 References)
Study found students high in both creativity and intelligence had
significantly higher scores in self-actualization than those obtained
by students high in either creativity or intelligence. The results
were interpreted as indicating that educational systems should stress
both intellectual and creative abilities to achieve the highest level
of psychological well-being.

1041   Dauw, Dean C.   "Personality self-descriptions of original thinkers
       and good elaborators."   Psychol Sch   3(1):   78-79, January, 1966.
       (12 References)
Tested all seniors in a middle-class Minnesota high school on Torrance's
Minnesota Tests of Creative Thinking.   Highly creative students had a
significantly higher creativity self-concept than low creative students.
There were no significant differences between original thinkers and good
elaborators.

1042   Degman, Ruth M.   "Creativity and disadvantaged children."   For
       a summary see: Diss Abstr Int   35A(3):   1423-24, September, 1974.
       (0 References)

1043   Drews, Elizabeth M., and Montgomery, Susan.   "Creative and academic
       performance in gifted adolescents."   High Sch J   48(2):   94-101,
       November, 1964.   (0 References)
Summarizes what authors found over 10 years research.   Creative intellectuals, they say, are independent, contemplative, and unrelentingly
curious.   Finds the majority of the gifted non-creative.   Says schools
should teach for creativity, and describes briefly a social studies
program which was designed to foster creativity.

1044   Elliott, Rosalie C.   "Creativity and the handling of conflict in
       bright sixth graders."   For a summary see: Diss Abstr Int   31B(12):
       7621-22, June, 1971.   (0 References)

1045   Farber, Seymour M.   Conflict and creativity.   New York: McGraw-
       Hill, 1963.   360p.
This book is a record of the second symposium Man and Civilization:
Control of the Mind, held at the University of California San Francisco
Medical Center in 1962.   The first section entitled Individual Potentialities contains the papers "Determinants of Intelligence", "Prediction
and Individual Behavior" and "Prediction of Creativity and Success",
of interest to those working with the gifted.

1046   Fleming, Elyse S., and Weintraub, Samuel.   "Attitudinal rigidity
       as a measure of creativity in gifted children."   J Educ Psychol
       53(2):   81-85, April, 1962.   (8 References)
This study found that a moderate negative relationship was found to
exist between rigidity and verbal creativity.   Chronological age appeared
to be related to verbal creativity.

1047   Gardner, Sheldon F.   "Creativity in children: a study of the
       relationship between temperament factors and aptitude factors
       involved in the creative ability of seventh grade children with
       suggestions for a theory of creativity."   For a summary see: Diss
       Abstr Int   24(2):   822, August, 1963.   (0 References)

1048   Garwood, Dorothy S.   "Personality factors related to creativity in
       young scientists."   J Abnorm Soc Psychol   68(4):   413-19, 1964.
       (36 References)
Male science majors designated as higher creatives scored high on
composite personality originality, cognitive flexibility, dominance,
sociability, social presence, and self-acceptance.   The highly creative
group showed greater integration of nonconscious material as pertaining
to concepts of self, father and mother.   The highly creative were less
consciously identifying with their mothers.

1049 Getzels, Jacob W., and Jackson, Philip W. Creativity and
      intelligence: exploration with gifted children. New York:
      Wiley, 1962. 293p.
The authors attempt to answer the persistent question "What is the
relationship between creativity and intelligence?", hoping thereby to
shed light on other issues involving creativity. The subjects of their
study were 6th - 12th grade students from a Chicago private school with
a mean I.Q. of 132. Within this intellectually talented population,
two groups were studied: the highly intelligent, here labeled "convergent thinkers," and the highly creative "divergent thinkers," of
lower intelligence.

1050 Ginsberg, Gerald P., and Whittemore, Robert G. "Creativity and
      verbal ability: a direct examination of their relationship."
      Br J Educ Psychol 38(2): 133-39, June, 1968. (21 References)
The threshold concept of the relation between creativity and intelligence
implies that measures of creativity begin to differ markedly from
measures of I.Q. only above a certain level of intelligence.

1051 Givens, Paul R. "Creativity and the gifted child." Educ Theory
      13(2): 128-31, April, 1963. (8 References)
Suggests that intelligence usually refers to the ability to deal with
abstract concepts and adapt to new situations. Proposes the idea of
two kinds of intelligence--adaptive and creative.

1052 Glover, John, and Gary A. L. "Procedures to increase some aspects
      of creativity." J Appl Behav Anal 9(1): 79-84, Spring, 1976.
      (13 References)
Shows how instructions, reinforcement, and practice improved bright
4th and 5th grade students' scores on tests of creativity.

1053 Gowan, John C. Development of the creative individual. San
      Diego, California: Knapp, 1972. 153p. (Bibliography)
Deals with various aspects of creativity, its developmental stages,
escalation, environmental stimulation, penalties of noncreativity and
self-actualization.

1054 ------. "The relationship between creativity and giftedness."
      Gifted Child Q 15(4): 239-43 Winter, 1971. (12 References)
Defines developmental creativity and stresses importance of continued
environmental stimulation. It is suggested that the I.Q. level for
giftedness be changed to 120 because below I.Q. of 120 creativity and
intelligence are highly correlated.

1055 ------. "What makes a gifted child creative?" Gifted Child Q
      9(1): 3-6, Spring, 1965. (0 References)
Examines four theories as to why intelligence and creativity are highly
correlated about 120 I.Q. and divergent above and below. Finds
creativity shows definite relationships to cognitive competence.

1056 Guilford, J. P. "Factors that aid and hinder creativity." Teach
      Coll Rec 63(5): 380-92, February, 1962. (24 References)
Talks about basic traits of creativity, fluency and flexibility factors
elaboration, quantity vs. quality, group vs. individual thinking, context, cognition and memory, and non-aptitude traits and differences.

1057   Guilford, J. P.   "Intellect and the gifted."   Gifted Child Q
       16(3): 175-84, 239-43, Fall, 1972. (5 References)
States that intelligence is a broader concept than creativity, but
includes creativity. As there are at least 120 intellectual abilities,
education must be multivariate in nature to afford the potentially
creative the opportunity to develop their diverse talents.

1058   ————.   Intelligence,creativity and their educational implications.
       San Diego, California: Knapp, 1968. 229p. (Bibliography)
Interested in new frontiers in the discovery and development of human
talent, the author presents 18 papers which were delivered at conferences
or appeared in psychological journals. The three sections include (1)
components of intelligence (2) aspects of creativity and (3) educational
implications.

1059   ————.   "Potentiality for creativity."   Gifted Child Q 6(3): 87-
       90, Autumn, 1962. (3 References)
Paper summarizing latest findings on creativity, dealing with selection,
and suggesting that overachievers might include the creative.

1060   Guilford, J. P., and Christensen, Paul R.   "The one-way relation
       between creative potential and I.Q."   J Creat Behav 7(4): 247-52,
       1973. (3 References)
Analyzes scores of children in grades 4 through 6 on several tests of
divergent thinking in relation to their I.Q.'s. Results showed no high
scores by low I.Q. students, but some low scores by high I.Q. children.

1061   Haddon, F. A., and Lytton, Hugh.   "Teaching approach and the
       development of divergent thinking abilities in primary schools."
       Br J Educ Psychol 38(2): 171-80, June, 1968. (10 References)
This research evaluated the effects of differing teaching approaches on
divergent thinking abilities. 211 children from formal subject centered
and informal progressive primary schools were matched for verbal reasoning
and socioeconomic background. The results showed that pupils from the
informal schools were significantly superior in divergent thinking
abilities.

1062   Halpin, W. Gerald; Payne, David A.; Ellett, Chad D.   "In search of
       the creative personality among gifted groups."   Gifted Child Q
       18(1): 31-33, Spring, 1974. (7 References)
The "What Kind of Person Are You?" test was given to 360 gifted high
school students in 8 academic and artistic areas. Creative personality
scores were highest for the social science, art, and science groups,
lowest for music and foreign language groups.

1063   ————.   "Biographical correlates of the creative personality:
       gifted adolescents."   Except Child 39(8): 652-53, May, 1973.
       (1 Reference)
The authors attempted to synthesize previous research results by using
a biographical inventory to study the relationship between past
experiences and the creative personality of highly gifted adolescents.
Results indicate that different background factors are likely to
influence the development of creative personality for boys and girls.

1064   Hamilton, Dorothy D.   "A comparison of school achievement, teachers'
       ratings, self-ratings, and a personality score as predictors of

creative thinking potential." For a summary see: Diss Abstr Int
30A(7): 2905, January, 1970. (0 References)

1065 Herr, Edwin L.; Moore, Gilbert D.; Hansen James C.   "Creativity,
    intelligence and values: a study of relationships." Except Child
    32(2): 114-15, October, 1965. (0 References)
Studied relationship of intelligence and creativity. Found that
teachers did not give the highest grades to either the most intelligent
or most creative; thereby showing teacher ratings to be inadequate
criteria for identifying talent.

1066 Hasan, Parmeen, and Butcher, H. J.   "Creativity and Intelligence:
    A partial replication with Scottish children of Getzels' and
    Jackson's Study." Br J Psychol 57(1 and 2): 129-35, May, 1966.
    (15 References)
Tests similar to those used by Getzels and Jackson were given to 175
Scottish children of average intelligence (mean I.Q. 102). Correlations
between I.Q. and measures of creativity were much higher than in the
previous study. Contrary to Getzel and Jacksons findings, the "high
creativity" group was lower in academic attainment. Possible reasons
for the discrepancies are discussed.

1067 Heist, Paul.   The creative college student: an unmet challenge.
    San Francisco: Jossey-Bass, 1968. 253p. (Bibliography)
A collection of papers originally presented at a conference of the
Center for Research and Development in Higher Education at U. C. at
Berkeley.

1068 Helson, Ravenna.   "Childhood interest clusters related to creativity
    in women." J Consult Psychol .29(4): 352-61, August, 1965. (25
    References)
Six clusters of childhood interests were obtained in data from women,
and they were analyzed as to masculine and feminine connotations.
Scores on the imaginary play and artistic expression cluster showed the
strongest association with indexes of creativity; the tomboy cluster
also showed consistent significant association, and the social interaction cluster was negatively associated.

1069   "Effect of sibling characteristics and parental values on
    creative interest and achievement." J Pers 36(4): 589-607,
    December, 1968. (31 References)
The first main result was that the creative women and their brothers all
had scores that were higher than those of comparison subjects on the
cognitive traits relevant to creativity. The questionnaire data from
siblings and parents indicated that the creative women and their brothers
had both felt pressures from sibling competition in a context of
demanding and idealistic parental values.

1070 ———.   "Women mathematicians and the creative personality."
    J Consult Clin Psychol 36(2): 210-20, April, 1971. (33
    References)
The findings offer no support for the idea that creative women mathematicians are "mutants" with cognitive abilities different from other
women PhD's in mathematics. Neither do the findings show the creative
women to be more masculine.

1071 Holland, John L. "Creative and academic performance among talented
      adolescents." J Educ Psychol 52(3): 136-47, June, 1961. (21
      References)
Study compares the relationships between three criteria of academic and
creative performance and 72 other variables in talented adolescents.
Suggests that creative performance occurs more frequently among independent, intellectual, expressive, asocial, consciously original and
aspiring students. Academic achievers are usually perservering, sociable,
responsible, and from authoritarian families.

1072 Holland, John L., and Baird, Leonard L. "The Preconscious Activity
      Scale: the development and validation of an originality measure."
      J Creat Behav 2(3): 217-25, Summer, 1968. (15 References)
Describes a new originality measure based on personality study rather
than product or task analysis. It consists of 38 true-false items, and
was validated by use with more than 7,000 college students.

1073 Jacobson, Leonard L.; Elenewski, Jeffrey J.; Lordahl, Daniel S.
      et. al. "Role of creativity and intelligence in conceptualization."
      J Pers Soc Psychol 10(4): 431-36, December, 1968.
The relationship of creativity and intelligence to the use of mediation
and associative process was examined. Intelligence was found to predict
mediated but not non-mediated conceptualization or rote learning.

1074 Johnson, Roger A. "Teacher and student perception of student
      creativity: Something about Myself Test." Gifted Child Q 20(2):
      164-67, Summer, 1976. (6 References)
Describes the salient features of the Something About Myself creativity
checklist which is based on the rationale that creativity is reflected
in an individual's personality characteristics, thinking strategies, and
creative productions. Requiring only 10-15 minutes to administer, it is
useful with pupils over age 13.

1075 Joncich, Geraldine "A culture-bound concept of creativity."
      Educ Theory 14(3): 133-43, July, 1964. (34 References)
This social historian warns that creativity is being defined (and
researched) from the same kind of culture-bound presuppositions and
biases so freely attributed to intelligence test makers. The terms
intelligence and creativity are survivors and continuations of an
historical tradition specific to the U.S. and are pertinent only for a
modern industrialized, urbanized, and science oriented society.
Giftedness in other cultures might have quite different attributes.

1076 Khatena, Joe. "Adolescents and the meeting of time deadlines in
      the production of original verbal images." Gifted Child Q 15(3):
      201-4, Fall, 1971. (11 References)
This study attempts to explore the effects of a varying time interval in
the presentation of word stimuli as deadlines to be met in the production
of original verbal images by high, average and low creative adolescents.
The high and middle creatives showed marked gain with the increase of
time interval.

1077 ———. "Imagination imagery of children and the production of
      analogy." Gifted Child Q 19(4): 310-15, Winter, 1975. (10
      References)

A study involving 122 boys and 126 girls (grades 3 to 12) scoring high
on originality was conducted to explore the patterns of analogy production
in relation to intellectual maturity.

1078 Khatena, Joe. "Major directions in creativity research." Gifted
      Child Q 20(3): 336-49, Fall, 1976. (62 References)
An extensive review of major studies of creativity, emphasizing the work
of Gowan and Rowton, as well as cross cultural research, and studies
of creative disabled and disadvantaged youth.

1079 Klausmeier, Herbert J., and Wiersma, William. "The effects of
      I.Q. level and sex on divergent thinking of seventh grade pupils
      of low, average, and high I.Q." J Educ Res 58(7): 300-302,
      March, 1965. (7 References)
On all of the researchers tests of divergent and convergent thinking,
the low I.Q. group performed less well than the average I.Q. group and
the average I.Q. group performed less well than the high I.Q. group.

1080 Klausmeier, Herbert J.; Harris, Chester W.; Ethnathios, Zackeria.
      "Relationships between divergent thinking abilities and teacher
      ratings of high school students." J Educ Psychol 53(2): 72-75,
      April, 1962. (5 References)
The stability of factors of divergent thinking in students of school age
and the relationship between factor scores and performances of the
students remain to be defined. Three factors of boys and girls were
found common to both sexes and relatively stable. Fifteen of twenty
eight relationships between factor scores and teacher ratings of DT
performances were low, positive, and significant. The DT factors and
their classroom expression varied according to sex and subject field.

1081 Kogan, Nathan. "Creativity and sex differences." J Creat Behav
      8(1): 1-14, 1974. (30 References)
An examination of the literature relating to creativity and sex
differences, with non-definitive summary conclusions. Qualitative studies
are suggested, in which the form and manner of creative expression and
sex differences are questioned.

1082 Kravetz, Nathan. "The creative child in the un-creative school."
      Educ Forum 34(2): 219-222, January, 1970. (6 References)
The creative child may experience conflict as he moves through his
school years, clashing often with his peers, his teachers, with the
school administration, and may receive little support from parents.

1083 Krippner, Stanley, and Arons, Myron. "Creativity: person, product,
      or process?" Gifted Child Q 17(2): 116-23, 129, Summer, 1973.
      (0 References)
Considered are the person, product, and process aspects of creativity
in terms of historical origins and Eastern and Western differences.

1084 Krippner, Stanley; Dreistadt, Roy; Hubbard, C. Clark. "The
      creative person and non-ordinary reality." Gifted Child Q 16(3):
      203-28, Fall, 1972. (62 References)
The authors are associated with the Dream Laboratory in a large urban
medical center. They speculate that the giftedness of creative
individuals reflects time that they spend at different levels of reality.
Here they discuss numerous studies of hypnosis, psychedelics, dreams and
extrasensory perception in relation to creativity.

1085   Laird, Albert W.   "Differential analysis of creativity and
       imagination between gifted and non-gifted high school students as
       ascertained by the Kinget Drawing-Completion Test."   For a summary
       see: Diss Abstr Int   25(6):   3399, December, 1964.   (0 References)

1086   MacKinnon, Donald W.   "The nature and nurture of creative talent."
       Am Psychol   17(7):   484-95, July, 1962.   (18 References)
Talks about qualities of creativity, states that we have over-
emphasized the relationship of intelligence to creativity, and makes
recommendations for fostering creativity.

1087   ———.   "Personality and the realization of creative potential."
       Am Psychol   20(4):   273-81, April, 1965.   (27 References)
Speech ties in Rank's theory with a study on highly creative architects.

1088   Mackworth, Norman H.   "Originality."   Am Psychol   20(1):   51-66,
       January, 1965.   (94 References)
An address which deals with finding problems, the nature of problem
solving, and research warns that scientific inflation, intellectual
dishonesty and bad papers proliferate.

1089   Marjoribanks, Keven.   "Academic achievement, intelligence, and
       creativity: a regression surface analysis."   Multivariate Behav
       Res   11(1):   105-18, January, 1976.   (21 References)
By means of complex multiple regression models the relationships between
academic achievement, creativity, and intelligence are examined.
Findings indicate that for certain academic subjects creativity is related
to achievement up to a threshold level of intelligence, but after the
threshold has been reached creativity is not associated with further
increments in achievement.

1090   March, R. W.   "A statistical re-analysis of Getzels and Jackson's
       data."   Br J Educ Psychol   34(1):   91-93, February, 1964.   (5
       References)
The author's analyses led him to contradict the Getzels-Jackson position
in regard to low relationship between creativity and intelligence.
He concludes that the conventional I.Q. remains the best single criterion
for creative potential.

1091   McGannon, Thomas.   "Creativity and mathematics education."   Sch
       Sci Math   72(1):   7-12, January, 1972.
After a discussion of mathematics and the creative process, reconsidera-
tion of the process in mathematics education is urged, particularly in
the identification and fostering of mathematical talent.

1092   McHenry, R. E., and Shouksmith, George, A.   "Creativity, visual
       imagination and suggestibility: their relationship in a group of
       10-year-old children."   Br J Educ Psychol   40(2):   154-60, June,
       1970.   (16 References)
An experiment is described in which 147 10-year-old children were tested
for their creative ability.   They were then placed in an experimental
situation and exposed to peer suggestion.   Results show that children
who were highly creative were very open to suggestion.   Those measured
high on visual imagination were not.

1093 McNemar Quinn. "Lost: our intelligence? why?" Am Psychol
      19(12): 871-82, December, 1964. (27 References)
In this address to the annual convention of the A.P.A. the author
analyzes the reasons for discarding the concept of general intelligence
in favor of multifactor theories. In addition, he discusses the design
and logic behind so-called creativity tests, and finds them faulty.

1094 Madaus, George F. "Divergent thinking and intelligence: another
      look at a controversial question." J Educ Meas 4(4): 227-35,
      Winter, 1967. (18 References)
The writer states that research in creativity is presently at a crucial
juncture. Until the amount of systematic variance attributable to
methods factors of content, scoring and context used to measure the
traits, are determined (as far as possible) the true relationship between
the constructs of intelligence and divergent thinking will remain clouded.

1095 Milgram, Roberta M., and Milgram, Norman A. "Group versus
      individual administration in the measurement of creative thinking
      in gifted and nongifted children." Child Dev 47(2): 563-65, June,
      1976.
Gifted and nongifted Israeli children in grades 4-8 were given a
creativity battery. Results suggest a requirement of average intellectual
ability for the production of creativity distinct from intelligence in
individual administration and a requirement of above average intellectual
ability in group administration.

1096 Nguyen, Giao H. "Reconstruction in creativity: a unified concep-
      tion of the creative person." For a summary see: Diss Abstr Int
      31A(5): 2194, November, 1970. (0 References)

1097 Quattrocki, Carolyn G. "Recognizing creative potential in preschool
      children." Gifted Child Q 18(2): 74-80, Summer, 1974. (20
      References)
Teachers used Torrance's checklist on pre-school youngsters and
assessed each child's creative potential. The study discovered that
creativity can be recognized by a perceptive and sensitive teacher.
Pointed up the need for teacher training to teach recognition of and
fostering of creativity.

1098 Rees, Marjorie E., and Goldman, Morton. "Some relationships between
      creativity and personality." J Gen Psychol 65(1): 145-61, July,
      1961. (13 References)
Produced results that indicate that certain personality characteristics
are related to creativity. Found that most creative are more impulsive,
more aggressive, domineering and ascendant. Further divided into arts
and science groups for personality factors.

1099 Renzulli, Joseph S., and Callahan, Carolyn, M. "Developing
      creativity training activities." Gifted Child Q 19(1): 38-45,
      Spring, 1975. (0 References)
Points out basic techniques for encouraging youngsters to think
creatively, including general strategies and specific activities.

1100 Rhodes, James M. "Creativity resides in mental concept." Educ
      Forum 27(4): 477-81, May, 1963. (6 References)
Recognizing that the semantic problem about creativity is still with us,

the author advocates several processes through which the educational program can guide and encourage the gifted student into the creative criteria.

1101   Richards, James M., Jr.; Cline,Victor B.; Needham, Walter E.
       "Creativity tests and teacher and self judgments of originality."
       J Exp Educ 32(3): 281-85, Spring, 1964. (6 References)
Describes a study done with 120 Utah high school juniors. Purpose was to explore their intellectual characteristics related to teacher ratings of originality, and to obtain data relevant to the question of teacher discrimination against creative children in making such ratings. Results do not bear out Getzels' and Jackson's findings.

1102   Ripple, Richard E., and May, Frank B. "Caution in comparing
       creativity and I.Q." Psychol Rep 10(1): 229-30, February, 1962.
       (4 References)
By correlating Otis I.Q.'s and scores on creative-thinking tests by members of several seventh grade groups, homogeneous or heterogeneous with respect to I.Q., it was demonstrated that the low correlation of these measures reported by other investigators may well be due in part to the restricted I.Q. ranges in their samples.

1103   Rosenberg, Harry E., and Ehrgott, Richard H. "Performance
       contracting, programmed learning and behavior modification may
       inhibit learning of the gifted." Gifted Child Q 17(4): 254-59,
       Winter, 1973. (12 References)
Although programmed learning and teaching machines can provide an invaluable tool in the training of specific academic and social behaviors, they may have severe limitations in dealing with divergent and creative productions, and may actually inhibit the learning rate of the gifted.

1104   Roweton, William E.; Farless, James E.; Donham, Richard. et.al.
       "Indices of classroom creativity." Child Study J 5(3): 151-62,
       Summer, 1975. (5 References)
This study measured the relationships among three classroom creativity assessment procedures: (1) student and teacher rating of each other's performance, (2) two subtests from Torrance Tests of Creative Thinking, and (3) judges' ratings of student produced classroom products.

1105   Schaefer, Charles E., and Anastasi, Anne. "A biographical
       inventory for identifying creativity in adolescent boys." J Appl
       Psychol 52(1): 42-48, February, 1968. (22 References)
A biographical inventory was developed and cross-validated in a sample of 400 high school boys in the New York metropolitan area, subdivided into creative and control groups in artistic and scientific fields. Similarities and differences between creative students in the two fields were noted.

1106   Schlicht, William J.; Anderson, Derwyn L.; Helin, William C. et.al.
       "Creativity and intelligence: further findings." J Clin Psychol
       24(4): 458, October, 1968. (3 References)
In this correlational study of the relationship between creativity and intelligence, 194 students were given the CCFIT and the RAT. The correlation between scores on the two tests gave evidence of a moderate relationship.

1107   Schmadel, Elnora; Merrifield, Philip R.; Bonsall, Marcella. "A
        comparison of performances of gifted and non-gifted children on
        selected measures of creativity." Calif J Educ Res 16(3): 123-28,
        May, 1965. (7 References)
Inasmuch as the performance of the gifted students, as they were identified in this study, exceeded the performance of the total group on the
selected creative thinking measures, it is evident that children of high
ability may be both gifted and creative. It is, however,equally evident
that "creativeness" is not necessarily an attribute of the "gifted"
child.

1108   Schulman, David. "Openness of perception as a condition for
        creativity." Except Child 33(2): 89-94, October, 1966. (3
        References)
A creativity test and two perceptual tests were given to 89 fourth grade
children. Significant correlations were found between the creativity
and perceptual openness tests, suggesting the need for developing tests
of creativity and providing perceptual experiences in school.

1109   Seitz, Theodore L. "The relationship between creativity and
        intelligence, personality, and value patterns in adolescence." For
        a summary see: Diss Abstr Int 25(6): 3679-80, December, 1964.

1110   Selinger, Armand W., and Stafford, Newton B. "Identification of
        creatively gifted students in a typical senior high school
        population." For a summary see: Diss Abstr Int 31A(5): 2197,
        November, 1970. (0 References)

1111   Shaycoft, Marion F.; Daily, John T.; Orr, David B. et.al. Project
        talent: studies of a complete age group - age 15. Pittsburgh:
        University of Pittsburgh, 1963.
Finds that one test bearing the label "creativity" is correlated with
I.Q. by the value of .67 (average for boys and girls) in a carefully
chosen sample of able 15-year-olds.

1112   Sisk, Dorothy A. "Relationship between self concept and creativity:
        theory into practice." Gifted Child Q 16(3): 229-34, Fall, 1972.
        (12 References)
Gifted students who were described by their teachers as "low creatives"
were taught in small groups by graduate students trained to enhance the
self concept. At the end of the training teachers reported subjects to
be strengthened psychologically and academically.

1113   Smith, Richard L. "The special theory of creativity." J Creat
        Behav 7(3): 165-73, 1973.
Formulated and interpreted is the special theory of creativity and a
procedure for its application. The four conditions of creativity are
said to be motivation, selectivity, receptivity and competence.

1114   Spieth, Phillip E. "Intelligence as it relates to three creativity
        categories: science, art, and literature." For a summary see:
        Diss Abstr Int 25(3): 1759-60, September, 1964. (0 References)

1115   Stern, Stanley. "Television and creativity: the effect of
        viewing certain categories of commercial television broadcasting on
        the divergent thinking abilities of intellectually gifted elementary

students." For a summary see: Diss Abstr Int 34A(7): 3716-17,
January, 1973. (0 References)

1116 Taylor, Calvin W. "Effects of instructional media on creativity."
      Educ Leadersh 19: 453-58, April, 1962. (4 References)
Taylor proposes that all of the known learning and thinking processes
should be utilized by students while they learn subject-matter content.
Consequently he feels a need for techniques and instructional media which
are most effective in developing each of the known intellectual characteristics, including creativity.

1117 Taylor, Irving A. "Creative production in gifted young adults
      through simultaneous sensory stimulation." Gifted Child Q 14(1):
      46-55, Spring, 1970. (21 References)
Seventeen students were exposed weekly to simultaneous sensory stimulation. Drawings before and after were compared. After drawings showed
significant improvement in creativity and "psychological openness."

1118 ————. "Developing creativity in gifted young adults." Education
      94(3): 266-68, February, 1974.
Describes a training program for gifted 17-year-old students which
focused on developing 9 variables related to the creative process.
Through such techniques as small-group dynamics and sensory enrichment,
students increased appreciably in all areas.

1119 Thorndike, Robert L. "The measurement of creativity." Teach Coll
      Rec 64(5): 422-24, February, 1963. (0 References)
The writer states that the extension of our appraisal instruments to
aspects of divergent and productive thinking is a promising field of
investigation. However, this field needs a good deal more of basic
inquiry before the structure of its domain will be clear to us.

1120 Torrance, E. Paul. "The creatively gifted are cause for concern."
      Gifted Child Q 5(3): 79-87+, Autumn, 1961. (10 References)
The author opines that mental illness, academic underachievement, and
vocational failure are found in those who cannot think creatively. The
obverse may be observed in creative thinkers.

1121 ————. "Cultural discontinuities and the development of original
      thinking." Except Child 29(1): 2-13, September, 1962. (6
      References)
Explains some reasons for the decline in creative thinking at the fourth-
grade level. Gives suggestions to deal with the cultural discontinuities
which inhibit creative thinking.

1122 ————. "Curiosity of gifted children and performance on timed
      and untimed tests of creativity." Gifted Child Q 13(3): 155-58,
      Fall, 1969.
Torrance Tests of Creative Thinking were administered both in 5 minute,
and 24 hour versions. Although the correlation was significant, the
forecasting power was only 3%. It is suggested something different was
measured by giving the test under 2 conditions.

1123 ————. "Dyadic interaction as a facilitator of gifted
      performance." Gifted Child Q 14(3): 139-143, Fall, 1970. (10
      References)

Presents four studies supporting the hypothesis that working in pairs facilitates creativity. Findings indicated that college students benefit more from interaction than 5 year olds, that college juniors benefit more from working in dyads than independently, and that children working in pairs attempted more difficult tasks than when working alone.

1124 Torrance, E. Paul. Guiding creative talent. Englewood Cliffs, New Jersey: Prentice-Hall, 1962. 278p. (Bibliography)
Author has drawn heavily upon his own research and that of colleagues concerning the creative thinking of children, adolescents, and adults. Of special interest to teachers of the gifted is chapter 3 which describes differences between groups labeled highly intelligent and those labeled highly creative.

1125 ———. "Interscholastic brainstorming and creative problem solving competition for the creatively gifted." Gifted Child Q 18(1): 3-7, Spring, 1974. (4 References)
In a creativity contest at a university summer school for the gifted ?-member teams of disadvantaged children scored significantly higher in creativity, both as to number and originality of ideas produced, than teams of gifted advantaged children.

1126 ———. Rewarding creative behavior. Englewood Cliffs, New Jersey: Prentice-Hall, 1965. 353p. (Bibliography)
Report of an experimental program involving more than 20,000 school-age children. Formulates and develops a set of principles by which to create an environment where high value is placed on individual creativity in the learning process.

1127 ———. "Retooling education for creative talent: how goes it?" Gifted Child Q 18(4): 233-39, Winter, 1974. (20 References)
Reviews the progress of the past 15 years in the areas in which he predicted changes in 1960: objectives of education, teaching methods, curriculum and instructional materials, procedures for identifying creativity, and assessment of creative achievement.

1128 ———. "Testing and creative talent." Educ Leadersh 20(1): 7-10, 72, October, 1962. (7 References)
Describes some tests for creativity and their application with able students.

1129 Torrance, E. Paul, and Torrance, J. Pansy. "Is creativity teachable?" Bloomington, Indiana: Phi Delta Kappa Educational Foundation, 1973. 50p.
Reviewed are 142 studies in nine categories which evaluated the effectiveness of teaching creativity. The opinion of many is that creativity is not a skill which can be learned.

1130 Vernon, Philip E. "Creativity and intelligence." Educ Res 6(3): 163-69, June, 1964. (13 References) (U.K.)
Discusses creativity broadly, including factorial work of Guilford and Taylor's and Mackinnon's studies of creative and inventive individuals.

1131 Ward, William C. "Creativity in young children." Child Dev 39(3): 737-54, September, 1968. (22 References)
Measures of divergent thinking were administered to 7 and 8 year old

boys. Individual differences were reliable across tests and independent
of I.Q. Suggests that a unitary creativity dimension is present in
kindergarten children but is not measured by the figural test at this
age. Reflection-impulsivity was unrelated to creativity, as was
artistic preference.

1132 Westland, Gordon. "The investigation of creativity." J Aesthet
      Art Crit 28(2): 127-31, Winter, 1969.
The psychologist collates descriptions given by eminent persons on how
they create, compares creators for personality characteristics,
studies creative conditions, and develops tests which purport to
measure creative potential.

1133 Williams, Charlotte L. "Divergent production characteristics of
      academically and artistically gifted adolescents." For a summary
      see: Diss Abstr Int 27A(8): 2412-13, February, 1967. (0
      References)

1134 Wallach, Michael A., and Kogan, Nathan. Cognitive originality,
      physiognomic sensitivity, and defensiveness in children. Durham,
      North Carolina: Duke University, 1965. 217p.
The investigators differentiated modes of thinking in children and
introduced a single dimension or characteristic of intelligence which
could be considered a facet of creativity. This characteristic was
defined as individual difference in the ability to produce many unique
cognitive associates. Correlations between measures of this ability
and intelligence tests proved to be very low.

1135 ————. "Creativity and intelligence in children's thinking."
      Trans-Action 4(3): 38-43, January/February, 1967. (2 References)
Authors claim that little solid evidence can be found to support the
claim that creativity can be distinguished from the more familiar
concept of intelligence. They present some examples from children's
unique responses to show the difference between common and original or
imaginative responses.

1136 ————. Modes of thinking in young children. New York: Holt,
      Rinehart and Winston, 1965. 357p. (Bibliography)
Subtitled "A Study of the Creativity-Intelligence Distinction" this
volume describes research done to determine, among other things, whether
minimal interrelationships can be shown to exist between creativity
measures on the one hand and general intelligence on the other.

1137 ————. "A new look at the creativity-intelligence distinction."
      J Pers 33(3): 348-69, September, 1965. (24 References)
From the findings obtained the present definition of creativity denotes
a mode of cognitive functioning. The writer considers critical the
consideration of the child's joint status with regard to the conventional
concept of general intelligence and creativity as herein defined.

1138 Wallach, Michael A., and Wing, Cliff W. The talented student: a
      validation of the creativity-intelligence distinction. New York:
      Holt, Rinehart, Winston, 1969. 142p. (Bibliography)
Although the authors recognize that intelligence is related to academic
grades, they found it irrelevant to the display of extracurricular
accomplishments during the high school careers of the subjects they

studied (freshmen at a selective college). Ideational resourcefulness was the important factor outside the classroom where innovation was the key.

1139 Yamamoto, Kaoru. "Creativity - a blind man's report on the ele-
      phant." J Couns Psychol 12(4): 428-34, Winter, 1965. (95
      References)
Reports that philosophical differences among research workers have been responsible for failure to agree about creativity.

1140 ———. "Effects of restriction of range and test unreliability
      on correlation between measures of intelligence and creative
      thinking." Br J Educ Psychol 35(3): 300-5, November, 1965.
      (20 References)
Investigators gave I.Q. and Creative Thinking Tests to nearly 1300 suburban 5th grade American children. Corrections for explicit selection and for unreliability of the creativity measures indicated that the true correlation of I.Q. and creativity might be as high as .88.

1141 ———. "Threshold of intelligence in academic achievement of
      highly creative students." J Exp Educ 32(4): 401-5, Summer, 1964.
      (10 References)
The concept of a threshold of intelligence in the relationship of creative thinking abilities and academic achievement was examined. A secondary and elementary group of the top 20 percent on creativity were classified into three subgroups. In the elementary subgroups there was no threshold. In the secondary population, the threshold phenomen was observed in the high (135+) and middle (120-135) groups.

1142 ———. "Validation of tests of creative thinking: a review of
      some studies." Except Child 31(6): 281-90, February, 1965.
      (26 References)
A review of recent validation studies in the area of creative thinking suggests that (1) investigators have not come to an agreement as to criteria (2) easily obtainable measures of creativity have shortcomings and (3) more validation studies are urgently needed.

1143 Yee, George F. "The influences of problem-solving instruction
      and personal-social adjustment upon creativity test scores of
      twelfth grade students." For a summary see: Diss Abstr Int
      26(2): 916, August, 1965. (0 References)

B. Comparative Studies

1144 Babad, Elisha Y., and Budoff, Milton. "Sensitivity and validity
      of learning-potential measurement in three levels of ability."
      J Educ Psychol 66(3): 439-47, June, 1974. (11 References)
Describes the use of an alternative to the traditional I.Q. test to assess the intellectual potential of disadvantaged children. The instrument described was administered to bright, average and dull children with training in relevant problem solving strategies interpo-lated. The lower intelligence groups profitted more than the bright from the training.

1145   Barbe, Walter B., and Horn, Raymond A. One in a thousand: a
comparative study of highly and moderately gifted elementary school
children. Columbus, Ohio: State Department of Education, 1964.
78p.
This study identifies two groups of children in grades 3-6: one highly
gifted (I.Q.'s above 148), the other moderately gifted (I.Q.'s 120-134).
It examines their adjustments, family backgrounds, achievements, and
educational programs, and discusses the significant differences between
the two groups.

1146   Bart, William M. "The effect of interest on horizontal decalage
at the stage of formal operations." J Psychol 78(2): 141-50,
July, 1971. (12 References)
Test administered to compare level of interest with level of formal
reasoning in biology, history and literature. Authors found two levels
have little association, thus concrete reasoning in a content area
must precede formal reasoning.

1147   Beamer, Robert H. "Transfer after training with single vs. multiple
tasks by individuals and pairs of low and high ability fifth
graders." For a summary see: Diss Abstr Int 31A(6): 2730,
December, 1970. (0 References)

1148   Blake, Kathryn A., and Williams, Charlotte L. "Induction and
deduction and retarded,normal and superior subjects concept
attainment." Am J Ment Defic 73(2): 226-31, September, 1968.
(23 References)
Retarded, normal and superior children from public school regular and
special classes were compared on their attainment of concepts by
deduction, induction-discovery, and induction-demonstration. With MA
held constant, the groups did not differ in level of concept attainment;
with CA held constant the score of the superior was double that of the
normal and four times that of the retarded. For all groups deduction
was the most effective means of learning with the two inductive methods
similarly effective.

1149   ————. "Retarded, normal, and superior subjects' attainment of
verbal concepts at two levels of inclusiveness." Psychol Rep
23(2): 535-40, October, 1968. (19 References)
Retarded, normal, and superior public school students were compared on
grouping object-level words by criteria at two levels of inclusiveness.
With CA held constant, the groups differed significantly: the superior
exceeded both others and the normal exceeded the retarded.

1150   ————. "Retarded, normal and superior subjects learning of paired
associates by whole and parts methods." Psychol Rep 25(1): 319-24,
August, 1969. (22 References)
Seventy-two subjects used whole, pure-parts, and progressive parts
methods in learning CVC trigramnumeral pairs. Groups equated for MA
did not differ in rote learning; groups equated for CA did differ with
superior group excelling. The groups did not react differentially to
the three methods.

1151   Blodgett, Elliott D. "A comparative study of intellectually gifted
and intellectually average children in a problem-solving situation."
For a summary see: Diss Abstr Int 21(12): 3699-3700, June, 1961.
(0 References)

1152   Broad, Robert D.   "Experimental modification of the moral judgement
        of intellectually gifted and average male students."   For a summary
        see: Diss Abstr Int 33B(7): 3279, January, 1973. (0 References)

1153   Brown, Frederick G., and DuBois, Thomas E.   "Correlates of
        academic success for high-ability freshmen men."   Pers Guide J
        42(6): 603-7, February, 1964. (12 References)
Results indicate that different characteristics of high ability students
were rewarded in two colleges having curricular emphasis. The engineers
were more hard working, energetic, conforming and efficient, while the
sciences and humanities students were more flexible and more oriented to
the general philosophy and goals of education.

1154   Caplan, Nathan S., and Powell, Marvin.   "A cross comparison of
        average and superior I.Q. deliquents."   J Psychol 57(2): 307-18,
        April, 1964. (0 References)
One hundred average I.Q. and one hundred superior I.Q. (120+) deliquents
in Cleveland were compared on numerous criteria. A much greater amount
of parent-child conflict was found among the superior children, as was
the amount of success in school.

1155   Cattell, Raymond B.   "The theory of fluid and crystallized general
        intelligence checked at the 5-6 year-old level."   Br J Educ Psychol
        37(2): 209-24, June, 1967. (19 References)
Under a grant from the National Institute of Mental Health, Cattell
tested the theory of fluid and crystallized general intelligence. He
states that crystallized intelligence, gc, depends upon culturally
acquired judgmental skills, while fluid ability, gf, encompasses insightful performances in which individual differences in learning
experience are unimportant.

1156   Clarke, H. Harrison, and Olson, Arne L.   "Characteristics of 15
        year-old boys who demonstrate various accomplishments or diffi-
        culties."   Child Dev 36(2): 559-67, June, 1965. (14 References)
This study contrasted with characteristics of other boys of their age
the physical, mental, and interest characteristics of 15-year-old boys
who had outstanding achievements in athletics, science, fine arts,
leadership, and scholarship or who were poor students or presented
deliquency manifestations. The only trait that was common to all
outstanding groups was intelligence.

1157   Cropley A. J.   "Creativity and intelligence."   Br J Educ Psychol
        36(3): 259-66, November, 1966. (46 References)
A battery of 13 tests, six "convergent" and seven "divergent" was
administered to 320 7th grade students and the divergent tests scored
for originality. Results showed that although the divergent tests
indicated a separate factor, creativity, there was a significant correlation with the factor defined by the more normal tests of intelligence.

1158   Danneffel, George J.   "A Comparison of the non-language multiple-
        choice problem solving ability of very bright, average, and high-
        grade mentally defective eight-year-old children."   For a summary
        see: Diss Abstr Int 33A(3): 1042, September, 1972. (0 References)

1159   Day, H. I., and Langevin, R.   "Curiosity and intelligence: two
        necessary conditions for a high level of curiosity."   J Spec Educ
        3(3): 263-68, Fall, 1969. (24 References)

Curiosity and I.Q. scores failed to correlate significantly, although the tendency to do so was in a positive direction.

1160 Dickerson, Windel L. "A study of illogical choice behavior on concept learning tasks among bright, normal and retarded children." For a summary see: <u>Diss Abstr Int</u> 27A(2): 386, August, 1966. (0 References)

1161 Dolezal, Charles H. "Short-term memory performance of superior, normal, and retarded children." For a summary see: <u>Diss Abstr Int</u> 29A(5): 1448, November, 1968. (0 References)

1162 Doughty, Earl, Jr. "Characteristic differences between pupils identified as gifted and non-gifted." For a summary see: <u>Diss Abstr Int</u> 26(10): 5908-9, April, 1966. (0 References)

1163 Drews, Elizabeth M. "Are intelligence and talent the same?" <u>NEAJ</u> 50(1): 40-41, January, 1961. (0 References)
Part of "Briefing for Parents" entitled "Your Child's Intelligence", this selection is couched in language the average layman can understand: it presents both sides of the creativity-intelligence controversy, and indicates the need for further research before saying with certainty how the two qualities are related.

1164 Edwards, Meredith P., and Tyler, Leona E. "Intelligence, creativity and achievement in a nonselective public junior high school." <u>J Educ Psychol</u> 56(2): 96-99, April, 1965. (5 References)
To test Torrance's threshold hypothesis, a twice-talented group, high on both School and College Achievement Test and creativity was compared with the high SCAT group. These groups did not differ in Sequential Tests of Educational Progress scores, but the twice-talented group was significantly lower than the high SCAT group on grade-point average.

1165 Eisenman, Russell, and Robinson, Nancy. "Complexity-simplicity, creativity, intelligence, and other correlates." <u>J Psychol</u> 67(2): 331-34, November, 1967. (8 References)
With 75 high school students as subjects it was found that (a) the paper and pencil personality measure of creativity, previously linked to originality; was related to preference for complexity; there was no significant correlation between I.Q. and the creativity test.

1166 Ferris, Robert W. "An investigation of high school senior participants and nonparticipants in honors courses with respect to certain nonintellective and cognitive factors." For a summary see: <u>Diss Abstr Int</u> 29A(4): 1102, October, 1968. (0 References)

1167 Gill, Newell T., and Messina, Robert. "Visual self-confrontation and the self-concept of the exceptional child." <u>Florida J Educ Res</u> 15(1): 18-36, 1973.
A pilot study of methods and effects (photography, mirrors, films, and videotape) of extending childrens' self-awareness during a 7 month period. Gifted subjects were compared with children with specific learning disabilities and EMR boys on self-recognition and self-concept measures. Post-tests showed improvement in all except the EMR subjects.

1168 Goldstein, Herbert, and Kass, Corinne. "Incidental learning of
      educable mentally retarded and gifted children." Am J Ment Defic
      66(2): 245-49, September, 1961. (5 References)
Compared gifted with mentally retarded as to incidental learning. Gifted
did acquire incidental learning and were accurate in naming from memory
and giving details.

1169 Groth, Norma J. "Achievement of autonomy and other developmental
      tasks in bright and average adolescents." Gifted Child Q 17(1):
      64-67, Spring, 1973. (4 References)
Study used gifted to test autonomy achievement, time perspective achievement, and leadership polarization achievement. Although bright adolescents develop autonomy and time perspective faster, it was not
significant in leadership polarization. Girls were ahead in that.
Boys indicated authority diffusion and insecurity.

1170 Hauck. Barbara B. "A comparison of gains in evaluation ability
      between gifted and non-gifted sixth grade students." Gifted
      Child Q 11(3): 166 71, Fall, 1967. (15 References)
Sixth grade experimental and control groups were equated on I.Q. scores,
sex, race, socioeconomic status, and pretest scores on semantic evaluation
tests. Subjects then experienced 18 daily 30-minute lessons emphasizing
mental set, game theory, role-playing, and feedback. Subjects showed a
significant gain over the controls on semantic evaluation tests.
Intellectual level was unrelated to test gain.

1171 Iscoe, Ira, and Pierce-Jones, John. "Divergent thinking, age and
      intelligence in white and Negro children." Child Dev 35(3):
      785-97, September, 1964. (23 References)
Ideational fluency and flexibility scores were obtained from 267 school
children. Overall, the divergent thinking scores were significantly
higher for Negroes. Fluency scores were dependent upon role and interaction with age.

1172 Iscoe, Ira; Williams, Martha; Harvey, Jerry. "Age, intelligence
      and sex as variables in the conformity behavior of Negro and white
      children." Child Dev 35(2): 451-60, June, 1964. (8 References)
In this study of Negro and white children subjected to simulated group
pressures, Negro females conformed less than white females. Age and
race were significant variables. The importance of criterion specificity
was emphasized. Results were discussed in terms of differential cultural
roles and the regression analysis model was recommended for investigation
of the relation between personality factors and conformity behavior.

1173 Jensen, Arthur R. "Learning ability in retarded, average, and
      gifted children." Merrill-Palmer Q 9(2): 123-40, April, 1963.
      (7 References)
Junior high pupils classified as EMR were compared with average and
gifted children in the same school on a learning task new to all. There
were highly significant differences between the groups and the rate of
learning correlated with I.Q. even within the retarded group. The
retarded showed greater improvement with practice on subsequent trials.

1174 Klausmeier, Herbert J., and Check, J. "Retention and transfer in
      children of low, average and high intelligence." J Educ Res
      55(7): 319-322, April, 1962. (12 References)

Retention and transfer abilities were compared among children of low,
average and high intelligence. No significant difference in retention of
arithmetic learning was found in children with the learning task graded
to each child's achievement level. Researchers suggest that classroom
teachers should find present achievement level of child, then offer
individualized instruction at that level, facilitating greater retention
and transfer.

1175 Krippner, Stanley. "Etiological factors in reading disability of
      the academically talented in comparison to pupils of average and
      slow-learning ability." J Educ Res 61(6): 275-79, February, 1968.
      (19 References)
A comparison of reading disabilities in high, middle, and low intelligence
groups found that the high intelligence group's disabilities were significantly more often functional in origin than those in the average and low
groups. Of help to those high intelligence disabled would be perceptual
training, dominance establishment and motor coordination.

1176 Kyte, George C., and Fornwalt, James E. "Comparison of superior
      children with normal children in the rate mastery of the multipli-
      cation of fractions." J Educ Res 60(8): 346-50, April, 1967.
      (0 References)
A superior group and an average group were taught multiplication of
fractions by the same person using the same instructional materials and
methods. The superior group mastered each step faster than the average
group and retained a higher degree of mastery.

1177 Laurence, Ronald, and Sutton-Smith, Brian. "Novel response to toys:
      a replication." Merrill-Palmer Q 14(2): 159-60, April, 1968.
      (7 References)
Head-start Negro children with mean I.Q.'s in the 80's were compared in
response to toys with high socioeconomic white children with a mean I.Q.
of 139. Each sex gave more response to its own sex toys. Boys gave more
unique responses than girls to all categories.

1178 Lindeman, Barbara, and Kling,Martin. "Bibliotherapy: Definitions,
      uses and studies." J Sch Psychol 7(2): 36-41, 1968/1969.
      (42 References)
Bibliotherapy, an interaction between the reader and literature useful
in aiding personal adjustment, is discussed in regard to gifted, average,
and retarded students.

1179 Lucito, Leonard J. "Independence-comformity behavior as a function
      of intellect: bright and dull children." Except Child 31(1):
      5-13, September, 1964. (7 References)
The author compared 55 bright sixth graders with 51 dull sixth graders
on a task testing independence-conformity behavior. The bright students
were significantly more independent in their decisions than were the
dull, although there was a wide range of behavior within the gifted group.

1180 Milgram, Norman A., and Milgram, Roberta M. "Dimensions of locus
      of control in children." Psychol Rep 37(2): 523-38, October,
      1975. (26 References)
Report of a multidimensional measure of locus of control which was
recently administered to non-gifted and gifted Israeli children in
grades 4 through 8. In comparison to non-gifted children, the gifted

assumed more personal responsibility and expressed more feelings of
competence in dealing with situations.

1181 Millner, Joan O. "A comparison of two groups of gifted high school
      seniors on the basis of participation or non-participation in
      experimental elementary school programs for the academically
      talented." For a summary see: Diss Abstr Int   28A(8):   3076-77,
      February, 1968. (0 References)

1182 Mosier, Jack A. "A study of parent occupational expectations for
      gifted and average children compared with the child's occupational
      goals and creativity." For a summary see: Diss Abstr Int   32A(8):
      4297, February, 1972. (0 References)

1183 Nipper, William A. "A comparison of certain aspects of categorizing
      behavior in retarded, normal and gifted children at two age levels."
      For a summary see: Diss Abstr Int   28A(7):   2563-64, January, 1968.

1184 Nolan, Mary Pat, and Fargen, J. Jerome. "Personality differences
      between able sophomore university students of 1961 and 1971."
      J Educ Res   69(1):   11-13, September, 1975. (6 References)
College males were chosen on the basis of three criteria for intelligence
and achievement. The Minnesota Personality Scale was administered to
131 subjects in 1961 and 174 in 1971. Results revealed significant
differences in socialization, self-possession, social and economic views,
and attitudes toward institutions over the decade of the sixties.

1185 Ogdon, Donald P. "Extrapolated WISC-R I.Q.'s for gifted and
      mentally retarded children." J Consult Clin Psychol   43(2):   216,
      April, 1975. (2 References)
Remarkably gifted and retarded children may earn a WISC-R scaled score
that is beyond Wechsler's norms. Ogdon derived regression equations for
the relationship between I.Q.'s and scaled scores at the upper and lower
extremes of Wechsler's data. Cautions regarding the clinical use of
these I.Q.'s are presented here.

1186 Palacino, Vincent. "A comparative study of the effectiveness of
      stimulation in changing regular classroom teachers' attitudes toward
      the integration of exceptional children into the regular classroom.
      Diss Abstr Int   34A(6):   3218, December, 1973. (0 References)

1187 Paraskevopoulos, Ioannis. "Developmental stages for decoding
      symmetry in retarded and gifted children." Am J Ment Defic
      73(3):   447-54, November, 1968. (23 References)
Gifted and EMR public school pupils reproduced from memory double,
bilateral, horizontal, and asymmetrical dot patterns. Multiple
comparisons revealed that the onset of the effective structures to decode
symmetry is a function of maturational and cognitive factors. While
gifted could decode double symmetry early in preschool age, EMR subjects
didn't master the skill until age 8. By age 11 the gifted decoded
horizontal symmetry, a task that remained beyond even the 16 year old
EMR pupils.

1188 Rhodes, Leland E. "The visual evoked response: a comparison of
      bright and dull children." For a summary see: Diss Abstr Int
      28B(7):   3079, January, 1968. (0 References)

1189   Steele, Joe M.; House, Ernest R.; Lapan, Stephen D.   et.al.
       "Cognitive and affective patterns of emphasis in gifted and average
       Illinois classes." Except Child 37(10):   757-59, Summer, 1971.
       (2 References)
In a representative sample of programs for the gifted, classes were shown
to be superior in several dimensions to a control group of suburban
classes of similar socioeconomic level.

1190   Sullivan, Joseph P., and Moran, Louis J.   "Association structures
       of bright children at age six." Child Dev 38(3):   793-800,
       September, 1967. (8 References)
The factor structure of free word associations of 101 bright 6-year-old
children was compared to the factor structure typically found with adult
samples. The only major difference in factor structure was attributed
to "functional" associates caused by more competing associations with
adults.

1191   Thompson, Jack M., and Finley, Carmen J.   "A further comparison of
       the intellectual patterns of gifted and mentally retarded children."
       Except Child 28(7):   379-81, March, 1962. (4 References)
Study looked at strengths and weaknesses of gifted on Weschler subtests.
The 400 gifted were highest in similarities, information, comprehension
in other words, verbal comprehension. They were weakest in perceptual
organization - coding, picture arrangement, and object assembly.

1192   Torrance, E. Paul, and Johnson, Richard T.   "Gifted thirteen-year-
       olds in two cultures: Greater London and Greater Twin Cities
       (U.S.A.)." Gifted Child Q 10(3):   125-31, Autumn, 1966. (4
       References)
Advocates of special provisions for the education of gifted children in
the U.S. have often cited the methods of the English school system as a
model to be emulated. This study compares the mathematics achievement
of gifted 13 year olds in the two cultures and tries to ascertain the
experiences and attitudes of the subjects that are hypothesized to
affect mathematics learning.

1193   Welsh, James A.   "Associative learning rates of bright, normal and
       retarded children using paired-associate lists of varying lengths."
       For a summary see: Diss Abstr Int 28A(6):   2106, December, 1967.
       (0 References)

1194   Williams, Charlotte L., and Blake,Kathryn A.   "Type of grouping
       criterion and retarded,normal, and superior subjects' verbal
       concept attainment." Train Sch Bull 65(2):   40-45, August, 1968.
       (19 References)
Compared selected retarded, normal, and superior subjects equated for
MA and CA on their use of 2 grouping criteria: (a) categorizing object-
level words on the basis of 1st-order concepts, and (b) grouping object-
level words on the basis of initial letters. The superior group exceeded
their age-mates on both variants, but when MA was equal, all subjects
had similar levels of concept attainment.

1195   Williams, Charlotte L., and Tillman, M. H.   "Associative character-
       istics of selected form classes for children varying in age and
       intelligence." Psychol Rep 22(2):   459-68, April, 1968. (12
       References)

Retarded, normal and superior children across four age levels were compared
on homogeneous responses for six form classes on word-association and
word-usage tasks. Results generally indicated that rates of development
were similar. Initial differences in performance level were maintained
or, in a few instances, increased.

1196 Williams, Eddie H. "Effects of readiness on incidental learning
       in EMR, normal, and gifted children." Am J Ment Defic 75(2):
       117-19, September, 1970. (6 References)
Investigated the effects of readiness on incidental learning on 30 EMR,
30 normal and 30 gifted. When readiness was given none of the groups
differed in incidental learning; when readiness was not given, they did.
Readiness had no effect on gifted.

1197 Yamamoto, Kaoru. "Creativity and unpredictability in school
       achievement." J Educ Res 60(7): 321-25. March, 1967. (22
       References)
In the 9th and 11th grades and on each subtest of the ITED battery,
overachieving and underachieving groups were identified. When these
two groups were compared on tests of creative thinking the mean scores
did not show any consistent trend across the different achievement areas
to favor either one of these groups.

1198 ————. "Role of creative thinking and intelligence in high school
       achievement." Psychol Rep 14(3): 783-89, June, 1964. (8
       References)
The author formed three special groups from 272 high school students at
a university laboratory school: a high I.Q. - low creativity group, a
high I.Q. - high creativity group, and a low I.Q. - high creativity
group. The performances of these three groups on the Iowa Tests of
Educational Development were then compared and no differences in
achievement level were found.

1199 Zimmerman, Irla L., and Woo-Sam, James. "The utility of the
       Wechsler Preschool and Primary Scale of Intelligence in the public
       school." J Clin Psychol 26(4): 472, October, 1970. (4 References)
Compared the test performances on the WPPSI and the Stanford-Binet LM
of referred kindergarteners and 1st graders. Results were similar from
both instruments below the superior level. I.Q.'s were significantly
higher for gifted children on the Stanford-Binet.

IX

Bibliographies

1200 Boston, Bruce, ed. A resource manual of information on educating
the gifted and talented. Reston, Virginia: The Council for
Exceptional Children, 1975. 97p.
The manual provides directories of federal, state and national resources,
seven papers on the state of gifted education, and information on such
other resources as films and state level parent organizations.

1201 Creativity: a selective bibliography. exceptional child
bibliography series no. 667. Reston, Virginia: The Council for
Exceptional Children, 1975. 33p.
Contains approximately 150 abstracts from CEC computer files and ERIC.
Citations are divided into five major topical groupings: general
creativity, research studies, creativity and the classroom, tests and
measurements, creativity and intelligence, and problem solving.

1202 Gifted children and the arts and humanities: a selective
bibliography. exceptional child bibliography series no. 661.
Reston, Virginia: The Council for Exceptional Children, 1975. 33p.
Contains approximately 200 abstracts from the computer files of CEC and
ERIC. References included treat aspects such as creative thinking,
creative expression, curriculum, instructional materials, teaching
methods, language arts, music, social studies, films and photography.

1203 Gifted: handicapped,disadvantaged and underachievers: a selective
bibliography. exceptional child bibliography series no. 660.
Reston, Virginia: The Council for Exceptional Children, 1975. 26p.
Contains approximately 100 abstracts and associated indexing information
for documents published from 1957 to 1974 and selected from the CEC
Information Services and ERIC.

1204 Gowan, John C. An annotated bibliography on the academically
talented. Washington, D.C.: National Education Association, 1961.
156p.
This publication of the NEA project on the Academically Talented Student
represents a resume of the more significant writing of the decade
1950-1960. Its objective is to provide maximum help to the knowledgeable
consumer of research, whether in the school system, the university, or
in other areas of life.

1205 ————. Annotated bibliography on creativity and giftedness.
Northridge, California: San Fernando Valley State College
Foundation, 1965. 197p.
This U.S. Office of Education Cooperative Research project represents a

resume of the more significant writing on creativity and gifted children since 1960.

1206 Grotberg, Edith H. "A selected bibliography on the gifted and creative child." Education 88(1): 52-56, September/October, 1967.
This annotated bibliography of literature on the gifted and creative child includes a variety of materials: studies, special reports, program descriptions, reviews of research and selected bibliographies, yearbooks, and texts.

1207 Job, Beverly J., and Campbell, Patricia B. "Language arts resources for the gifted: an annotated bibliography." Gifted Child Q 20(2): 205-23, Summer, 1976.
From the many excellent resources available the authors have chosen a few current, teacher-tested examples which are with listed with an evaluation from an experienced user. Categories include 1. creative writing 2. dramatics 3. thinking skills 4. humanities 5. values clarification 6. professional 7. miscellaneous.

1208 Mathematics and science for gifted children: a selective bibliography. exceptional child bibliography series no. 656.
Reston, Virginia: The Council for Exceptional Children, 1975. 16p.
Contains approximately 70 abstracts from CEC computer files and ERIC. References included treat aspects such as talent identification, creativity, enrichment, program descriptions, curriculum guides, instructional materials, teaching methods, advanced placement and acceleration.

1209 Programming for the gifted: a selective bibliography. exceptional child bibliography series no. 609. Reston, Virginia: The Council for Exceptional Children, 1975. 22p.
Contains approximately 85 abstracts from CEC computer files and ERIC. References included treat aspects such as enrichment, acceleration, creativity, curriculum, educational programs, special classes, teaching methods, class activities, inservice teacher education, and instructional materials.

1210 Start, Ann. Gifted child; a selected annotated bibliography. Windsor, Ontario: National Foundation for Educational Research, 1972. 40p.
An annotated bibliography of 113 items from British and American publications on the gifted. It is divided into six sections: (1) deals with a general reading list; (2) definition of giftedness; (3) identification of gifted children; (4) description of gifted children; (5) underachievement; and (6) programs for working with gifted children.

1211 Stievater, Susan M. "Bibliography of recent books on creativity and problem solving." J Creat Behav 7(3): 208-13, 1973.
Presents a list of 61 recent books relating to creativity and problem solving, classified according to primary interest areas.

1212 Treffinger, Donald J.; Borgers, Sherry B.; Render, Gary F. et.al.
"Encouraging affective development: a compendium of techniques and resources." Gifted Child Q 20(1): 47-65, Spring, 1976.

Included in the compendium are approximately 175 references to books,
journal articles, instructional materials, filmstrips, or films
concerned with encouraging affective development in gifted and other
children.

1213   Verbeke, Maurice G., and Verbeke, Karen A.   The education of the
       gifted child, 1965-1971: an annotated bibliography. Glassboro,
       New Jersey: Glassboro State College; New Jersey Department of
       Educational Administration, 1973. 127p.
Presents some 400 citations intended for use by teachers, parents and
administrators. They represent the period of the late 60's, a time of
diminished interest in the gifted and stress upon creativity.

1214   Witty, Paul A. "Recent publications concerning the gifted and
       the creative student." Phi Delta Kappan 46(4): 221-24, January,
       1965.
A summary of materials recently published on the gifted. References
would be of great value to those wanting to survey other writings in
the field.

1215   Witty, Paul A., and De Boer, Dorothy L. "A selected bibliography
       of studies and research on the gifted and on the creative
       individual." Education 82(8): 496-9, April, 1962.
A list of books and articles dealing primarily with the gifted but also
covering the creative individual.

1216   Zelenik, Mary E. An annotated bibliography of math materials.
       Los Angeles: University of Southern California Instructional
       Materials Center for Special Education, 1973. 52p.
Provides information on approximately 500 math materials appropriate for
students from pre-school through high school. Many are suitable for
enrichment of the gifted.

X

Miscellaneous

1217 Astin, Alexander W. "College preferences of very able students."
   Coll Univ 40(3): 282-97, Spring, 1965. (18 References)
Examines the college preferences of a national sample of 120,458
exceptionally able high school students. Estimates the "popularity" of
each of 1,013 accredited 4-year colleges and universities by checking
the total number of those scholars who named the institution as either
their first or second choice.

1218 Beswich, N. W. "The school library and the highly gifted child."
   Sch Libr 17(4): 349-55, December, 1969.
The author, feeling that the gifted child presents a particular challenge
to the school librarian, offers a variety of suggestions for the
provision of suitable books.

1219 Blumenfeld, Warren S. "College preferences of able Negro students:
   a comparison of those naming predominantly Negro institutions and
   those naming predominantly white institutions." Coll Univ 43(3):
   330-41, Spring, 1968. (9 References)
This study is part of the research done by the National Merit Scholarship
Corporation. A survey of the 938 Negro students who were finalists
in the 1966 National Achievement Scholarship program showed that only
14% preferred a predominantly Negro college. Most preferred the most
selective Eastern private colleges that are chosen by able white
students.

1220 Boag, Audrey K. "Special services - are they increasing in our
   schools?" NY State Educ 53(8): 21, 37, May, 1966.
In responding affirmatively to this question, the author provides a
brief review of services needed by exceptional children.

1221 Boyd, David E. "The mad scientist." Sch Act 40: 16-17,
   November, 1968. (0 References)
Personal account by a teacher of a student who was considered a "problem
child", but was found to be a highly gifted individual.

1222 Burke, Margaret J. "A case-study approach to the development of
   self-concepts among a group of superior students." For a summary
   see: Diss Abstr Int 29A(1): 54, July, 1968. (0 References)

1223 Davis, Ruth K. "A study of the factors affecting congruent or
   incongruent college choice among highly gifted girls." For a
   summary see: Diss Abstr Int 32A(10): 5543, April, 1972. (0
   References)

1224   Dreistadt, Roy. "The prophetic achievements of geniuses and
       types of extrasensory perception." Psychology 8(2): 27-40,
       May, 1971. (14 References)
This theoretical and speculative study attempts to describe the prophetic
nature of genius. It is further theorized that insofar as the prophetic
achievements of genius are aided by precognition, the three main types
of geniuses, - artistic, scientific and inventive - are aided by
telepathy, clairvoyance, and mixed clairvoyance and telepathy respectively.

1225   Drews, Elizabeth M. "What every able woman should know." J Natl
       Assoc Women Deans Couns 25(1): 14-20, October, 1961. (23
       References)
Describes the able woman as to ability, achievement, school attitudes,
activities, values, interests, aspirations, adjustment and health.

1226   Dulit, Everett. "Adolescent thinking a la Piaget: the formal
       stage." J Youth Adolesc 1(4): 281-301, December, 1972. (5
       References)
Replicated two of Piaget and B. Inhelder's 1958 formal-stage experiments.
Relevant Piagetian concepts are described in the context. The methods
and findings of this study are given.

1227   Eissler, K. R. Talent and genius. New York: Quadrangle, 1971,
       403p.
Discussed are psychoanalytic differences between talent and genius.
Locates the source of genius in early identification with hero figures,
and the energy derived from frustrations in other areas.

1228   Ertl, J. P. "Intelligence testing by brainwaves." Mensa Bull
       110: 3-6, April, 1968.
The director of the Center of Cybernetic Studies at the University of
Ottawa presents findings showing a high degree of relationship between
the electrical activity of the human brain and intelligence as measured
by psychological tests.

1229   Fox, Gudelia A. "The gifted: how are they viewed?" Gifted Child
       Q 12(1): 23-33, Spring, 1968. (53 References)
Discusses the factors influencing the anti-intellectualism traditional
in our society. Gives thorough coverage to research studies at the
elementary, secondary, and college level which attempted to assess
attitudes toward the intellectually gifted.

1230   Frederickson, Ronald H., and Rothney, John W., eds. Recognizing
       and assisting multipotential youth. Columbus, Ohio: Charles E.
       Merrill, 1972. 181p.
Contains nine articles on the creative, the multipotential female, bright
black youth, vocational decision-makers, evidence of multipotentiality,
national, regional and state programs for youth, and education for the
multipotentialed.

1231   Gedo, John E. "On the psychology of genius." Int J Psychoanal
       53(2): 199-203, May, 1972. (22 References)
Presents a paper read at the 27th International Psycho-Analytical Congress
discussing the origins of human creativity. The similarity and difference
between the mental life of one genius and a number of talented men is
described. The need to conceptualize a typology of genius is discussed.

1232 The gifted: educational resources. Boston: Sargent, 1961. 285p.
A preliminary survey of primary and secondary schools in the United
States which seek through inspiring teaching to realize the capabilities
of mentally superior students.

1233 Goertzel, Victor, and Goertzel, Mildred G. Cradles of eminence.
    Boston: Little, Brown, 1962. 362p.
While not pretending to be a scientific study, this highly readable book
presents the authors' findings as a result of a survey of the emotional
and intellectual climates in which 400 eminent people of the 20th
century were reared. They use the term "eminent" to mean "standing high
in comparison with others."

1234 Gowan, John C. "Issues in the education of disadvantaged gifted
    students." Gifted Child Q 12(2): 115-19, Summer, 1968. (11
    References)
Identifies six issues in the education of gifted disadvantaged children
which need much further discussion and research. These are identification, individual and type differences, nature, time and results of
intervention, and special aspects of guidance.

1235 Graves, William H. "How misleading the fifty years? a reply to
    Jacobs." Gifted Child Q 17(4): 268-71, Winter, 1973. (11
    References)
Criticizes an earlier article by Jacobs which reported a significant
drop in I.Q. for gifted children after one year in elementary school.
Argues that "statistical regression" was probably responsible for the
drop, not miseducation.

1236 Gregory, Robert J. "International students: resources for
    exceptional children." Except Child 34(4): 282-83, December,
    1967. (1 Reference)
Emphasizes that most exceptional children benefit tremendously from a
learning experience involving foreign students and international ideas.

1237 Guilford, J. P. "Intelligence: 1965 model." Am Psychol 21(1):
    20-26, January, 1966. (18 References)
Describes the author's structure-of-intellect model, with its five
operation categories intersecting with its four content categories, and
these, in turn, intersecting with its six product categories. Cites
progress in terms of many new intellectual abilities to occupy cells of
the model, and a few movings of abilities within the model to give
better logical fits to theory.

1238 Hausdorff, Henry, and Farr, S. David. "Effect of grading practices
    on the marks of gifted sixth grade children." J Educ Res 59(4):
    169-72, December, 1965. (3 References)
Study finds that a dual marking system does not produce higher marks
than a single marking system. Gifted children marked on standards for
a heterogeneous group received significantly higher marks than gifted
children marked on standards for a homogeneous group.

1239 Holland, John L. "The National Merit Research program." Education
    82(8): 477-81, April, 1962. (0 References)
Discusses identification of talent, forecasting achievement, conservation of talent, influence of colleges, climates, - all in relation to the

National Merit program.   Contains summaries of merit research projects in
progress during 1960-61.

1240   Holland, John L., and Richards, James M., Jr.   "The many faces of
        talent: a reply to Werts."   J Educ Psychol   58(4):   205-9,
        August, 1967.   (15 References)
Authors feel that grades are an inefficient way to select for non-
academic talents and have little relationship with other talents.

1241   Isaacs, Ann F.   "Discipline: perspective prescription for
        giftedness."   Gifted Child Q   17(1):   10-35, Spring, 1973.   (37
        References)
Presents a review and discussion of the literature on mental health,
discipline, an opinion survey of psychologists in a search for the best
modes of discipline and character development.   Also gives examples of
discipline as manifested both negatively and positively in the lives of
gifted people, plus recommendations emphasizing the need for knowledge
of sound mental health principles and practices to promote maximum
growth of the gifted individuals'potentialities.

1242   Jaramillo, Mari L.   "Cultural conflict curriculum and the
        exceptional child."   Except Child   40(8):   585-87, May, 1974.   (0
        References)
Argues that the American educational system must be changed to reflect
the growing recognition of the value of the many cultural groups in
our society.   It is stressed that the special education classroom
teacher and the culturally different child both have important contributions to make in molding this new educational system.

1243   Joesting, Joan.   "Why must we waste talents of one-half the
        gifted?"   Gifted Child Q   14(4):   252-54, Winter, 1970.   (3
        References)
Author suggests that talented women denied constructive outlets in male
dominated society may try to destroy society's structures.

1244   Jones, Ralph H.   "Legal provisions for educating gifted and slow
        learning children in elementary schools in Indiana and in other
        selected states."   For a summary see: Diss Abstr Int   26(8):
        4336-37, February, 1966.

1245   Jones, Reginald L.   "The hierarchical structure of attitudes
        toward the exceptional."   Except Child   40(6):   430-35, March, 1974.
        (13 References)
The author investigated the structure of attitudes toward the exceptional
among 264 male and female undergraduate students at Berkeley.   Results
on a 78-item social distance questionnaire reveal a common core of
attitudes which cut across categories of disability and interpersonal
situation.   Attitudes toward the gifted emerged as a separate factor
isolated in virtually all instances from those held toward the disabled.

1246   Kahn, P. M.   "Education of the academically gifted: a Trojan
        horse?"   Natl Assoc Second Sch Princ Bull   No. 287:   22-25, December,
        1963.
Deals with problems inherent in education of the gifted, including
neglect of the majority, neglect of under- and over-achievers, neglect of
possible mental health aspects in segregation, and other possible areas
of neglect.

1247   Keaster, Charles W.   "Development of California school district
       programs for mentally gifted minors and special state aid."   For a
       summary see: Diss Abstr Int   29A(12):   4231, June, 1969.   (0
       References)

1248   Kennedy, Wallace A., and Willicutt, Herman C.   "A factorial study
       of praise and blame."   Psychol Rep   17(2):   511-17, October, 1965.
       (10 References)
The effectiveness of praise and blame on the discrimination performance
of 720 students as a function of race, grade, intelligence and sex was
studied by the authors.   Reproof had a debilitating effect on performance,
while praise resulted in an increase in performance larger than that
associated with practice alone.

1249   Krippner, Stanley.   "Boy who read at eighteen months."   Except
       Child   30(3):   105-109, November, 1963.
Discusses testing results of a four-year-old who read on a second-grade
level.   Important factors were superior general intelligence, visual
memory, listening vocabulary, social maturity, speech and hearing
development and home background.   Although subject had an I.Q. of 157,
another study found that one-third of a group of preschool readers had
an I.Q. of 110 or less.

1250   Lake, Thomas P.   "We're all about the exceptional child."   Volta
       Rev   77(2):   141-42, February, 1975.   (0 References)
Reports services of the Council for Exceptional Children's Information
Center on Handicapped and Gifted Children.   Computer searches of the
literature and product planning and development provide materials
available to those in special education.

1251   Lauten, Doris A.   "The relationship between intelligence and motor
       proficiency in the intellectually gifted child."   For a summary see:
       Diss Abstr Int   31B(3):   1521, September, 1970.   (0 References)

1252   Lazar, Alfred L.   "Reasons cited by college students in teacher
       training for taking an elective course on the education of the
       gifted."   Gifted Child Q   17(4):   274-78, Winter, 1973.   (2
       References)
The 30 students enrolled in an introductory course on the gifted were
asked their reason for taking the course.   "Interest in the gifted" was
the chief reason given.

1253   Leavell, Alfred.   "Survey of reimbursement centers in the Illinois
       state program for the gifted."   For a summary see: Diss Abstr Int
       33A(9):   4983, March, 1973.   (0 References)

1254   Litterst, Milton R.   "An approach to meeting the educational needs
       of the gifted."   For a summary see: Diss Abstr Int   21(8):   2161,
       February, 1961.   (0 References)

1255   Lyon, Harold C., Jr.   "Popular myths about the gifted."   Kootenay
       Cent Gifted J   1(1):   3-5, June, 1973.
Twelve popular myths concerning gifted students are presented, and facts
are cited to refute them.   Discusses the presence of gifted pupils in
various racial and socioeconomic groups, needs of the gifted for quality
career education programs and for intergration of cognitive and affective
programs.

1256   Marks, Russel. "Lewis M. Terman: individual differences and the
     construction of social reality." Educ Theory 24(4):   336-55, Fall,
     1974. (77 References)
The writer reveals how Terman's work on intelligence tests not only was
conditioned by the social mileu, but also helped to change the social
order. Furthermore, he prescribed what the social implications of these
differences were for the social order and was thus involved in the
construction of social reality.

1257   Martindale, Colin. "Degeneration, disinhibition, and genius."
     J Hist Behav Sci 7(2): 177-82, April, 1971. (24 References)
The concern of this paper is with the claim that the supposed traits of
degeneration are present in men of genius. The total rejection of the
degeneration model actually led to a setback in the understanding of
creativity.

1258   Mills, Barbara N. "Attitudes of decision-making groups toward
     gifted children and public school programs for the gifted." For
     a summary see: Diss Abstr Int 34A(4): 1739-40, October, 1973.
     (0 References)

1259   Newland, T. Ernest. "A critique of research on the gifted."
     Except Child 29(8): 391-98, April, 1963. (0 References)
Newland concludes that researchers must pay more attention to uniform
nomenclature, validity and reliability, sound theory, precise writing,
and other factors.

1260   Noyes, Margaret E. "A study of programs for gifted children in
     school systems of 50,000 to 99,999 population with emphasis on
     establishing a model for gifted children in a heterogeneous setting
     for the Mobile County schools." For a summary see: Diss Abstr Int
     32A(9): 5074, March, 1972. (0 References)

1261   Parnes, Sidney J., and Harding, Harold F., ed. A source book for
     creative thinking. New York: Scribner's, 1962. 393p.
This useful guide and source book contains many interesting problems and
exercises for use with gifted and creative students in the classroom.

1262   Paulus, Vimala. "A study of the levels of aspiration of gifted
     pupils and their parents with reference to the achievement of the
     gifted pupils." For a summary see: Diss Abstr Int 23(6): 2015,
     December, 1962. (0 References)

1263   Payne, James S.; Kauffman, James M.; Brown, Gweneth. et.al.
     Exceptional children in focus. Columbus, Ohio: Merrill, 1974.
     129p. (Bibliography)
In Chapter 8 the authors conclude: "As we begin to think about the
gifted as a human resource to solve society's problems, we must be aware
that we have no right to harness their intellectual talents at the cost
of their basic freedoms."

1264   Pines, Maya. Revolution in learning: the years from birth to
     six. New York: Harper and Row, 1967. 244p. (Bibliography)
The author's report on a number of projects in compensatory education.
A result of her research on how man's experiences in earliest childhood
affect his intellectual growth. Her journey through selected universities,

laboratories, and experimental schools led to a discovery of a violent controversy among the experts as to the best methods of facilitating early learning.

1265   Purdy, Ruth S.   "The developmental process, the inhibition process, and the production of human movement on the Kinget Drawing Completion Test."   For a summary see: Diss Abstr Int   27A(6):   1680, December, 1966.   (0 References)

1266   Richards, James M.; Holland, John L.; Lutz, Sandra W.   "Prediction of student accomplishment in college."   J Educ Psychol   58(6): 343-55, December, 1967.   (40 References)
Results indicate that nonacademic accomplishment can be assessed with moderate reliability, that both academic and non-academic accomplishment can be predicted to a useful degree, and that nonacademic accomplishment is largely independent of academic potential and achievement.

1267   Roberts, Joseph P.   "Intellectually gifted adolescents: a multivariate analysis of certain educationally relevant attributes." For a summary see: Diss Abstr Int   31A(9):   4588-89, March, 1971. (0 References)

1268   Roberts, Roy J.   "Prediction of college performance of superior students."   Natl Merit Scholarsh Corp Res Rep   1(5):   1-24, 1965. (11 References)
Prediction is made of the college performance of the nation's most gifted high school students, the National Merit Scholarship winners.

1269   Ross, John.   "Three cognitive dimensions."   Psychol Rep   17(1): 291-300, August, 1965.   (5 References)
A logical space developed by Oppenheim to differentiate and locate publications was used to construct a self-report questionnaire.   Factor analysis of responses to the questionnaire gave reason to suppose that Oppenheim's dimensional scheme may provide a basis for cognitive styles each corresponding to a different dimension.

1270   Rossi, Ernest L.   "Growth, change and transformation in dreams." J Humanistic Psychol   11(2):   147-69, Fall, 1971.   (36 References)
Author outlines 10 hypotheses about dreaming for the gifted.   Says that what is important for the psychotherapist is to be sensitive to any signs of change and transformation that take place in the dreamer since they represent efforts to cope with developmental blocks.

1271   Rowland-Jones, Tim L.   "English educator studying the gifted reports on his visit to America."   Gifted Child Q   17(3):   211-14, Fall, 1973.   (0 References)
An English educator comments on general aspects of American education and specific efforts to educate gifted students.

1272   Rubovits, Pamela C., and Maehr, Martin L.   "Pygmalion black and white."   J Pers Soc Psychol   25(2):   210-18, February, 1973. (21 References)
After being rated for dogmatism, a group of white female teacher trainees were assigned to teach white and black 7th and 8th graders who had randomly been given labels of gifted or nongifted.   As noted before, subjects gave preferential treatment to "gifted" students.

1273   Schere, Richard A.   "Differential reinforcement with exceptional
       children."   For a summary see: Diss Abstr Int   31A(3): 1088,
       September, 1970.   (0 References)

1274   Schimmels, Cliff.   "New cloth for old tunics."   J Thought   9(3):
       191-94, July, 1974.
Discusses how the educational voucher system would answer the educational
needs of contemporary society and how today's educational problems
parallel those of earlier times.

1275   Seagoe, May V.   "Terman and the gifted."   Natl Elem Princ   51(5):
       76-78, February, 1972.   (0 References)
Terman's lifelong work with gifted children convinced him that they
should work at their own pace, be accelerated beyond their age group,
work independently much of the time, develop persistence and creativity,
meet and work with other gifted children, and have ample access to
guidance in reaching life decisions.

1276   ———.   Terman and the gifted.   Los Altos, California: Kaufmann,
       1975. 258p.   (Bibliography)
This biography of Terman focuses on his pioneering work in mental testing,
education of the gifted, personality research and social reform.   Among
five appendixes are lists of his publications and unpublished
manuscripts.

1277   Sexton, Thomas G., and Poling, Donald R.   Can intelligence be
       taught?"   Bloomington, Indiana: Phi Delta Kappa Educational
       Foundation, 1973. 34p.   (Bibliography)
The authors cite evidence indicating that intelligence can be trained,
given a physiologically normal student and an intensely persistent tutor.
The purpose of increasing human intelligence, competence, or potential
is to insure that the human race will continue to evolve in a positive
direction, solving any problems which may present themselves as a threat
to comfort or survival.

1278   Shepardson, Marie E.   "Some factors related to level of achievement
       and level of educational and vocational goals of intellectually
       gifted children."   For a summary see: Diss Abstr Int   25(3): 1758,
       September, 1964.   (0 References)

1279   Smidchens, Uldis, and Sellin, Donald.   "Attitudes toward mentally
       gifted learners."   Gifted Child Q   20(1): 109-13, Spring, 1976.
       (11 References)
Study involved the responses of 116 graudate students in education toward
questions about mentally gifted learners.   Correlates of attitude were
defined as sex, curriculum preparation, previous experience, and
perceived traits of the gifted.   Special training and services for
regular classroom teachers are recommended.

1280   Smith, Gjertrud H.   "Professional and lay attitudes toward the
       education of the intellectually gifted high school student."   For
       a summary see: Diss Abstr Int   20(3): 939-40, September, 1959.
       (0 References)

1281   Stahl, Martin L.   "Program opportunities and per-pupil costs of
       services for the academically gifted."   For a summary see: Diss
       Abstr Int   27A(1): 88-89, July, 1966.   (0 References)

1282   Stanley, William H.   "The relationship of certain conative factors
       of intellectually gifted children to academic success."   For a
       summary see: <u>Diss Abstr Int</u>   25(8):   4512-13, February, 1965.   (0
       References)

1283   Swing, Elizabeth A.   "Public school elitist education in a
       revolutionary era."   <u>Engl J</u> 62(9):   1223-24, 1304-7, December, 1973.
       (7 References)
Describes the many problems and stresses which the academically talented
have to bear.   The teacher-author offers the thesis that the obsession
with excellence in post-sputnik America has had the effect of foreclosing
to the young a voice in their future by denying them an opportunity to
live fully within their present.

1284   Tannenbaum, Abraham J.   <u>Adolescent attitudes toward academic</u>
       <u>brilliance</u>.   New York: Bureau of Publications, Teachers College,
       Columbia University, 1962.   100p.
This monograph explores the status of intelligence in the adolescent
world.   It also tries to identify influences on those attitudes and
concludes that gifted students generally have an advantage in social
standing, although students with I.Q.'s above 150 "show signs of serious
difficulty in their relationships with schoolmates."   Adolescents were
more favorable toward gifted students who showed athletic aptitude.   The
study also suggested that schools could do more to strengthen incentives
toward scholarship.

1285   Tauss, Vita C.   "A proposed evaluation of a program for gifted
       children in New York City junior high schools based upon the needs
       of the school system and a survey of modern theory and practice."
       For a summary see: <u>Diss Abstr Int</u>   28A(11):   4394-95, May, 1968.
       (0 References)

1286   Thomas, Donald.   "Gifted and talented children: the neglected
       minority."   <u>Natl Assoc Second Sch Princ Bull</u>   60(1):   21-24,
       October, 1976.
Gifted children are not receiving the kind of education they need and
deserve.   In overlooking the needs of such students, Thomas states,
our schools are allowing a great natural resource to go to waste.   He
surveys the situation in this article by answering the question he
poses.

1287   Tomasson, Verna.   "Gifted children in a bind."   <u>Nation</u>   217:
       688-91, December 24, 1971.
Cites the 1971 Office of Education report that more than two million
talented students are suffering from neglect in U.S. elementary and
secondary schools.   Some suggested programs to correct this situation
are described.

1288   Toynbee, Arnold.   "Is America neglecting her creative minority?"
       <u>Accent Talent</u>   2(2):   1-3, January, 1968.   (0 References)
Declares that an overly egalitarian misconception about demoncracy and
an excessive conservatism are inhibiting our youths' creativity.   Offers
suggestions on how to utilize the talents and creativity of our
brightest youth.

1289   Tracey, Ellen K.   "A survey of the characteristics of the intellectually gifted child and the educational facilities for the gifted student in several carefully selected secondary schools on Long Island."   For a summary see: Diss Abstr Int 24(2): 635, August, 1963.   (0 References)

1290   Vitelli, Raymond J.   "Non-cognitive correlates of academic achievement of gifted adolescent males."   For a summary see: Diss Abstr Int 33A(10): 5569, April, 1973.   (0 References)

1291   "What on earth is Mensa?" Phi Delta Kappan 52(8): 480-81, April, 1971.
Questions and answers about Mensa, an international organization made up of 18,000 members, all of whom scored at the 98th percentile on a standardized I.Q. test.   Mensa's interest in identifying and aiding gifted children is noted.

1292   Wiener, Jean L.   "Attitudes of psychologists and psychometrists toward gifted children and programs for the gifted." Except Child 34(5): 354, January, 1968.   (0 References)
A comparison of the attitudes of psychologists in a study with those of teachers and other educators indicates that psychologists and psychometrists were less inclined to favor the gifted.

1293   Wiener, Jean L., and O'Shea, Harriet E.   "Attitudes of university faculty, administrators, teachers, supervisors, and university students toward the gifted." Except Child 30(4): 163-65, December, 1963.   (3 References)
Questionnaire showed that supervisors were most favorable to gifted, followed by administrators, university faculty, and teachers. University students were least favorable.

1294   Zehrback, Richard R.   "A study of intellectual maturity in gifted elementary school boys."   For a summary see: Diss Abstr Int 24(5): 1927, November, 1963.   (0 References)

XI

Addendum

1295 Aring, Charles D. "Creativity requires nurture." <u>JAMA</u> 237(12): 1205, March 21, 1977. (2 References)

1296 Bailey, Donald B., and Leonard, Judith. "Model for adapting Bloom's taxonomy to a preschool curriculum for the gifted." <u>Gifted Child Q</u> 21(1): 97-103, Spring, 1977. (10 References)

1297 Collis, Henry. "The First World Conference on Gifted Children." <u>International Journal of Early Childhood</u> 7(2): 167-68, 1975.

1298 ———. "Recognizing the gifted child." <u>Practitioner</u> 218(1304): 213-16, February, 1977. (0 References)

1299 Daddario, E. O. "Science, the future, and the gifted child." <u>Gifted Child Q</u> 21(1): 32-36, Spring, 1977. (0 References)

1300 Fine, R. "The uncommunicative genius." <u>Psychoanal Rev</u> 63(3): 409-25, Fall, 1976.

1301 Finley, E. R. "Program for the academically talented." <u>Sch Community</u> 63(6): 10+, February, 1977.

1302 Gresson, A. D., and Carter, D. G. "In search of the potentially gifted: suggestions for the school administrator." <u>Clearing House</u> 50: 503-71, April, 1977.

1303 Hall, Thomas R. "A study of situational problem solving by gifted high school mathematics students." For a summary see: <u>Diss Abstr Int</u> 37A(2): 906-7, August, 1976. (0 References)

1304 "Informal listing of names and addresses of the gifted child establishment." <u>Gifted Child Q</u> 21(1): 17-20, Spring, 1977.

1305 Jankowski, P., and Jankowski, F. <u>Accelerated programs for the gifted music student</u>. Englewood Cliffs, New Jersey: Parker, 1976.

1306 Ketcham, Bunty, and Snyder, Robert T. "Self-attitudes of the intellectually and socially advantaged student: normative study of the Piers-Harris Children's Self-Concept Scale." <u>Psychol Rep</u> 40(1): 111-16, February, 1977. (23 References)

1307   Koukeyan, Berjouhi B. "Evaluation of a vertical-horizontal
enrichment program for the math-gifted students fourth, fifth and
sixth grades." For a summary see: Diss Abstr Int 37A(9): 5587,
March, 1977. (0 References)

1308   Lane, William K. "The relationship between personality and differential academic achievement within a group of highly gifted and
high achieving children." For a summary see: Diss Abstr Int
37A(5): 2746, November, 1976. (0 References)

1309   LaSalle, Don P. "In pursuit of a pattern for scientists." Gifted
Child Q 21(1): 1-11, Spring, 1977. (6 References)

1310   Lombard, Thomas J. "Economical and simplified alternative for
providing educational opportunities to intellectually talented
students." Contemporary Education 48(2): 85-89, Winter, 1977.
(0 References)

1311   McClintock, J. "Edith Project: raising a child to be a genius."
Harpers 254: 21-24, March, 1977.

1312   McCormack, Robert E. "A study to determine the effectiveness of
an enrichment program for selected, highly gifted and talented
seventh grade students." For a summary see: Diss Abstr Int 37A(11):
6878-79, May, 1977. (0 References)

1313   Musgrove, Walter J., and Estroff, Elsie H. "Scale to measure
attitudes of intellectually gifted toward an enrichment program."
Except Child 43(6): 375-77, March, 1977. (0 References)

1314   National network directory newsletter: a directory of parent
organizations for parents of the gifted. Oakland, New Jersey:
Gifted Child Society, Inc., 1976. 60p.

1315   Olson, Meredith B. "Right or left hemispheric information
processing in gifted students." Gifted Child Q 21(1): 116-21,
Spring, 1977. (10 References)

1316   Passow, A. Harry. "Fostering creativity in the gifted child."
Except Child 43(6): 358-64, March, 1977. (20 References)

1317   Pledgie, Thomas K. "A comparison of program characteristics found
in theoretical and operational supplementary educational programs
for gifted students." For a summary see: Diss Abstr Int 37A(9):
5750, March, 1977. (0 References)

1318   "Professional bibliography for giftedness." Gifted Child Q 21(1):
inside back cover, Spring, 1977. (14 References)

1319   Rader, John R. "An evaluation of a simulation on the identification of the gifted and talented." For a summary see: Diss Abstr
Int 37A(8): 5002, February, 1977. (0 References)

1320   Renzulli, Joseph S., and Smith, Linda H. "Two approaches to
identification of gifted students." Except Child 43(8): 512-18,
May, 1977. (7 References)

1321 Rimm, Sylvia.   "Gift--an instrument for the identification and measurement of creativity." For a summary see: _Diss Abstr Int_ 37A(5): 2804, November, 1976.

1322 Ruscett, Sylvia P.   "Program development for gifted and academically talented children as conducted under the auspices of Ottawa area intermediate school district." For a summary see: _Diss Abstr Int_ 37A(10): 6201, April, 1977. (0 References)

1323 Scott, John.   "Don't make me walk when I want to fly." _Instructor_ 86(5): 68-72, January, 1977. (0 References)

1324 Sharon, Jared B.   "College for kids." _Community and Junior College Journal_ 47(6): 22-24, March, 1977. (0 References)

1325 Tabackman, Marc J.   "A study of family psycho-social environment and its relationship to academic achievement in gifted adolescents." For a summary see: _Diss Abstr Int_ 37A(10): 6381, April, 1977. (0 References)

1326 "Who are the gifted?" _Instructor_ 86(8): 55, April, 1977.

1327 Wolf, Joan S.   "The effect of modeling on reading selections of gifted and non-gifted students." For a summary see: _Diss Abstr Int_ 37A(5): 2791, November, 1976.

1328 Wright, Donna G.   "A model for the planning and management of programs for gifted students." For a summary see: _Diss Abstr Int_ 37A(8): 4775, February, 1977. (0 References)

1329 Zaffrann, Ronald T.   "A case study approach to an understanding of factors affecting the development of locus-of-control in gifted and talented adolescents." For a summary see: _Diss Abstr Int_ 37A(10): 6288, April, 1977. (0 References)

Appendix A: Some Individuals and Organizations Concerned with the Gifted

1. Barbe, Walter - Highlights for Children, Honesdale, Pennsylvania.

2. Biondi, Angelo - J Creative Behavior, Creative Education Foundation SUC-B, 1300 Elmwood Avenue, Buffalo, New York 14222.

3. Bruch, Kay - V.P. TAG, 185 Tuxedo Road, Athens, Georgia 30602.

4. Craig, Marjorie - Executive Secretary AAGC, 15 Gramercy Park, New York 10003.

5. Drews, Elizabeth - Portland State University, Oregon.

6. Feldhusen, John - Purdue University, West Lafayette, Indiana.

7. Fogel, Max - MENSA, 340 Brighton Road, Norristown, Pennsylvania 19403.

8. Freehill, Maurice - University of Washington, Seattle.

9. French, Joseph - Pennsylvania State University, State College, Pennsylvania.

10. Gallagher, James J. - 625 West Cameron Drive, Chapel Hill, North Carolina 25714.

11. Gensley, Juliana - Elementary Education California State University, Long Beach, California 90840.

12. Gifted Students Foundation, 12810 Hillcrest #120, Dallas, Texas 75230.

13. Gold, Marvin - TAG Newsletter, University of Southern Alabama, Mobile, Alabama 36688.

14. Gowan, John C. - President NAGC and Editor Gifted Child Quarterly, 9030 Darby Avenue, Northridge, California 91324.

15. Groth, Norma J. - Fort Lewis College, Durango, Colorado.

16. Holland, John - Johns Hopkins University, Baltimore, Maryland.

17. Isaacs, Ann - 8080 Springvalley Road, Cincinnati, Ohio 45236.

18. Jackson, Philip - ERIC-TAG, CEC, 1920 Association Drive, Reston, Virginia 22901.

19. Khatena, Joe - Marshall University, Huntington, West Virginia.

20. Krippner, Stanley - Humanistic Psych.Assn, 325 9th Street, San
     Francisco, California 44103.

21. Lazer, Al - California State University, Long Beach, California
     90840.

22. Malone, Charlotte - 7121 Wandermere Drive, San Diego, California
     92119.

23. Martinson, Ruth - California State University, Long Beach, California
     90840.

24. Meeker, Mary - SOI Institute, 214 Main Street, El Segundo, California
     90245.

25. Personnel Press (Torrance Tests) 191 Spring Street, Lexington,
     Massachusetts 02173.

26. Parnes, Sidney - Creative Education Foundation SUC, Buffalo, New
     York 14222.

27. Planec, Peter - Operations Research, 1400 Spring Street, Silver
     Springs, Maryland 20910.

28. Plowman, Paul - Director Gifted Child Programs, 721 Capital Mall,
     Sacramento, California 95814.

29. Renzulli, Joseph - President, TAG, University of Connecticut,
     Storrs, Connecticut 06268.

30. Rogers, Alan - Gifted Children's Research Institute, 300 West 55th
     Street #4-W, New York City 10019.

31. Sanborn, Marshall - (guidance) University of Wisconsin, Madison,
     Wisconsin 53705.

32. Sato, Irving - Director LTI, 316 West 2nd Street, Ph 0, Los Angeles,
     California 90012.

33. Sheridan Psych Services (Guilford Tests), P.O. Box 6101, Orange,
     California 92667.

34. Sisk, Dorothy - USOE Consultant for the Gifted Child, Room 2100,
     ROB-3, General Services Building, 7th and D Streets, Washington,
     D.C. 20202.

35. Stanley, Julian - Psychology, Johns Hopkins University, Baltimore,
     Maryland.

36. Tannenbaum Abraham - Teachers College, Columbia University, New
     York City 10025.

37. Taylor, Calvin - University of Utah, Salt Lake City, Utah.

38.   Torrance, E. Paul – Educational Psych, University of Georgia, Athens, Georgia 30601.

39.   Vassar, William – Consultant for Gifted, Box 2219, Hartford, Connecticut 06115.

40.   Ward, Virgil – University of Virginia, Charlottesville, Virginia 22903.

Appendix B: List of Instruments Useful in Identifying the Gifted

1. Stanford-Binet Intelligence Scale

2. Wechsler Intelligence Scale for Children

3. Wechsler-Bellevue Intelligence Scale

4. Wechsler Adult Intelligence Scale

5. College Board Scholastic Aptitude Test

6. Progressive Matrices

7. Goodenough-Harris Drawing Test

8. Torrance Tests of Creative Thinking

9. Cooperative School and College Ability Tests

10. Peabody Picture Vocabulary Test

11. California Test of Mental Maturity

12. Otis Self-Administering Tests of Mental Ability

13. Porteus Maze Test

14. Otis Quick-Scoring Mental Ability Tests

15. Ohio State University Psychological Test

16. Lorge-Thorndike Intelligence Tests

17. Miller Analogies Test

18. Kuhlmann-Anderson Test

19. Remote Associates Test

20. Wonderlic Personnel Test

21. Gesell Developmental Schedules

22. Henmon-Nelson Tests of Mental Ability

23. Alternate Uses

24. Benton Visual Retention Test

25. California Short-Form Test of Mental Maturity

26. Culture Fair Intelligence Test

27. Wechsler Memory Scale

28. Wechsler Preschool and Primary Scale of Intelligence

29. Graduate Record Examinations Aptitude Test

30. Consequences

31. Army General Classification Test

32. Columbia Mental Maturity Scale

33. Block-Design Test

34. Full-Range Picture Vocabulary Test

35. Arthur Point Scale of Performance Tests

36. Leiter International Performance Scale

37. Revised Beta Examination

38. Kent Series of Emergency Scales

39. Mill Hill Vocabulary Scale

40. Christensen-Guilford Fluency Tests

41. College Qualification Tests

42. Cattell Infant Intelligence Scale

43. Hidden Figures Tests

44. Quick Test

45. Merrill-Palmer Scale of Mental Tests

46. AH4, AH5, and AH6 Tests

47. Slosson Intelligence Test

48. Pintner-Cunningham Primary Test

49. Concept Mastery Test

50. Moray House Verbal Reasoning Tests

* 50 Tests Most Frequently Cited in the Literature (in order of
  frequency)

Appendix C: Audio-Visual Materials for Professional Use

Filmstrips

Title	Area	Source	Audience
"Alternative Measurement Tactics for Educational Evaluation"	testing	VIMSET	T and A
"Bringing the Community to the Classroom"	methods	WSU	T and A
"Grouping Students for Effective Learning"	methods	BMF	T and A
"How Pupils and Teachers Plan Together"	methods	WSU	T
"How to Confer Successfully With Your Childs Teacher"	methods	NEA	T and G
"Individualized Instruction"	methods	VIMCET	T
"Testing, Testing, Testing"	testing	Part I & II GA	T and G
"The Whys and How of Student Filmaking"	methods	UMM	T

Films

Title	Area	Source	Audience
"Angry Boy"	psych.	IFB	T, G, A
"Challenge of the Gifted"	methods	McGraw-Hill	T and G
"Child Language: Learning without Teaching"	psych.	Sterling Ed. Films	T
"Children's Aggression: Its Origin and Control"	psych.	Sterling Ed. Films	T and G
"Child's Play and the Real World"	psych.	Sterling Ed. Films	T and G
"Cognitive Development"	psych.	McGraw-Hill	T and G, A
"A Desk for Billie"	methods	NEA	T and A, G
"Education for Excellence"	methods	Board of Education New York City	T and A
"Ego Development: The Core of a Healthy Personality"	psych.	Sterling Ed. Films	T and G
"Enrichment Unit"	methods	OSUMPD	T
"Experiment in Excellence"	methods	McGraw-Hill Part I and Part II	T and A
"The Gifted Child"	psych.	NET Indiana U.	T and G
"The Gifted Ones"	methods	NFBC	T and A
"Heredity and Environment"	genetics	Coronet	T and G
"I Walk Away in The Rain"	psych.	Calvin Prod.	T and G
"The Impact of the Classroom Environment in Child Development"	methods	Sterling Ed. Films	T and P

Appendix D: Media Aids for Student Use

Filmstrips

Title	Area	Source	Audience
"Careers in Science"	careers	Popsi	S
"Careers That Matter"	careers	Coksby	S
"Choosing a College"	guidance	GA	S
"The College Dropout – Six Out of Every Ten"	guidance	GA	S
"Cooperative Way to A College Education"	guidance	GA	S
"Counseling in Vocational Decision"	guidance	QED	S
"Developing Your Study Skills"	guidance	Part I and II GA	S
"Education and College Planning"	guidance	A Series GA	S
"Freshman Year at College"	guidance	GA	S
"Getting Ready for College" Part I "How to Choose the Right College" Part II "How to Read the College Catalogue" Part III "How to Get Ready For College"	guidance	EFS	S
"High School Course Selection and Your Career"	guidance	Part I and II GA	E and S
"How to Take Notes"	language arts	Aims	E
"How to Write a Report"	language arts	Aims	E
"How We Learn"	guidance	Aims	E
"How We Study"	guidance	Aims	E
"The Meaning of Success"	guidance	Popsci	S
"The Meaning of Work"	careers	Popsci	S
"The Right Road"	guidance	IFB	S
"Should You Go To College?"	guidance	GA	S
"Study Abroad"	guidance	USNCU	S
"To Be Somebody"	guidance	Popsci	S
"What Is Your Future in the Changing World of Work?"	careers	EGH	S
"When You Visit a College"	guidance	GA	S
"Where to Find It"	research	Aims	S
"Who Should Go To College"	guidance	GA	S

Title	Area	Source	Audience
"In a Class by Himself"	methods	WVIZ-TV	T and A, G
"An Intellectual Caste System"	testing	NET Indiana U.	T and G
"The I.Q. Myth"	testing	CBS News	T and G
"The Learning Process"	psych.	CTV Television	T, G and A
"Less Far Than the Arrow"	methods	Calvin Prod.	T
"Let's Get to Work"	voc.guid.	EBEC	T, G and A
"No Two Alike"	testing	NET Indiana U.	T, G and A
"One Step at a Time: An Introduction to Behavior Modification"	psych.	McGraw-Hill	T and G
"Piaget's Developmental Theory: Classification"	psych.	Sterling Ed. Films	T and G
"Piaget's Developmental Theory: The Growth of Intelligence in the Pre-School Years"	psych.	Sterling Ed. Films	T and G
"Principles of Development"	psych.	McGraw-Hill	T and G
"Problem of Pupil Adjustment-The Drop-Out"	psych.	McGraw-Hill	T and G
"Providing for Individual Differences"	methods	IASTC	T
"Questioning Skills I: Fluency in Asking Questions"	methods	General Learning Corp.	T
"Questioning Skills II Probing Questions"	methods	General Learning Corp.	T
"Questioning Skills III Higher Order Questions"	methods	General Learning Corp.	T
"Questioning Skills IV Divergent Questions"	methods	General Learning Corp.	T
"Rafe: Developing Giftedness in the Educationally Disadvantaged"	psych.	NEA	T and G
"The Test"	guidance	McGraw-Hill	T and G
"Testing Intelligence with the Stanford Binet"	testing	Indiana University	T and G
"Understanding the Gifted"	psych.	Churchill	T and G
"And Wonders Never Cease"	A-V educ.	NEA	T and A
"A World to Perceive"	precep.	NET Indiana U.	T and G

A = Administrator

G = Guidance Counselor

P = Parents

T = Teacher

Title	Area	Source	Audience
"You and Your College Entrance Examination" GA Part I and Part II	guidance	GA	S
"You and Your Guidance Counselor"	guidance	Popsi	S
"Your First Year in High School"	guidance	Part I and II GA	E and S

Films

"Antonia: A Portrait of the Woman"	careers	Phoenix	S
"The Bright Young Newcomer"	guidance	Contemporary/ McGraw-Hill	S
"College Ahead"	guidance	Guidf	S
"College-Your Challenge"	guidance	Corf	S
"The Dehumanizing City and Hymie Schultz"	values	LCA	S
"Everybody Rides the Carousel"	psychology	Pyramid	S
"The Fine Art of Aggression"	values	LCA	S
"Going to School Is Your Job"	guidance	Journal	E
"Groupthink"	psychology	McGraw-Hill	S
"Guidance for the Seventies: The Blame Game"	guidance	BFA	S
"Guidance for the Seventies: Putting Yourself Together"	guidance	BFA	S
"Higher Education - Who Needs It?"	guidance	Carouf	S
"How's Your New Friend"	guidance	McGraw-Hill	S
"I Am How I Feel"	guidance	Churchill	E
"I Am How I Look"	guidance	Churchill	E
"I Am What I Know"	guidance	Churchill	E
"I Only Want You to Be Happy"	guidance	McGraw-Hill	S
"I Who Am, Who Am I?"	values	LCA	S
"I'm Mad at Me"	guidance	Churchill	E
"I'm Mad at You"	guidance	Churchill	E
"It's Easy If You Know How"	guidance	Disney	E
"Jobs and Their Environments: On the Job"	careers	McGraw-Hill	S
"Jobs for Men: Where Am I Going?"	careers	McGraw-Hill	S
"Jobs for Women: Where Are You Going Virginia?"	careers	McGraw-Hill	S
"Jobs in the City: Mass Media"	careers	Centron	E
"Jobs in the City - Medical and Health"	careers	Centron	E
"Jobs in the City: Women at Work"	careers	Centron	E
"Joys of Kinetic Art"	art	Daneli International Films	S

Title	Area	Source	Audience
"Leadership: Style or Circumstances"	psychology	McGraw-Hill	S
"Making a Decision Is..."	guidance	Churchill	S
"A Matter of Choice"	ethics	ABC: Xerox	S
"Modern Women: The Uneasy Life"	guidance	NET	S
"The Most Important Thing"	careers	NVETA	S
"My Friend"	guidance	Utah State Board of Education	S
"Next Year Is Now"	guidance	Guggenheim Prod.	S
"Of Skates and Elephants"	guidance	TFC	E
"Problem Solvers"	reasoning	Churchill	S
"Responsibility: What Are Its Limits?"	guidance	Disney	E
"See-Touch-Feel: A Report on the Artist in the School"	art	ACI	S
"A Sense of Purpose"	values	LCA	S
"The Social Animal"	psychology	Net	S
"Try Out"	careers	NVETA	S
"Trying Times"	guidance	NVETA	S
"What's the Good of a Test?"	guidance	Journal	E and S
"Woman's Place"	values	ABC: Xerox	S

E = Elementary
S = Secondary

Appendix E: Basic Bibliographic Tools

1. Bibliographic Index

2. Books in Print

3. British Education Index

4. Child Development Abstracts

5. Cumulative Book Index

6. Current Index to Journals in Education

7. Dissertation Abstracts International

8. Education Index

9. Exceptional Child Education Abstracts

10. Index Medicus

11. Mechanized Information Center (O.S.U.)

12. Monthly Catalog of U.S. Government Publications

13. National Union Catalog

14. Psychological Abstracts

15. Public Affairs Information Service

16. Readers' Guide to Periodical Literature

17. Research Relating to Children

18. Resources in Education

19. Social Sciences Citation Index

20. Social Sciences Index

21. Sociological Abstracts

Author Index

In the list below, the numbers after each name

refer to item numbers in the Bibliography.

A

Abraham, Willard, 1, 15, 908
Ackerman, Paul R., 712
Adalbert, Sister Mary, 586
Adams, Henry L., 281, 282
Addy, Sandra T., 486
Adler, Manfred, 16, 81, 82, 83
Adler, Marilynne J., 456
Ahr, A. Edward, 306
Aiken, Lewis R., Jr., 115
Alam, Sami J., 413
Albert, Robert S., 166, 191
Aldous, Joan, 167
Alexakos, C. E., 976
Alexander, Karl L., 977
Alkema, Chester J., 666
Allen, Arthur T., 414
Allen, Bonnie, 672
Alves, Gerald J., 956
Anastasi, Anne, 116, 1023, 1105
Anastasiow, Nicholas J., 246, 361, 965
Anderson, Derwyn L., 1106
Anderson, Joy, 302
Anderson, Kenneth E., 17
Anderson, Robert, 679
Andrews, Frank M., 337
Andrews, Henry B., 228
Anzalone, Patricia, 779
Aring, Charles D., 1295
Armstrong, Charles M., 938
Armstrong, H. G., 168
Armstrong, Kenneth, 713
Arnold, Carole R., 33
Arons, Myron, 1083
Ashley, Rosalind M., 780
Ashner, Mary J., 803
Ashpole, Kenneth M., 714
Astin, Alexander W., 990, 1217
Astin, Helen S., 117
Auger, John G., 978
Austin, C. Grey, 415

Axford, Lavonne B., 416

B

Babad, Elisha Y., 1144
Bachtold, Louise M., 118, 247, 248, 249, 301, 439, 909, 1024, 1025
Bailey, Donald B., 1296
Bailey, Kent G., 250
Bailey, Roger C., 250
Baird, Leonard L., 1072
Balcerak, Carl, 417
Baldwin, Joseph W., 307
Ball, Helen H., 510
Balow, Bruce, 418
Bamman, Henry A., 587
Banks, George, 527, 568
Barbe, Walter B., 18, 19, 20, 21, 192, 374, 487, 588, 685, 781, 837, 1145
Barber, Prudence S., 303
Barnard, James W., 211
Barnes, Fred P., 22
Barney, David, 458
Barnickle, Donald W., 457
Barron, Frank, 23, 153
Bart, William M., 1146
Beamer, Robert H., 1147
Beck, Joan, 878
Beck, Madeline H., 782
Becker, Leonard J., 419
Bedmar, Richard L., 1026
Beery, Richard D., 838
Beggs, Berenice B., 1027
Bell, Hugh M., 957
Bennett, Frances, 420
Bereday, George Z., 533, 534
Berk, Ron, 421
Berkowitz, Harry, 488
Bernal, Ernest M., Jr., 169, 375
Besdine, Matthew, 170

Selective Key Word Subject Index

In the list below, the numbers after each word

refer to item numbers in the Bibliography.

A

Ability, -ies 11, 62, 95, 115, 128, 132, 138, 147, 168, 201, 250, 272, 284, 302, 312, 323, 334, 368, 371, 373, 392, 418, 423, 431, 433, 434, 546, 866, 893, 897, 909, 998, 1013, 1038, 1061, 1080, 1144, 1158, 1170, 1173, 1175

Academically Talented Project 26

Accelerate, -d, -ing, -ion, -s 150, 326, 456, 461, 465, 466, 467, 468, 471, 475, 477, 479, 483, 630, 643, 644, 969, 993, 1305

Acceptance - Rejection 107, 975

Achievement, -s 100, 105, 120, 173, 178, 203, 204, 206, 220, 238, 292, 316, 317, 382, 383, 419, 429, 447, 503, 695, 846, 872, 875, 876, 934, 943, 948, 950, 962, 976, 981, 986, 994, 998, 1000, 1001, 1003, 1007, 1012, 1037, 1064, 1089, 1141, 1164, 1169, 1197, 1198, 1262, 1270, 1290, 1296

Act (Legislation) 718, 769, 770, 773 See also: Bill; Laws; Legislation

Actualization 929

Adjective Check List 957

Adjustment, -s 483, 524, 968, 1143

Administration, -tive 737, 738, 765, 1095

Administrator, -s 743, 1293, 1302

Adolescent, -s 147, 156, 177, 178, 183, 186, 199, 241, 247, 266, 275, 299, 301, 357, 844, 964, 1038, 1043, 1071, 1076, 1105, 1109, 1133, 1169, 1226, 1267, 1284, 1290, 1325, 1329

Adult, -s 217, 388, 461, 1000, 1001, 1117, 1118

Advanced Placement (Program) 435, 448, 775, 978

Advisors 874

Affective 123, 214, 217, 264, 855, 1189, 1212

Age 217, 943, 1111, 1171, 1172, 1183, 1190, 1195

Alternative 382, 387, 525

American 30, 111, 251, 494, 1271

Analysis (Psycho) 223

Antecedents 266

Anxiety 148, 203, 204, 206, 255, 317, 931

Aptitude, -s 144, 311, 317, 335, 1047

Art, -s 163, 164, 260, 261, 277, 357, 649, 666, 667, 668, 669, 670, 671, 672, 673, 674, 675, 676, 677, 1114, 1202

Artist, -s 155, 158, 676

Artistic, -ally 159, 163, 289, 678, 1133

Asian 172

Aspiration, -s 209, 1010, 1262

Assessing, -ment 29, 316, 320, 352, 910

Association 1190

Associative 1193, 1195

Atchison (Kansas) 888

Attainment 201, 1194

Attitude, -s 183, 267, 269, 278, 279, 292, 298, 465, 505, 530, 550, 669, 766, 782, 789, 808, 841, 885, 888, 896, 901, 1046, 1186, 1245, 1258, 1279, 1280, 1284, 1292, 1293, 1313

Average 124, 204, 225, 359, 362, 364, 1151, 1152, 1154, 1158, 1169, 1173, 1174, 1175, 1182, 1189

List of Journal Abbreviations

Abbreviation	Title
Accent Talent	Accent on Talent
Acta Paedopsychiatr	Acta Paedopsychiatrica
Adv Sci	Advancement of Science
Am Biol Teach	American Biology Teacher
Am Correct Ther J	American Corrective Therapy Journal
Am Educ	American Education
Am Educ Res J	American Educational Research Journal
Am J Ment Defic	American Journal of Mental Deficiency
Am J Orthopsychiatry	American Journal of Orthopsychiatry
Am Psychol	American Psychologist
Am Sch Board J	American School Board Journal
Am Sociol Rev	American Sociological Review
Arch Gen Psychiatry	Archives of General Psychiatry
Arith Teach	Arithmetic Teacher
Art Act	Arts and Activities
Art Educ	Art Education
Art Psychother	Art Psychotherapy
Assoc Educ Psychol J Newsl	Association of Educational Psychologists Journal and Newsletter
Athene	Athene
Aust Math Teach	Australian Mathematics Teacher
Behav Sci	Behavioral Science
Br J Criminol	British Journal of Criminology
Br J Educ Psychol	British Journal of Educational Psychology
Br J Psychol	British Journal of Psychology
Br J Stat Psychol	British Journal of Statistical Psychology
Bus Educ World	Business Education World
Calif J Educ Res	California Journal of Educational Research
Cathol Educ Rev	Catholic Educational Review
Cathol Sch J	Catholic School Journal
Child Dev	Child Development
Child Educ	Childhood Education
Child Study J	Child Study Journal
Child Today	Children Today
Clearing House	Clearing House
Clin Pediatr	Clinical Pediatrics

Coll Board Rev — College Board Review
Coll Educ Rec — College of Education Record: University of Washington

Coll Univ — College and University
Couns Psychol — Counseling Psychologist
Daedalus — Daedalus
Del Med J — Delaware Medical Journal
Diss Abstr Int — Dissertation Abstracts International

Early Years — Early Years
Educ Dig — Education Digest
Educ Forum — Educational Forum
Educ Leadersh — Educational Leadership
Educ Psychol — Educational Psychologist
Educ Psychol Meas — Educational and Psychological Measurement

Educ Rec — Educational Record
Educ Res (U.K.) — Educational Research
Educ Res (U.S.) — Educational Researcher
Educ Theory — Educational Theory
Education — Education
Electroencephalogr Clin Neurophysiol — Electroencephalography and Clinical Neurophysiology
Elem Eng — Elementary English
Elem Sch Guid Couns — Elementary School Guidance and Counseling

Elem Sch J — Elementary School Journal
Engl J — English Journal
Except Child — Exceptional Children
Florida J Educ Res — Florida Journal of Educational Research

Genet Psychol Monogr — Genetic Psychology Monographs
Gifted Child Q — Gifted Child Quarterly
Grade Teach — Grade Teacher
Hahinukh — Hahinukh: Review for Educational Thoughts

High Points — High Points
High Sch J — High School Journal
Highlights Teach — Highlights for Teachers
Hist Educ Q — History of Educational Quarterly
Horizon — Horizon
Hum Behav — Human Behavior
Hum Dev — Human Development
Ill J Educ — Illinois Journal of Education
Ill Med J — Illinois Medical Journal
Ill Sch Res — Illinois School Research
Indep Sch Bull — Independent School Bulletin
Indian Educ Rev — Indian Educational Review
Innovator — Innovator
Instructor — Instructor
Int J Psychoanal — International Journal of Psychoanalysis

Int Psychiatry Clin — International Psychiatry Clinics
Intellect — Intellect
J Abnorm Soc Psychol — Journal of Abnormal and Social Psychology

J Aesthet Art Crit	Journal of Aesthetics and Art Criticism
J Am Psychoanal Assoc	Journal of the American Psychoanalytic Association
J Appl Behav Anal	Journal of Applied Behavioral Analysis
J Appl Psychol	Journal of Applied Psychology
J Appl Sci	Journal of Applied Science
J Chem Educ	Journal of Chemical Education
J Child Psychol Psychiatry	Journal of Child Psychology and Psychiatry
J Clin Psychol	Journal of Clinical Psychology
J Coll Stud Pers	Journal of College Student Personnel
J Consult Clin Psychol	Journal of Consulting and Clinical Psychology
J Consult Psychol	Journal of Consulting Psychology
J Couns Psychol	Journal of Counseling Psychology
J Creat Behav	Journal of Creative Behavior
J Educ Meas	Journal of Educational Measurement
J Educ Psychol	Journal of Educational Psychology
J Educ Res	Journal of Educational Research
J Educ Sociol	Journal of Educational Sociology
J Emot Educ	Journal of Emotional Education
J Exp Educ	Journal of Experimental Education
J Gen Educ	Journal of General Education
J Genet Psychol	Journal of Genetic Psychology
J Health Phys Educ Recreat	Journal of Health, Physical Education and Recreation
J Hist Behav Sci	Journal of the History of the Behavioral Sciences
J Humanistic Psychol	Journal of Humanistic Psychology
J Ind Arts Educ	Journal of Industrial Arts Education
J Individ Psychol	Journal of Individual Psychology
J Learn Disabil	Journal of Learning Disabilities
J Natl Assoc Women Deans Couns	Journal of the National Association of Women Deans and Counselors
J Negro Educ	Journal of Negro Education
J Nurs Educ	Journal of Nursery Education
J Parapsychol	Journal of Parapsychology
J Pers	Journal of Personality
J Pers Soc Psychol	Journal of Personality and Social Psychology
J Psychol	Journal of Psychology
J Res Sci Teach	Journal of Research in Science Teaching
J Sch Psychol	Journal of School Psychology
J Second Educ	Journal of Secondary Education
J Soc Issues	Journal of Social Issues
J Spec Educ	Journal of Special Education
J Teach Educ	Journal of Teacher Education
J Thought	Journal of Thought

J Vocat Behav	Journal of Vocational Behavior
J Vocat Educ Guid	Journal of Vocational and Educational Guidance
J Youth Adolesc	Journal of Youth and Adolescence
Kappa Delta Pi Rec	Kappa Delta Pi Record
Kootenay Cent Gifted J	Kootenay Centre for the Gifted Journal
Learning	Learning
Math Sch	Mathematics in School
Math Teach	Mathematics Teacher
Meas Eval Guid	Measurement and Evaluation in Guidance
Mensa Bull	Mensa Bulletin
Mensan	Mensan
Merrill-Palmer Q	Merrill-Palmer Quarterly
Mich J Second Educ	Michigan Journal of Secondary Education
Multivariate Behav Res	Multivariate Behavioral Research
Music Educ J	Music Educator's Journal
Nation	Nation
Nations Sch Coll	Nation's Schools and Colleges
Natl Assoc Second Sch Princ Bull	National Association of Secondary School Principals Bulletin
Natl Cathol Educ Assoc Bull	National Catholic Education Association Bulletin
Natl Elem Princ	National Elementary Principal
Natl Merit Scholarsh Corp Res Rep	National Merit Scholarship Corporation Research Reports
NEA J	NEA Journal
Neurology	Neurology
NJEA Rev	New Jersey Education Association Review
North Carolina Med J	North Carolina Medical Journal
Nurs Times	Nursing Times
NY State Educ	New York State Education
Ohio Sch	Ohio Schools
Ontario J Educ Res	Ontario Journal of Educational Research
Orbit	ORBIT
Parents Mag	Parents Magazine
Peabody J Educ	Peabody Journal of Education
Pedagog Forsk	Pedagogisk Forskning: Scandinavian Journal of Educational Research
Pediatr Clin North Am	Pediatric Clinics of North America
Percept Mot Skills	Perceptual and Motor Skills
Pers Guid J	Personnel and Guidance Journal
Phi Delta Kappan	Phi Delta Kappan
Plan Higher Educ	Planning for Higher Education
Practitioner	Practitioner
Proc R Soc Med	Proceedings of the Royal Society of Medicine
Psychoanal Study Child	Psychoanalytic Study of the Child
Psychol Rec	Psychological Record
Psychol Rep	Psychological Reports

Psychol Sch	Psychology in the Schools
Psychol Today	Psychology Today
Psychology	Psychology
PTA Mag	P. T. A. Magazine
Pupil Pers Serv J	Pupil Personnel Services Journal
Read Dig	Reader's Digest
Read Teach	Reading Teacher
Relig Educ	Religion in Education
Rev Educ Res	Review of Educational Research
Saturday Rev	Saturday Review
Sch Act	School Activities
Sch Arts	School Arts
Sch Community	School and Community
Sch Couns	School Counselor
Sch Libr	School Librarian
Sch Life	School Life
Sch Sci Math	School Science and Mathematics
Sch Soc	School and Society
Scholastic Teach	Scholastic Teacher Junior/Senior High
Sci Art	Sciences de l'Art
Sci Educ	Science Education
Science	Science
South J Educ Res	Southern Journal of Educational Research
Spec Educ Can	Special Education in Canada
Spec Educ: Forward Trends	Special Education: Forward Trends
Stud Art Educ	Studies in Art Education
Super Stud	The Superior Student
Talents Gifts	Talents and Gifts
Teach Coll Rec	Teachers College Record
Teach Except Child	Teaching Exceptional Children
Teacher	Teacher
Tex Outlook	Texas Outlook
Times Educ Suppl	Times (London) Educational Supplement
Todays Educ	Today's Education
Todays Health	Today's Health
Top News	Top of the News
Train Sch Bull	Training School Bulletin
Trans-action	Trans-action
US News World Rep	U. S. News and World Report
Va J Educ	Virginia Journal of Education
Va Med Mon	Virginia Medical Monthly
Viewpoints	Viewpoints
Vocat Guid Q	Vocational Guidance Quarterly
Volta Rev	Volta Review

ABOUT THE COMPILER

Jean Laubenfels has a B.A. from Stanford University and an M.A. and Ph.D from Ohio State University. She has had experience in teaching and counseling able students at the elementary, secondary, and college levels in both public and private schools. She is presently employed by the Department of Exceptional Children at the Ohio State University as a curriculum writer.